# Countercultural Conservatives

# Countercultural Conservatives

*American Evangelicalism
from the Postwar Revival
to the New Christian Right*

## Axel R. Schäfer

THE UNIVERSITY OF WISCONSIN PRESS

Publication of this volume has been made possible, in part, through support from the **Anonymous Fund of the College of Letters and Science** at the University of Wisconsin–Madison.


The University of Wisconsin Press
1930 Monroe Street, 3rd Floor
Madison, Wisconsin 53711-2059
uwpress.wisc.edu

3 Henrietta Street
London WC2E 8LU, England
eurospanbookstore.com

Printed in the United States of America

Library of Congress Cataloging-in-Publication Data
Schäfer, Axel R.
Countercultural conservatives: American evangelicalism from the postwar revival to the New Christian Right / Axel R. Schäfer.
p.     cm.—(Studies in American thought and culture)
Includes bibliographical references and index.
ISBN 978-0-299-28524-1 (pbk.: alk. paper)
ISBN 978-0-299-28523-4 (e-book)
1. Evangelicalism—United States—History—20th century.
2. Christian conservatism—United States—History—20th century.
3. Christianity and politics—United States—History—20th century.
I. Title.   II. Series: Studies in American thought and culture.
BR1642.U5S33 2011
277.308′2—dc22
2011012634

*For*
*Dave White*

# Contents

# Acknowledgments

The nineteenth-century German historian Leopold von Ranke's famous dictum for the historian to write *wie es eigentlich gewesen [ist]* is commonly translated as "what actually happened." Far from simply being an admonition not to go beyond what the sources tell us and to be a recorder of real events, however, Ranke's sentence implicitly describes the ambivalence at the center of the historian's task: "Eigentlich" can mean both "actually" and "in its essence." The writing of history thus requires not just the historical actuary, who reconstructs the details of past events, but also the storyteller, who gives us a sense of their momentousness and puts it all in perspective.

This task to weave a coherent story out of the tangled web of history, however, is fraught with serious danger. At best it yields a feat of the historical imagination steeped in a profound knowledge of the past. At worst, the historian becomes complicit in the narrative justification of the dominant socioeconomic order and distribution of power. Indeed, Ranke himself knew a thing or two about myth-making in the age of the nation-state. The saving grace is the historian's own pesky antinomian mood and inclination. Temperamentally inclined to detect nuances and discrepancies, and to engage in petulant detective work among dusty records of interest to maybe two or three other twisted souls, the historicizing mind distrusts all master narratives that claim to "make sense of experience." While meaning is desired, confusion and contradictions prevail. While lessons are sought, frightening repetition of errors is found. While motivations and intentions are studied, actions and outcomes bear little resemblance to them. In other words, at the beginning of a research project there are probing questions and tentative answers. At the end it's the other way around.

The tension between the painstaking reconstruction of historical detail and the search for the all-encompassing story is nowhere more palpable than in writings about subjects that have both deep cultural resonance and are constantly present in contemporary public debates. The resurgence of evangelicalism in the United States is such a theme, because it deals with both a specific social movement and a temper suffusing American culture. Hence, this book is both a close-up story of intramovement conflicts, maneuvers, and machinations, and an attempt to make a "larger point" that queries established assumptions about modern conservative Protestantism. This includes challenging the notion that resurgent evangelicalism is primarily a movement of religious and moral orthodoxy, that it is naturally in alliance with conservative politics, and that it should be understood as a reaction to the turmoils of the 1960s.

It is in the hope that I have been able to strike a balance between the two dimensions of the historian's craft, and avoided most of the pitfalls inherent in them, that I express my gratitude to friends, colleagues, and acquaintances from whose comments and reflections I have benefited to no end. Michaela Hoenicke Moore, Alan Lessoff, Marcus Graeser, Knud Krakau, Celeste-Marie Bernier, Howard Brick, Thomas Fuchs, and David K. Adams in many different ways have been part of the book's germination and design over the years. Some read chapters, drafts, or the whole manuscript, and were generous with their insights and feedback. Others encouraged me to continue simply on the basis of their fiery brilliance, sympathetic understanding, intuitive warmth, obstinate insistence, or patient tolerance of my bizarre ramblings. All of them, through their friendship, thoughtful engagement, and incisive criticism, have been on my mind throughout the writing process as a sort of mental audience and panel of critics. They have helped me think more deeply about what it means to be a historian by showing me how to feel my way into the past while at the same time remaining a detached critic and observer.

Other colleagues and friends in the profession generously shared their thoughts and insights, and pushed me along in this endeavor. They include Hans-Jürgen Grabbe, Mark Noll, Hugh Wilford, David Weeks, Daniel K. Williams, Kendrick Oliver, Iwan Morgan, Jonathan Bell, Daniel Scroop, Richard King, Robert Mason, and Daniel Geary. My colleagues in American Studies at Keele Unversity, particularly John Dumbrell, Robert Garson, Martin Crawford, and Steve Mills, as well as the staff at the Research Institute for the Humanities at Keele, made sure that I was surrounded by a collegial and convivial atmosphere. A David Bruce Centre for American Studies Research Grant, two sabbatical leave grants from Keele University, and a research fellowship from the John F. Kennedy Institute of the Free University Berlin provided generous institutional and financial support. Without the excellent assistance of the staff at the archives I visited, the professionalism of the editorial team at the University of Wisconsin Press, and the helpful suggestions and generous sharing of knowledge by the anonymous readers, this book would not have been possible. For all this I am profoundly grateful to each and every one of the people involved. My particular thanks, however, is reserved for Paul Boyer, the series editor, who went beyond the call of duty in identifying and obtaining illustrations, editing chapters, and being a friend and a mentor for this project.

There are many other people I owe a debt of gratitude to. Some might not remember that they made a contribution, others were unwittingly complicit in this book, and a few will know without being mentioned how much they meant to me. I particularly want to thank Petra and Carsten Tismer, Helga Tismer, and Brigitte and Holger Fleischer for keeping me sane and offering me a place for rest and respite during difficult times. Most importantly, however, I want to thank my wife Brenda, who had to live with this project for far too long and whose patience I tested to the limits. Without her love, wisdom, and straight talk I would have been utterly lost in the fog of self-doubt and circular reasoning that can engulf the historian in the postmodern age.

This book is dedicated to the memory of David Olds White, Sr., whose knowledge, passion, experience, and humor left a mark on this project in innumerable ways. Dave and his wife Janice were generous to a fault when they offered me their friendship and invited me to share in the intellectual atmosphere of their beautiful home (not to mention in all the banana pancakes and gin and tonics). It is in affectionate recognition of his deep moral earnestness and intellectual commitment that I dedicate this study of a religious movement to someone so profoundly critical of religious belief.

# Countercultural Conservatives

# Introduction

## *Beyond the "Backlash"*

The notion that religious orthodoxy feeds naturally into socioeconomic and political conservatism is arguably one of the most widespread and rarely questioned assumptions among observers of resurgent evangelicalism in the United States. Indeed, the scholarly attention lavished on the apostles of the New Christian Right, ranging from James Robison to Pat Robertson, has made it difficult to separate modern religious revivalism from the image of an intrinsic alliance between Christian fundamentalists, conservative Republicans, and disaffected southern Democrats that is characterized by market fetishism, a hawkish foreign policy, and moral absolutism. It tends to reduce evangelical politics to pro-life demonstrations and anti-gay initiatives, and evangelical thought to denunciations of rampant secularization and moral permissiveness.

Evidence to the contrary has had little success in challenging this pervasive image. Yet this evidence is compelling, particularly when the analytical scope is broadened from the exclusive focus on the New Christian Right since the late 1970s to the broader postwar evangelical resurgence. A few examples may suffice. Many moderate evangelicals viewed American capitalism as corrupted by corporate welfare and expressed concerns about the lack of moral values in laissez-faire economics, and even among conservatives in the movement support for the capitalistic ethos was not always as fervent as one might expect. In 1967 Harold Lindsell, soon-to-be editor of the leading evangelical magazine *Christianity Today* and a key figure in taking it in a more rightwing direction, criticized other denominations for having "thrown boldly the mantle of the church . . . over democracy, capitalism, the status quo, and opposition to left wing and communistic causes of all kinds." He insisted that the church should not commit itself

3

to either a free market or a managed economy, warning that it was otherwise in danger of becoming "the voice of those who have managed to seize control of the power structures."[1]

Likewise, a tough stance on defense policy rarely met with unanimous approval within the wider evangelical movement. In a 1956 *Christianity Today* poll of evangelical clergy, the majority of those surveyed called for "less nationalism, more world vision." Many also demanded "less emphasis on bombs and materials for war," more international disarmament negotiations, and new efforts to strengthen international relations.[2] In 1977 the National Association of Evangelicals (NAE) reaffirmed its 1952 resolution against "the militarization of the nation in peacetime" and spoke out against universal military training and the proliferation of nuclear weapons.[3] And a confidential 1986 poll of *Christianity Today* subscribers showed that the readership's top priorities were "pursuing increased nuclear disarmament treaties with the Soviets" and "making substantial cuts in the overall defense budget." Moreover, "cutting defense spending to reduce the federal deficit" received the support of 50 percent of those polled.[4] Indeed, manifestations of pacifism so worried conservatives that in April 1977 Colorado Congressman William L. Armstrong, a key figure in engineering links between the Republican party and the NAE, warned about "the evident decline in the willingness of our people to support an adequate national defense."[5] Likewise, the equally conservative director of the NAE's Office of Public Affairs, Robert Dugan, felt it necessary to assure Ronald Reagan's chief of staff in 1983 that his office was "working behind the scenes to counteract some of the drift toward the nuclear freeze position" among evangelicals.[6]

Finally, even on supposedly clear-cut moral issues, evangelicals remained divided. As late as 1989 a Gallup survey found that a majority of white evangelicals believed abortion should be legal and backed the Equal Rights Amendment. There was also a significant amount of consensus across religious lines in regard to more public funding for schools, AIDS education, civil rights, and increased government spending for social programs. While religious traditionalists were generally more conservative than modernists on issues of sexuality, reproductive rights, and gender divisions, they were often more progressive on issues of economic equality and no more conservative on racial issues.[7]

Although by the late 1990s conservative Protestants clearly formed one of the most loyally Republican groups in the religious spectrum, these examples suggest that evangelicalism remained a highly diverse movement that consisted of a wide variety of groups with often antagonistic views. Moreover, they point to an underlying problem in research on conservative Protestantism. As religious historian Jon Butler has noted, scholarship frequently discusses the rise of the

Christian Right, but rarely provides a *historical* explanation for it. Instead, most analysts talk about the New Christian Right solely in terms of a defensive "backlash" against the secularizing effects of sociocultural change, sixties radical- ism, and the growth of the liberal welfare state. In doing so, they never really explain how and why evangelicals, whose egalitarian, democratic, and even anticapitalist impulses had played such a significant role in abolitionism, the women's suffrage movement, Populism, and American socialism, could ally themselves so solidly with political and economic conservatism. After all, evangeli- cals traditionally constitute an electorate that, for all intents and purposes, feels closer to William Jennings Bryan than to Milton Friedman.[8]

Over the past two decades, however, a number of books have shifted the analytical focus in the study of this multifaceted movement to the period prior to the 1980s. In contrast to conceptualizing resurgent evangelicalism purely in terms of "episodes of revival" and "political insurgency," they highlight its long-term engagement and complex relationship with Cold War politics and culture.[9] Building upon these findings, this book offers a fresh interpretation of the broader movement's organizational resurgence, sociocultural repositioning, political ideology, and partisan affiliation. It connects an analysis of newly acces- sible archival materials to a broad interpretive history of postwar evangelicalism.

In a nutshell, this study advances three main arguments. First, by interpreting resurgent evangelicalism in light of social movement theory, it suggests that modern conservative Protestantism was characterized less by the effort to assert fixed traditional moral and theological concepts than by the attempt to reconcile conflicting impulses. Christian conservatives, though often regarded as staunch traditionalists, were both remarkably modern and remarkably worldly. In particular, evangelicals sought to mediate between religious piety and growing worldliness, theological orthodoxy and therapeutic conversionism, and moral traditionalism and consumer society. On the one hand, evangelicalism was characterized by new ecumenical impulses, the domestication of its born-again theology, and cultural accommodation to liberal capitalism. On the other hand, the resurgence was accompanied by separatist institution building, the emergence of deep religious divides, and an uncompromising politics of morality. Moreover, as I have argued elsewhere, the emerging evangelical political ideology was characterized by a kind of "antistatist statism" that combined denunciations of liberal public policy with growing support for the national security state, the politics of economic growth, and public aid for religious agencies.[10] In short, the processes by which evangelicals navigated tensions and contradictions in their relationship with other denominations, the state, and society were as important for their political and cultural orientation as their theological beliefs.

Second, the findings show that conservative Protestantism is not a monolithic player in a culture war but a disparate movement whose political allegiances are tentative and negotiable. In shifting the focus toward the period of neo-evangelical organizing in the 1940s and 1950s, the rise of leftwing and liberal evangelicalism in the 1960s and 1970s, and the internal fragmentation and purges that preceded the dominance of the conservative wing since the late 1970s, the study suggests that conservative Protestantism's politics remained contested. Evangelical political and cultural orientations were frequently shaped by internal power struggles and external coalition building. Seen from this angle, the dominance of the Christian Right within the movement was not primarily based on a natural affinity between religious and secular conservatism. Instead, it was the contingent result of a complex process of reconciling conflicting ideological positions, marginalizing intramovement adversaries, and linking up with non-evangelical groups. In this process the Christian Right built upon both the postwar neo-evangelical return to the cultural mainstream and the social action focus of the evangelical Left in the 1960s and 1970s.

Third, the book interrogates the "backlash" theory of the evangelical resurgence, which locates the mobilization of evangelicals primarily in the hostile reaction against the political and cultural liberalism of the 1960s. In contrast, it suggests that the organizational strength, cultural attractiveness, and political efficacy of the New Christian Right was predicated less upon resentment against the cultural changes of the 1960s than upon the ability to merge the insurgent styles and rhetoric of the period with a forceful and unambiguous embrace of the dominant liberal capitalist order. The Christian Right's "soft conversionism" integrated the psychology and language of personal liberation, authenticity, and self-actualization derived from the 1960s into a traditional narrative of spiritual transformation that affirmed the bourgeois individual. Its "moralistic materialism" co-opted the language of cultural transvaluation, but also affirmed consumer society. And its "countercultural capitalism" combined a traditionalist notion of moral order based on market relations with a libertarian emphasis on individual self-expression. Evangelicalism was thus a catalyst for integrating the anti-establishment impulses of the insurgencies into the mainstream of American society while effectively sidelining their radical socioeconomic content. This became evangelicalism's central ideological contribution to the broader conservative resurgence.

Chapter 1 outlines the theories and concepts that form the analytical basis of this book. It does this by juxtaposing the key interpretations of evangelicalism's

more recent political mobilization with analyses of its broader postwar resurgence. In seeking to understand the rise of evangelical rightwing partisanship
since the 1970s, scholars have largely concentrated on three main phenomena.
First, they have shown that the growth of conservative Protestantism went
hand in hand with the partial realignment of traditional ecclesiastical divisions
along a broader liberal-orthodox divide. As a result, evangelical Protestants,
who believe in the inerrancy of the Bible, salvation through faith, the born-
again experience, and a premillennialist eschatology, felt closer to conservative
Catholics and Jews than to liberal members of their own theological tradition,
who emphasized the historical constructedness of sacred texts.

Second, researchers have suggested that moralistic campaigns centered on
issues such as abortion, gay rights, pornography, and welfare reform facilitated
new transdenominational coalitions based on shared perceptions of social reality
and moral truth. These helped align the orthodox, with their belief in fixed and
universal moral norms, against the liberals, who had a relativistic worldview.
Since the 1970s, these identities rooted in moral outlooks, lifestyles, and social
values have arguably sidelined traditional socioeconomic, regional, and ethno-
religious divisions as key determinants of partisan political affiliation. Despite
being traditionally known for their virulent anti-Semitism and anti-Catholicism,
evangelicals, for example, began to avidly embrace alliances across denominational boundaries by promoting a broad-church approach centered on a
campaign against secular humanism and moral iniquity.

Finally, scholars have argued that this normative realignment in the
religious sphere spilled over into politics and reshaped the partisan divide along
traditionalist-modernist lines. In this process the GOP became largely a party
of the devout and committed members of the evangelical, mainline Protestant,
and Catholic traditions. By the same token, the Democratic party saw a substantial increase in support among those with no religious affiliation, a steady loyalty
among those with low levels of religious commitment, and a substantial decline
in the presence of conservative Protestants and committed Catholics.

While these findings by political scientists offer important insights into the
partisan mobilization of evangelicals, however, research from a variety of other
disciplines suggests that the dominant focus on the New Christian Right has
tended to obscure the broader meaning of the religio-political resurgence. In
shifting the emphasis toward evangelicalism's postwar organizational resurgence,
these studies in part complement and in part question the findings of political
mobilization theorists. Sociologists of religion, for example, see evangelicalism's
renewed cultural legitimacy and influence as rooted in its accommodation to

modernity, rather than in its assertion of moral traditionalism. In their view, the movement's emphasis on individualism, choice, voluntarism, flexibility, and immediate individual access to spiritual knowledge reflected modern social conditions. This played an integral part in the modernization process by promoting the norms and values underlying consumer capitalism.

Meanwhile, analysts in the functionalist tradition link the resurgence of postwar evangelicalism to its ability to meet the social challenges of war-related dislocation. The highly flexible and mobile evangelical churches often provided the social and community services that were lacking in the new suburban tract developments of the burgeoning South and West. Moreover, many researchers credit the internal organizational resources of conservative Protestantism with providing the institutional basis for the postwar resurgence. They also note the movement's competitive advantage in a society characterized by spiritual pluralism and market orientation.

In contrast to the literature on political mobilization, these "resurgence theories" therefore suggest that processes of postwar adjustment, adaptation, and even secularization explain the cultural and political resonance of the movement. They cast doubt on the notion that a new cultural divide easily sidelined traditional denominational and ethno-religious identities and their commensurate political affiliations. They query the thesis that theological divisions between traditionalists and modernists translated into a "culture war" that manifested itself in partisan divisions. And they dispute the assertion that moral orientation replaced socioeconomic concerns in shaping partisan loyalty.

This analytical divergence, the chapter concludes, indicates the need for an interpretive model that locates the substance of postwar evangelicalism not only in firm theological beliefs, but also in its engagement with the specific institutional contexts and ideological settings of Cold War politics and society. The story of the evangelical resurgence in general, and the rise of the Right in particular, is neither solely one of a countermovement, as political mobilization analysts suggest, nor simply one of adjustment to modernity, as resurgence theorists tend to argue. Instead, the evangelical "essence" is located in the effort to balance conflicting aspirations. These include the tensions between an insurgent message and sociocultural integration, and between political militancy and securing a place in the mainstream. They also extend to contradictions between antimodern traditionalism and consumer capitalism, theological orthodoxy and ecumenism, and organizational fragmentation and unity.

The remaining chapters move from the theory to testing the interpretive model on the basis of a closer examination of the three key stages in the postwar evangelical journey. Chapter 2 looks at the period from the early 1940s to the mid-1960s when the movement re-entered mainstream society. As Robert Fowler has pointed out, "evangelicalism underwent a historical inner change at exactly the time that it stepped into the larger American culture."[11] Spurred on by the challenges and opportunities of wartime and postwar American culture, a new generation of evangelicals re-engaged with the world, seeking to establish an effective organizational presence, intellectual respectability, cultural relevance, and political influence. Institutionally, they embarked upon a flurry of new ventures, ranging from magazines and seminaries to charities and missionary organizations. In these efforts they were supported by conservatives who had remained in the mainline Protestant denominations. While neo-evangelicals distanced themselves from prewar fundamentalism, many mainline believers, scarred by the ravages of war and totalitarianism, questioned modernism and its postmillennial identification of the Kingdom of God with a specific social program.

Ideologically, the postwar neo-evangelical movement offered a religious identity that was both distinct from traditional fundamentalism and outside liberal secular society. Neo-evangelicals sought to restore legitimacy to theological orthodoxy, yet pioneered a form of therapeutic conversionism that was no longer at odds with consumer culture. They sought to sharpen the divide between liberal and orthodox forms of religion, but also softened their image in order to engage in transdenominational coalition building. They accommodated to the technological and cultural expressions of liberal society, yet rejected liberal epistemology. And although they sought to reawaken the spirit of social involvement, they remained wedded to separatist pietism.

The chapter shows that the postwar evangelical resurgence cannot be separated from the dramatic social and economic changes in postwar American society, namely suburbanization and the shift in economic power from the commercial centers of the Northeast to the military-industrial complex of the South and the West. Texas, California, Florida, Arizona, and other evangelical strongholds profited significantly from the sociodemographic shifts ushered in by the buildup of military industries, the politics of economic growth, and the Cold War welfare state. This resulted in the upward mobility of many evangelicals. Socioculturally, the revival thus saw moral traditionalism and fundamentalist religion being embraced by an increasingly suburban, educated, and modern group of people in an environment characterized by corporate high-tech industries, consumer culture, and lavish subsidies provided by postwar government. In turn, evangelicals simultaneously espoused the old-time religion and modern technology, moral conservatism and the norms of consumer capitalism, the fruits of social ascent and the expectation of cataclysmic collapse.

All these developments helped evangelicals attain a measure of theological, cultural, and socioeconomic success within the broader postwar consensus. However, their rabid anti-Catholicism, racist legacy, and residual anti-Semitism continued to mark their distance from the pluralist currents of American culture. Though on the one hand "firmly representative of the world of the American middle class," conservative Protestants were engaged in "a rather strange dance, so to speak, in which conservative evangelicals emulate many trends of popular culture while continuing to denounce America's transgressions."[12] This duality seeped into the marrow of the neo-evangelical institutions, particularly the NAE. While it has received little attention from scholars, the NAE emerged as the most important national organization of the postwar resurgence between the 1940s and the 1960s. It served as a clearinghouse, offered resources, spawned a plethora of successful affiliates, and helped open inroads into government. The NAE provided a broad organizational umbrella and experienced rapid institutional growth. Yet it remained theologically divided and organizationally shaky as denominations both inside and outside the association continued to establish their own institutions. Likewise, many NAE commissions and affiliates became more successful than the mother organization, and parachurch and single-interest groups pulled at its seams. The NAE thus thrived on its broad, inclusive appeal, but also contained the germs of theological infighting, institutional fragmentation, and political division.

Postwar neo-evangelicalism, therefore, constituted an unstable compound as a self-declared "third force" in American Protestantism. Relying upon decentralized and centrifugal structures, it sought to unify a diverse fundamentalist clientele and disillusioned liberals. While deepening religious divisions, it aspired to be theologically inclusive and ecumenical. And while seeking sociocultural relevance within the postwar liberal order, it remained institutionally separatist and doctrinally uncompromising. The combination of organizational consolidation, theological domestication, and cultural accommodation on the one hand, with institutional fragmentation, biblical orthodoxy, and a subcultural identity on the other, fixed the parameters for the movement's later political positioning.

Based on this analysis, chapter 3 examines the period of "mobilization" from roughly the mid-1960s to the mid-1970s. This section paints a very different picture of evangelicalism than is commonly found in media depictions of a resurgent Christian Right. In the 1960s and 1970s, a restless generation of liberal and leftwing "new evangelicals," motivated by the unfulfilled social action aspirations of postwar neo-evangelicalism, challenged the theological orthodoxies, economic conservatism, and cultural traditionalism of the evangelical establishment. By this time even Billy Graham had conceded that in the 1950s he had frequently confused the Kingdom of God with the American way of life. Spearheaded by groups such as Evangelicals for McGovern, Evangelicals for Social Action, the People's Christian Coalition, and the Christian World Liberation Front, the newly resurgent evangelical Left championed women's liberation, pacifism, progressive social justice, and civil rights. Leftwing evangelicals also established links with the insurgent movements of the 1960s, including the civil rights groups and the counterculture. Their public presence ranged from the theological iconoclasm of a Paul Jewett via the principled pacifism of a Jim Wallis to the dedicated antiwar activism of a Mark Hatfield.

Left evangelical hopes for adding a progressive social platform to the postwar revival, however, soon gave way to despair, for a variety of internal and external reasons. Acrimonious debates about sociopolitical involvement and divisive battles over scriptural authority created deep rifts. Moreover, schisms within the Left over race and gender issues, and over political participation and grassroots action, showed that a commitment to redistributive social justice was not a strong enough tie to bind the movement together. Rather than enabling evangelicals to forge a unified agenda, the leftwing resurgence ended up exacerbating the movement's deep ideological and organizational divisions. By the mid-1970s the NAE was weakened from a decade of infighting, and an inward-looking focus on renewing the spiritual mission had replaced substantive sociopolitical activity within the organization.

Nonetheless, the radical evangelicals left a profound imprint on the larger movement. This is illustrated by the development of links between sixties evangelicalism and the counterculture. Cognitive and organizational similarities between revivalist religion and the counterculture meant that left-leaning evangelicals were in the vanguard of the latter's spiritual infiltration. Although opposed to the excesses and moral relativism of the period, the evangelical Left frequently shared the spirit of the sixties: reliance on intuitive knowledge and the ecstatic experience of the divine; emotional spontaneity; a desire for personal conversion; and an aversion to consensus liberalism, large-scale bureaucracies, and technological rationality. Particularly in the 1970s it was not uncommon to see hippies in granny dresses talking about "getting high" on Jesus.

Left evangelical inroads into the counterculture resulted in two crucial developments. On the one hand they paved the way for reintegrating the sixties into the cultural mainstream. In offering loose church structures in combination with a moral critique of liberal capitalism, consumerism, and superpatriotism, left-leaning evangelicals appealed to a generation disenchanted with the Cold War order and attracted by decentralized, unstructured communities. While church organizations were casual, however, their moral message was strict and provided a crucial normative framework for the resocialization of recovering hippies. On the other hand, the appropriation of sixties modes and sentiments further domesticated traditional evangelical conversionism by emphasizing the experiential and therapeutic aspects of Christianity. It promoted the replacement of theological dogma with mystical meaning systems in which the unmediated experience of the divine was the primary way of constructing identity.[13] This found expression in the growth of pentecostal and charismatic groups within the evangelical family at the expense of Calvinist and reformist denominations. The evangelical revival of the 1970s, rather than being nurtured by the rejection of the 1960s, was thus in many ways a "Jesus trip" that grew out of flower power culture. In merging countercultural styles with biblical traditionalism, the evangelical Left carried the distinctive combination of subcultural identity and cultural integration that had been at the core of conservative Protestantism in the 1940s and 1950s into the later period of unrest and upheaval.

Chapter 4 looks at the formation of a rightwing challenge to this leftist and liberal evangelicalism from the mid-1970s to the early 1990s. This period of "militancy" saw the consolidation of the New Christian Right as a dominant, though by no means exclusive, voice of conservative Protestantism. Throughout the postwar neo-evangelical resurgence and the liberal rumblings of the 1960s and 1970s, conservatives had vied for influence within the movement. While left evangelicals denounced the complicity of the churches in oppression and exploitation, the Right condemned social gospel tendencies and demanded a return to a focus on individual soul-saving. It emphasized doctrinal purity over social engagement and the inerrant word over the mystical experience. With their strongholds in the Jim Crow South, conservatives felt increasingly threatened by desegregation, the civil rights movement, and the anti–Vietnam War protests. Among the main rightwing political operators were televangelists such as Oral Roberts, Jimmy Swaggart, Jim Bakker, and Pat Robertson, as well as "neo-fundamentalist" organizations, such as Christian Voice, Religious Roundtable, Moral Majority, American Coalition for Traditional Values, and Concerned Women for America.

Scholars commonly trace the revival of neo-fundamentalism among evangelicals back to separatist institution building and an angry reaction to the sixties. While both the institutional subculture and backlash sentiments were important, however, the conservative wing within the movement had by the 1970s undergone a profound transformation. It had broken out of its cultural confines and entered the political scene with a message that was both militant and moderate, countercultural and conservative, traditionalist and modern. Conservatives developed salience within the movement by appropriating both the integrative and the insurgent impulses of postwar and sixties evangelicalism. Their agenda of socially involved pietism, ecumenical orthodoxy, and single-issue moralism amounted less to an assertion of biblically based religion than to a this-worldly taming of fundamentalism. This set the intellectual and institutional stage for their effort to co-opt establishment evangelicals and sideline the evangelical Left in a series of raucous internal controversies over social action, biblical inerrancy, and the virtues of capitalism. With the evangelical center immobilized and the evangelical Left hopelessly divided, neo-fundamentalists offered an effective response to the wider religious constituency's desire for a unified political and theological voice.

In the same vein, neo-fundamentalism thrived on the appropriation of countercultural themes, rather than their rejection. The Right's political lobbying relied heavily on the rhetoric and organizational techniques gleaned from the insurgent movements, as the right-to-life campaign indicates. Indeed, the boundaries between evangelicalism and the insurgencies were rather more fluid than is commonly assumed. In many ways the Right provided a space for culturally acceptable forms of hippie hedonism, yet discarded the movement's potential for meaningful socioeconomic change. While the Right channeled the hippie search for cultural authenticity into a libertarian ethic of entrepreneurial self-actualization, many hippies-turned-fundamentalists retained a subcultural identity centered on ritualized ecstasy and nonrational systems of knowledge.

Meanwhile the growing ties between neo-fundamentalists and a newly energized secular conservative movement turned the former from an inner-evangelical insurgency into a key player in the wider conservative resurgence. In particular, the positioning of rightwing evangelicalism as both a carrier of anti-establishment sentiments and a culture religion for the liberal capitalist order appealed to those outside the evangelical fold. While returning to a traditional moral home base, the Right's focus on "social issues," such as homosexuality, abortion, busing, and school prayer, broadened its popular appeal beyond the sectarian base. As David H. Watt has noted, the focus on "family values" made it possible for people who would have been puzzled by talk about the Second Advent and the Rapture to sympathize with evangelical concerns.[14] Though rhetorically harking back to the old-time religion, rightwing evangelicalism's scaled-down conversionist theology emphasized secular therapeutic effects and translated business success into a religious drama for an audience not familiar with the intricacies of evangelical liturgy. Likewise, the Right's economic conservatism had a broader allure. It symbolically revived the emancipatory and egalitarian rhetoric of nineteenth-century republican producer-class ideology, with its faith in the link between hard work, self-discipline, economic self-sufficiency, and moral development. At the same time, however, it sanctioned the consumer capitalism, suburbanization, defense-related economic growth, and Sunbelt affluence that had shaped the lives of many in the middle and working classes.

On this basis conservative evangelicals provided a newly energized secular conservative movement with the populist ideology and constituency necessary for electoral success. The Christian Right's combination of radicalism and reaction appealed to both the insurgent mood and the desire for moral certainty after a period of cultural questioning and political disillusionment. Its advocacy of "social issues" provided the Republican party with an effective tool to build a popular base among an electorate that had traditionally eluded its appeal. The politics of morality gave voice to the cultural fears and economic aspirations of the lower-middle and working classes in a post-sixties climate defined by de-industrialization, the decline of unions, the collapse of old-style party machines, and the fraying of traditional structures of social solidarity.

Finally, the conclusion summarizes the book's contribution to the continuing debate about conservative Protestantism, which has raised as many questions as it has answered. It highlights the ways in which the book's findings revise entrenched analytical concepts in the study of postwar evangelicalism, resurgent conservatism, and the relationship between orthodox religion and sociocultural modernity. In common parlance, the "New Right" and "evangelical Christianity" are often used interchangeably, especially by liberal opponents who conjure up the specter of an unholy alliance of fundamentalists, conservative Republicans, wayward southern Democrats, and the extreme Right fringe. In contrast, this book suggests that in order to comprehend evangelicalism, we need to take into account its highly diverse and conflictual nature, its complex relationship with postwar American society and culture, its sustained engagement with the insurgent movements of the 1960s, and the tentativeness of its rightwing affiliation. By the same token, it suggests that the New Christian Right, despite its self-declared hostility to the secular liberal order, constituted another kind of "liberalism," resulting in an attachment to the very socioeconomic and political system that had created the alleged immoralities against which conservatism railed.

# 1

# The Enigma
# of Conservative Protestantism

The dramatic resurgence of white evangelical and fundamentalist Christianity in the United States since the 1940s has left a generation of academics scrambling for explanations. Subscribing to an Enlightenment paradigm that links the appearance of "modernity" to a weakening of religious ideas and institutions, most scholars predicted that religious orthodoxy would ultimately cease to be important. Building upon the theories of seminal thinkers ranging from Karl Marx via Max Weber to Émile Durkheim, researchers expected religion to recede from public life. They attributed this retreat not just to abstract processes of urbanization and industrialization, the spread of science and technology, and the rise of the bureaucratic nation-state, but also to particular secularization agents, such as educators, scientists, bureaucrats, social reformers, and even religious leaders themselves. As religious historian Jon Butler has lamented, scholars subsequently treated religious mobilization merely as a historical "jack-in-the-box" that, when popping up, offered the occasional religious scare in an otherwise largely secular story.[1]

Yet, as the *Economist* reported in 2003, "three times as many Americans believe in the virgin birth as in evolution."[2] What is more, the religious revival was not confined to the spiritual sphere but spilled over into partisan politics, particularly as conservative Protestants mobilized in the aftermath of the cultural and political upheaval of the 1960s and 1970s. In turn, after largely downplaying the political relevance of the evangelical resurgence until this time, scholars subsequently placed conservative Protestantism squarely at the center of momentous sociocultural and political shifts in the United States.[3] Exploring once again the extent to which partisan political changes were rooted in religious realignments, a new generation of historians and social scientists found that religious issues were often the strongest single factor in determining voter behavior.[4] Their research indicated that twentieth-century religious developments prefigured political divides rather as changes in the religious landscape in the eighteenth and nineteenth centuries had shaped the political alignments leading up to the American Revolution and the Civil War. In short, they suggested that the resurgence of evangelicalism as a significant political and cultural force in American society constituted not only one of the most significant developments in American religion since the 1930s, but also one of the most important influences in U.S. politics since the 1960s.[5]

This chapter reviews the key postwar religio-political changes and outlines the main scholarly explanations for the organizational resurgence and political mobilization of conservative Protestants. It critically examines both resurgence and mobilization theories and, in the process, suggests an alternative interpretive approach to understanding the theological, institutional, cultural, and sociopolitical features of postwar evangelicalism.

## Religiosity and the Growth of Evangelicalism after World War II

American society is characterized by a high level of religious belief, which has remained largely stable since the 1940s. About 96 percent of Americans believe in God; 87 percent consider themselves Christians; roughly 60 percent of Americans are churched; nine out of ten Americans never doubted the existence of God; eight in ten say they believe in miracles and will have to answer for their sins on Judgment Day; seven out of ten believe in life after death; and a third have had a particularly powerful religious insight or awakening. In short, the "baseline of religious belief is remarkably high" in the United States, certainly the highest in the Western world.[6]

The two decades after the Second World War were boom times for American Christianity. These years were marked by sustained church growth across the board that either mirrored or outpaced population growth. Between 1940 and 1960, the population grew from 132 million to 178 million, an increase of about 35 percent. During the same period, membership in the United Methodist Church rose from 8.0 to 10.6 million (32 percent). The number of Presbyterians increased from 2.6 to 4.1 million (57.7 percent), and that of Episcopalians from 2.0 to 3.3 million (65 percent). The respective figures for the mainline Evangelical Lutherans are 3.1 to 5.3 million, an increase of 71 percent. The number of Southern Baptists, the largest of the evangelical Protestant denominations, rose from almost 5 million to 9.7 million, an increase of more than 90 percent. The equally theologically conservative Missouri Synod Lutherans grew from 1.3 million to 2.4 million (85 percent). Meanwhile, Roman Catholic numbers doubled from 21 million to 42 million. The wide range of smaller evangelical, pentecostal, and fundamentalist denominations was also part and parcel of this overall expansion. The Assemblies of God grew from a membership of 200,000 to over 500,000 (150 percent), and the Christian Reformed Church from 122,000 to 236,000 (93 percent). Overall, church membership grew from 57.0 percent of the U.S. population in 1940 to 63.3 percent in 1959.[7]

In contrast to the decades immediately after the war, church growth between the 1960s and the 1990s was marked by a distinct disparity. First, the number of self-described secularists, ranging from atheists and agnostics to those not affiliated with any organized religion, roughly doubled. Second, the percentage of Catholics increased from 20 to 27 percent of the population between the 1940s and the late 1980s, while the percentage of Protestants fell from 69 percent to 56 percent. By 1988 the Catholics, the largest single denomination, had grown to 55 million, an increase of another 31 percent.[8] The most dramatic changes, however, took place within the Protestant fold. While mainline Protestant churches experienced either an absolute or a net loss, evangelical and fundamentalist churches saw their membership increase considerably in these decades.

By 1988 the American population had increased from 178 million to 246 million (38 percent), yet United Methodist membership had dropped from 10.6 to slightly over 9 million, a loss of 18 percent. The respective numbers for other mainline churches reveal a similar picture. Although Evangelical Lutheran membership remained roughly the same at 5.3 million, Presbyterians went from 4.1 to 2.9 million (–29 percent), Episcopalians from 3.2 to 2.5 million (–22 percent), and Congregationalists from 2.2 million to 1.6 million (–27 percent). Meanwhile, at the other end of the Protestant spectrum, theologically orthodox denominations thrived. The Southern Baptists solidified their position as the largest Protestant denomination with a membership increase from 9.7 to 14.8 million (53 percent). The Assemblies of God grew from half a million in 1960 to over 2.1 million in 1988 (300 percent). The Church of the Nazarene went from 300,000 to 550,000 (83 percent). And the number of Mormons, the fastest-growing newer religion, increased by a whopping 471 percent from 700,000 to 4 million between 1940 and 1988. In overall terms, by the 1990s about 44 percent of white Protestants were "born-again" Christians. Depending on specific criteria, this translated into a core evangelical constituency of between 20 and 30 percent of the population.[9]

As clear-cut as these figures might appear, however, they fail to reveal the often mind-boggling diversity and complexity of conservative Protestantism and the ongoing controversies about what constitutes an evangelical. The media reports on the New Christian Right and its political influence in recent decades have tended to regard evangelicalism as a unified force in the "culture war." Conservative Protestantism, however, encompasses a much wider variety of doctrinal positions, political viewpoints, religious sentiments, and denominational traditions than is commonly recognized outside the religious fold.

Theologically, the term "evangelical" describes an array of groups and liturgical styles shaped by a plethora of historical events and movements. Both the theologically liberal Evangelical Lutheran Church of America and the theologically orthodox National Association of Evangelicals identify with the term. Even within the orthodox fold, at least a dozen distinct and frequently antagonistic traditions are typically grouped under this umbrella term, ranging from Baptists and Methodists to pentecostals and the Holiness movement. Socioculturally, evangelicals can be found amidst the rich and powerful in the Sunbelt, poor whites of Appalachia, and deprived African American inner-city dwellers. Politically, evangelicalism consists of numerous groups with distinct social and economic views. George Bush and Pat Robertson are evangelicals, but so are Bill Clinton and Jesse Jackson. In the 1980 presidential elections all three main candidates—Ronald Reagan, Jimmy Carter, and John Anderson— were self-declared evangelicals. Conservative Protestants can be found in both the Sanctuary Movement and the Christian Coalition, and there are profound political differences between the neo-fundamentalism of a Jerry Falwell, the mainstream evangelicalism of a Billy Graham, and the leftwing evangelicalism of a Jim Wallis. While Reagan emerged as the most admired man among evangelicals in the authoritative Gallup survey on religion in the late 1980s, he was followed closely by Jesse Jackson and Billy Graham.[10]

This diversity indicates that there is little consensus on defining the term "evangelical." George Gallup's famous finding that 31 percent of Americans and 44 percent of Protestants are "born-again" Christians is intriguing but remains controversial. The number of committed evangelicals already drops significantly when qualifiers are added, such as encouraging others to believe in Christ, and belief in the literal truth of the Bible.[11] Thomas Askew, for example, regards affirmation of the Bible as the sole authority, salvation through faith, a personal conversion experience, the self-conscious nurturing of spirituality, and both evangelical mission and social witness as the basics of evangelical conviction.[12] Meanwhile, James Davison Hunter argues that biblical inerrancy, belief in the divinity of Christ, faith in Jesus as the only hope for salvation, and/or a powerful religious experience are the marks of evangelical identification.[13] In contrast, conservative evangelical Donald Bloesch rejects biblical absolutism because it places God's word "in the power of man, since words and propositions can be mastered by reason." For him, the fundamentalist assumption of inerrancy runs counter to evangelical mysticism.[14] Likewise, conservative political scientist Stuart Rothenberg doubts that belief in the inerrancy of the Bible is useful as a defining criterion. He found that 52 percent of born-again Christians and 54 percent of fundamentalists did not agree with a strict interpretation of the Bible. He also questions whether the status of being "born-again" is necessary for classifying evangelicals.[15]

To add to the confusion, the terms "evangelical" and "fundamentalist" do not encompass the same people. Fundamentalists are evangelical, Joel Carpenter concludes, but not all evangelicals are fundamentalists.[16] Furthermore, evangelicals do not particularly enjoy being called fundamentalists, and vice versa. Fundamentalists tend to be the more militant wing within evangelicalism. They emphasize doctrinal purity over social action, the inerrant word over the mystical experience, and separatism over inclusiveness. Whereas modern American evangelicalism was formed in the upheavals of the Great Awakenings of the eighteenth and nineteenth centuries, fundamentalism emerged from the fierce cultural battles of the early twentieth century, when new immigrants threatened Protestant domination in America, industrialization and urbanization challenged the norms of traditional Christianity, and higher criticism questioned the literal truth of the Bible. All definitions of evangelicalism thus remain problematic; indeed, Donald Dayton has called the term an "essentially contested concept" and suggested that we do away with it completely.[17]

While defining evangelicalism is thus tantamount to stepping into a cognitive minefield, we can nonetheless identify its main components by looking at the diversity of its roots. Indeed, I would agree with Mark Noll that the term retains its usefulness in designating a particular strand of Protestantism located somewhere between fundamentalists and mainline moderates.[18] Historically, modern American evangelicalism is a descendant of seventeenth-century Puritanism, the Great Awakenings of the eighteenth and nineteenth centuries, and the fundamentalist-modernist debates of the early twentieth century. Puritan reformation theology insisted on the supreme authority of the Bible for belief and practice. It advocated justification by faith alone, without any merits from good works, emphasized scriptural Christocentrism and Christ's atonement for our sins, and asserted the priesthood of all believers. Its Augustinian anthropology and Calvinist doctrines of predestination and election placed the emphasis on man's depravity, the need for repentance and conversion, and the search for spiritual purity through separation of the believer from worldly and sensual pleasures.

In the ensuing centuries, Great Awakening revivalism sought to bridge the gap between the personal, emotional experience of God in popular frontier religion and the highly rationalized forms of highbrow Protestantism. This brought a new emphasis on personal regeneration (being "born again") and a commitment to the doctrine of sanctification and personal appropriation of grace. It also unleashed a postmillennial optimism that generated a wave of mass evangelization, world mission, and social activism, ranging from the temperance movement to abolitionism. In the words of Michael Kazin, a "messianic, anti-hierarchical, Jesus-centered faith" became the dominant expression of American Protestantism. It also promoted congregational or democratic forms of government and a proneness to sectarian divisions.[19]

The first half of the twentieth century added yet another dimension to evangelicalism. The modernist critique of the Bible as a culture-bound work of literature, and sociocultural challenges to Protestant dominance, spawned a militant reaction. In turn, fundamentalism constituted itself as a movement against higher criticism. By the same token, its adherents rallied in opposition to the social gospel, which pursued societal change on the basis of postmillennialist beliefs and liberal theology. Fundamentalists embraced biblical inerrancy, premillennial notions of decline and destruction prior to Christ's Second Coming, and strict biblical morality. They also sought to separate themselves from what they considered liberal apostasy, while simultaneously pursuing an alliance with political and social conservatism. The ensuing modernist-fundamentalist controversies were the culmination of the "great reversal" of evangelicalism away from social action and toward separatist piety. They decoupled the social gospel from orthodox traditions and effectively split evangelicalism into a conservative and a liberal camp.[20]

The resurgence of conservative Protestantism since World War II can be divided into three further stages. The period from the early 1940s to the mid-1960s, dominated by moderate neo-evangelicalism, saw the fledgling recovery of theological respectability, institutional cohesion, and cultural engagement. At the same time, the rift between fundamentalism and evangelicalism was institutionalized in the formation of competing organizations. On the one hand, Carl McIntire's American Council of Christian Churches (ACCC, founded in 1941) demanded strict separatism and doctrinal purity. On the other hand, Harold John Ockenga, Carl F. H. Henry, Billy Graham, and other leading lights in the National Association of Evangelicals (NAE, 1942) focused on evangelism and on creating a broad interdenominational evangelical base.

This was followed by a second stage from roughly the mid-1960s to the mid-1970s, a period of renewed evangelical social activism, political involvement, and cultural recognition beyond the orthodox fold. At the same time, however, the decade was characterized by fragmentation and purges. It saw the rise of leftwing and liberal evangelicalism and the intensification of theological battles within evangelical denominations, particularly over the issue of inerrancy. A third stage began in the mid-1970s. It was marked by neo-fundamentalist consolidation and the rise of the New Christian Right as the main, though not exclusive, voice of conservative Protestantism.[21]

Although rightwing evangelicals dominate the political arena as a result of a tremendous organizational effort and skillful lobbying, radical and liberal groups in the movement continue to vie with conservatives for theological, cultural, and political influence. What is more, the abovementioned defining components of evangelical theological identity not only form a historical sequence, but also remain present in the contemporary movement. Hence, the legacy of the Reformation in the United States is embodied in the churches in the reformed (Calvinist) tradition and its ties to Puritanism. The spirit of revivalism is most clearly expressed in (Wesleyan) Methodism and Baptism, as well as in the newer pentecostal and charismatic churches. And fundamentalist sentiments can mainly be found in the churches organized in the ACCC, a range of conservative parachurch organizations, and the New Christian Right.

## Religious Realignments and the Political Mobilization of Evangelicals

Underneath these remarkable religious growth dynamics, another development reshaped the sectarian landscape in the United States. In the decades after the Second World War, a new split cut across the traditional religious triad of Protestant–Catholic–Jew in the United States. Dividing these groups along liberal-conservative lines, it defined differences in ideological rather than denominational terms. In turn, a new form of cultural conflict emerged, based less on membership in a faith tradition and more on levels of religious commitment, the orthodoxy of religious belief, and diametrically opposed moral assumptions.[22] While the "orthodox" believed in fixed and universal moral norms and located authority in a transcendent source outside human society, the "progressives" regarded moral codes as socially and historically constructed and located authority in human reason, science, and culture.[23]

Resurgent evangelicalism lay at the heart of this new divide. Believing in absolute moral codes and orthodox Biblicism, conservative Protestants increasingly felt that they had more in common with conservative Catholics and Jews than with liberal members of their own theological tradition, who had a more relativistic understanding of morality and emphasized the historicity of sacred texts. This had a dual effect on evangelicalism. On the one hand it deepened the estrangement evangelicals felt from the mainstream Protestant denominations. On the other hand, however, it opened up new opportunities for ecumenism among conservative Catholics, Protestants, and Jews. While the diminishing role of denominational differences helped evangelicals to break out of their theological confines and soften their harsh doctrinal and separatist image, the new appeal of orthodox forms of religion allowed conservative Protestants to present themselves as defenders of the true faith against the onslaught of theological liberalism and secular humanism.[24]

In turn, evangelicalism gained new cultural influence. Two developments were at the center of this process. First, the conversion experience that formed evangelicalism's "conceptual core" (Michael Lienesch) worked itself into the broader religio-cultural texture of postwar American society as a "mood, a perspective, an approach grounded in biblical theology" (Thomas Askew).[25] Understood as a general inner transformation subsequent to the intuitive and heart-wrenching realization of God's presence, conversionism was no longer exclusively wedded to an evangelical theological doctrine and liturgical tradition, but was increasingly appropriated by all denominations. Second, although the conversion experience in twentieth-century conservative Protestantism emphasized the redemption of individuals, it could easily shift toward "a way of thinking that can be applied not only to oneself but also to society."[26] Conversionism's tenet that the sinful heart and mind are the root cause of both personal and social ills means that the moral quality of society will change if individuals are "born again." It conceptualizes a revival not only as an individual spiritual renewal, but also as a collective return to traditional biblical values in a public rite of repenting and humbling oneself before God in search of salvation.[27]

What is more, this division along liberal-orthodox lines, many political analysts argue, did not remain confined to the religious realm. It also had tangible political consequences as the sociocultural upheaval of the 1960s and 1970s translated the split into a broader partisan conflict and changed the religious composition of the political parties. By the late twentieth century, a new political divide based on divergent moral values, lifestyles, and levels of religious orthodoxy and commitment had in part replaced class, race, ethnicity, region, and denomination as the main determinants of partisan identity. In short, the postwar religious realignment led to a starker normative profile of the feuding political camps that manifested itself in the "culture war." The two-party system within American religion was thus extended into the world of politics and government.

Using the findings of the National Election Studies, political scientist Geoffrey Layman in particular put forward an elaborate model showing that religious changes prefigured major political shifts and that partisan identities were increasingly defined by fundamentally different assumptions about moral authority.[28] Since the 1960s, Layman notes, the alignment of party loyalties has been undergoing significant change. Traditionally, both mainline and evangelical Protestants outside the South were predominantly Republican, while Catholics, Jews, and southern white Protestants identified with the Democratic party. By the 1990s, however, things had changed dramatically. Among Protestants, the presence of mainline religionists had declined in the Republican coalition, while southern evangelicals, once the religious backbone of the Democratic coalition, were likely to vote Republican. Among Catholics, traditionally a solid Democratic clientele, liberals continued to identify with the Democrats, while traditionalists had switched to the Republicans. Broadly speaking, while the Democratic coalition had a higher overall level of religious orthodoxy in the 1960s than did the Republican coalition, by the late 1990s the Republicans had become much more religiously orthodox than the Democrats. This divide between traditionalists and modernists gradually weakened the established ethno-religious and denominational structure of partisanship. In short, the more orthodox and committed members of religious groups were, the more Republican they tended to be. Conversely, those who were more liberal and less committed tended to identify with the Democratic party.[29]

The most striking example of this change was the seminal shift in the political identification of southern and western evangelicals from overwhelmingly Democratic in the 1960s and most of the 1970s to increasingly more Republican in the 1980s and 1990s.[30] In 1952 and 1956, evangelicals disproportionately supported liberal Democrat Adlai Stevenson.[31] The traditional link between evangelicals and the Democratic party, however, began to unravel in the 1960s. The religiously charged 1960 presidential elections, which resulted in the first Roman Catholic president, saw the first major defection of evangelical Protestants to the Republicans. During the 1964 Goldwater campaign, evangelicals also flexed their political muscle. Likewise, George McGovern's strong commitment to political and racial liberalism in the 1972 presidential election pushed many evangelicals into voting for Richard Nixon.[32] Nonetheless, well into the 1970s evangelicals remained politically split. While the majority of northern evangelicals voted Republican, their counterparts in the South and the West largely continued to be a loyal Democratic constituency. Indeed, Jimmy Carter in 1976 temporarily succeeded in halting the trend away from the Democratic party.[33]

In the ensuing decades, however, not only did evangelicals become more politically engaged, but their support for the Republican party steadily increased. A majority voted for Ronald Reagan in 1980, and despite their misgivings about his lukewarm approach to social issues, they cemented this political alliance in the 1984 elections. Four years later George H. W. Bush received overwhelming evangelical support.[34] By the end of the twentieth century, evangelicals, previously at least in part an important component of the New Deal coalition, were one of the most strongly Republican groups in the broader religious spectrum. Whereas less than 20 percent of devout evangelicals identified themselves as Republican in 1966, the figure had risen to well above 50 percent by 1996. Likewise, their identification with the Democratic party, which climaxed in 1964 with close to 60 percent, had dropped to about 25 percent by 1996.[35]

The religious divide itself, however, does not explain why evangelicals became increasingly involved in partisan politics. Indeed, theological orthodoxy and high levels of moral commitment could equally have been channeled into anything ranging from apolitical pietism to radical social activism. In seeking to clarify how and why the patterns of the postwar religious resurgence manifested themselves in party politics, Layman and others focus on the interplay of two specific mobilizing agents: changes in the political salience of religion, and changes in the nature, institutional structures, and strategic incentives of the party system.

First, they argue that the political salience of religion in general increased as the devoutness and commitment of religionists, especially the clergy, translated into political activism and, in turn, became an important source of organizational skills and resources. Indeed, a study of election data between 1952 and 1996 identified religion as the second most important "cleavage" separating American voters after race and ahead of class and gender.[36] Although the specific political effects of this phenomenon differed across the religious traditions, the relationship between religious orthodoxy, commitment, and support for the Republican party could be seen in all of them. In the case of evangelical Protestants, the major change was a large increase in the connection between religious commitment and Republicanism, whereas among mainline Protestants and Catholics, it was doctrinal orthodoxy that translated into support for the GOP.[37]

Second, they suggest that the changing party system turned these issues into partisan divides. The increasingly porous character of American parties in the twentieth century, supported by changes ranging from the introduction of open primaries to the reforms of the 1970s, took control away from party leaders. It opened up opportunities for motivated grassroots activists to shape the party platform, and provided strategic incentives to champion divisive cultural issues. In many cases suburban churches even replaced traditional urban party machines as get-out-the-vote organizations. Rather than being channeled into the formation of interest groups, protest movements, or third-party organizations, the religious cleavage was thus transposed into the established partisan political realm.[38]

In the end, the liberal-orthodox divide and the concomitant shift in the religious composition of the partisan coalitions meant that the determinants of political identification had changed profoundly in the United States. Between the end of the Second World War and the 1970s, partisan affiliation had largely revolved around socioeconomic issues. As the new liberal-orthodox divide manifested itself politically, however, partisanship became increasingly dominated by religiously based differences in the electorate's perception of social reality and moral truth. By the 1990s, as issues such as abortion rights, homosexuality, teenage pregnancy, drugs, family values, welfare reform, busing, and school prayer gained political salience, levels of religious orthodoxy and commitment became more reliable indicators of partisan affiliation than ethnic background, religious denomination, or socioeconomic status.

Rooted in fundamental divisions in moral views, the realignments of the "culture war" also meant that the class basis of the party system had weakened. Lower-status citizens identified themselves much less with the Democrats. Meanwhile, the Republican ties of the upper class had become slightly weaker. Indeed, the Republican mobilization of evangelicals, particularly via the New Christian Right, was part of the emergence of a new populist conservatism that constituted a "momentous break with an elitist conservatism unable to shed its association with the smug and wealthy."[39] In offering a populist agenda that embraced strict morality, the traditional work ethic, and American patriotism, it addressed the anxieties of working- and lower-middle-class voters aroused by insurgent groups such as the feminist movement, civil rights activists, and student demonstrators. This significantly strengthened the electoral fortunes of conservatism by providing the party with a socioeconomic base beyond its affluent upper-middle-class and business clientele. By achieving the elusive goal of mobilizing lower- and middle-class voters who had traditionally viewed Republicans as unfriendly to their economic interests, the party was finally able to overcome one of its fundamental obstacles to electoral success in the postwar period.[40]

## Explaining the Resurgence of Evangelicalism

The growth of evangelicalism, its theological realignment, the emergence of the "politics of morality," and the partisan mobilization of conservative Protestants outlined above are widely recognized phenomena among scholars of religion and politics. Nonetheless, there is little consensus about their causes. Indeed, the concomitant rise of modernity and of conservative Protestantism not only defied many of the basic assumptions about the secularism of modern industrial societies; it also contradicted established notions about religiosity as a dependent variable of socioeconomic status. Most scholars had traditionally associated upward social mobility with more ecumenical and culture-affirming forms of religious expression, and a lower socioeconomic status with more orthodox religious orientations. On this basis they viewed followers of conservative religion as socially, economically, and culturally liminal people. They depicted them as living predominantly in rural areas or small towns, and as belonging to lower educational, income, and occupational groups.[41] Now confronting them, however, was a thoroughly modernized, upwardly mobile, and organizationally cutting-edge group of people who embraced not only religious revivalism, but its most orthodox and conservative expressions. In the South and the West in particular, evangelicals thrived in a setting that combined military and high-tech industries, the emergence of affluent white-collar suburbs, and a proclivity for staunch moral and religious conservatism.[42]

In seeking to explain the perseverance of orthodox forms of religion despite manifestations of socioeconomic ascent and processes of modernization, scholars have advanced five main interpretations. First, sociologists of religion in particular link evangelicalism's renewed cultural legitimacy and influence to its accommodation to modernity, rather than its assertion of traditionalism. A second school of thought sees the resurgence as rooted in evangelicalism's functional role in postwar American society. Third, economistic models link the movement's successes to its competitiveness in a society characterized by spiritual pluralism and market orientation. A fourth analysis focuses on the "subcultural" internal organizational resources of conservative Protestants and their engagement in transdenominational coalition building. Finally, some researchers suggest that if population growth and church membership are controlled for, the religious landscape in the United States, rather than revealing an increased level of religiousness, hides a trend toward secularization. What follows is a brief critical review of these main interpretive strands.

## Modernization

Modernization theorists initially brought into play the concept of status anxiety as a way of explaining the evangelical resurgence. While they no longer regarded evangelicals as economically marginal, they nonetheless located their religious fervor in the reactions of an uprooted suburban middle class and upwardly mobile blue-collar workers against the cultural and economic upheaval caused by processes of modernization.[43] This concept of status anxiety, however, did not address the fundamental theoretical problems posed by the coexistence of conservative religion and modernity. Instead, it continued to construct modernizing processes as a normative baseline in which evangelicalism was little more than an epiphenomenon of deeper social realities. Rather than being understood on its own terms, orthodox religion was defined as a reaction against, a deviation from, or an adjustment to the given modern setting. As historian Jon Butler has noted, this ignored the continued salience of theological traditions and their long-term pragmatic engagement with the secular realm.[44]

Seeking to overcome this dilemma, sociologists of religion in particular began to explore more thoroughly the link between evangelicalism and modernization. Rather than understanding conservative Protestantism as being at odds with and reacting against modernity, Peter Berger, James Davison Hunter, Martin Marty, Mark Shibley, and others located its renewed cultural influence in its compatibility with and promotion of key modernizing trends of postwar American society. Evangelicalism, they maintained, was not an outdated and backward-looking religion. Instead, it was characterized by the appropriation of the cognitive assumptions of modernity and the norms of consumer culture. Rather than being in an adversarial relationship with modernity, evangelicalism found itself in a symbiotic one.[45] The popular postwar Youth for Christ movement, for example, copied the youth culture of the time with its fashions and celebrities, pepped-up music, fast-paced shows, and radio-style intensity.[46] Famed evangelist Billy Graham combined cultural modernity, use of the latest communications technology, and up-to-date personnel mobilization with an apocalyptic and countercultural message.[47] And theologian Carl F. H. Henry saw in the postwar resurgence a "strategic opportunity" to overcome evangelicalism's "hesitant attitude toward scientific endeavor" and to "stress the realities of a rational, purposive universe that coheres in the Logos as the agent in creation, preservation, redemption, sanctification and judgement."[48] Moreover, evangelical churches often acted as social and cultural innovators. Some, particularly pentecostalism and the Holiness traditions, were in the vanguard of the ordination of women, had a high percentage of female ministers, and introduced innovative and creative church practices.[49]

Many observers thus argued that neo-evangelicalism's prominent place within the mainstream of American culture by the end of the 1950s attested to its power of cultural assimilation, rather than to the assertion of evangelical distinctiveness. They regarded its main concepts and features as integral parts of the processes of modernization and secularization. These included the emphasis on the individual faith experience as an actively chosen status, the promise of spontaneous and personal access to supernatural knowledge, and the denial of hierarchical authority. Moreover, the absence of strong traditions and institutional ties in evangelicalism, and its high level of organizational mobility, made it a distinctly modern phenomenon.[50] Likewise, the possibility of complete personal change offered in conversion theology could be easily reconciled with, for example, the Enlightenment faith in what Thomas Paine had famously called the ability to "make the world over again." In James Davison Hunter's view, the personalization of the religious message in evangelicalism constituted a shift from "a concern with the proclamation of an objective and universal truth to a concern with the subjective applicability of truth," and thus embodied an alignment to the normative codes of modern pluralism.[51] As Robert Ellwood put it, the emphasis on the individual in popular evangelicalism had its origin in the existentialist focus on subjectivity and the heroic rebel.[52]

This symbiosis of modernity and traditionalism ultimately blunted the jagged theological edges of the movement. Adopting modern advertising techniques, using state-of-the art technology, relying on modern organizational and managerial principles, and catering to the tastes of new audiences influenced the evangelical message itself. In turn, evangelicals increasingly identified with the more materialistic, market-driven, and individualistic trajectories of American society. They abandoned the humility, self-doubt, and "tortured millennialism" (Hugh Heclo) of their Puritan forebears. Instead, they embraced a triumphalist and self-congratulatory "God-is-on-our-side" rhetoric that sanctified the American social order and promoted a therapeutic Christianity that primarily asked "what God can do for you."[53] Even as sympathetic an observer as Joel Carpenter linked aspects of Carl Henry's theology, such as his rejection of dispensationalism, to social ascent and middle-class respectability.[54]

As part of this "cognitive contamination" of evangelicalism, the conversion experience, a crucial component in orthodox identity, became less associated with self-denial, awareness of sin, and tough moral codes than with health, business success, and self-esteem. Conversion came to mean psychological healing. Promising prosperity and well-being through faith, it used Jesus as a "kind of theological chaser, making it all go down easier."[55] Evangelical leaders stressed broad principles and emphasized the functional and therapeutic dimensions of belief in the supernatural. Specific liturgies and denominational exclusiveness increasingly gave way to sermons on how faith empowered people and helped them become more affluent and better integrated. Carpenter and others called this "cheap grace." Evangelist Tammy Bakker, however, simply stated: "Today we take vitamins, trust God, and eat well."[56]

The NAE's postwar foray into the field of "industrial chaplaincy" provides a good example of the way in which religious concepts were rephrased in therapeutic terms. Seeking to build upon the growing postwar interest in personnel counseling, the chairman of the Industrial Chaplaincy Commission, A. Herman Armerding, explicitly touted religion as a means to a secular end—namely, to boost worker morale, efficiency, and productivity.[57] He located the causes of industrial unrest in individual maladjustment and a "lack of experience of conversion." In response, he put forth the concepts of "theo-psychotherapy" and "pneumatology," which regarded religion as the key to employee happiness and success. He also called on scientifically trained counselors "with a working knowledge of both mental and social hygiene" to address individual moral and adjustment problems.[58]

Evangelical content was thus transformed into an acceptable cultural expression "firmly representative of the world of the American middle class."[59] In evangelical beliefs and practices, piety gave way to moralism, and theology to ethics.[60] By elevating choice, flexibility, individual sovereignty, and free enterprise, evangelicalism provided spiritual sanctioning for business success and translated it into a religious drama in which the awakening constituted a relegitimation of the core myths of the American way of life. The converted individual was thus ultimately the bourgeois individual.[61]

## Functionalism

Meanwhile, a second influential school of thought drew upon the functionalist and social-relational theories developed by Talcott Parsons and others in order to explain the evangelical phenomenon. Its advocates linked the resurgence of evangelicalism to religion's role in norm maintenance and social integration under the conditions of weak public institutions and large-scale socioeconomic change. During and after World War II, Texas, Florida, California, Arizona, and other states where evangelicals had their traditional strongholds benefited disproportionally from both the buildup of military industries and a range of middle-class benefits, including the GI Bill, Social Security, housing subsidies, and mortgage support. By the 1960s conservative Protestantism in parts of the South and the West had become largely a suburban phenomenon. Evangelicals were no longer significantly more rural, older, poorer, or less educated than the average American. Indeed, those who had relocated from the Midwest to the Sunbelt to work in military-related industries often experienced a significant improvement of their economic fortunes in a government-subsidized technocratic setting.[62]

In spite of these potentially secularizing socioeconomic trends, however, evangelical churches were able to thrive amidst the social challenges of war-related dislocation. Postwar social and economic changes eroded loyalties to particular faiths, hastened the decline of denominational religion, and encouraged loose church structures and individualized searches for spiritual communities. Less tied to an established institutional heritage than mainline churches, trans-denominational organizations therefore had an advantage over traditional denominational identities. In turn, evangelical forms of instantaneous religious community, such as parachurches, free-standing congregations, and special purpose groups, became highly attractive in the postwar suburban setting, where people were mobile and separated from their traditional sociocultural contexts but frequently retained their religious habits and moral conservatism. Sparkling suburban churches, such as Robert Schuller's Crystal Cathedral, frequently predated enclosed shopping malls and their car-centered architecture.[63] Indeed, anecdotal evidence indicates "an engagement between religion and suburbanization so strong that it accounts for the exceptional rise in church membership among Americans between 1945 and 1970."[64]

Seen from a functionalist perspective, churches provided the social services that were lacking in the Sunbelt as private developers, encouraged by public subsidies, put up one suburban tract development after another without providing proper spaces for playgrounds, recreation facilities, schools, community centers, and the like. Offering nurseries, counseling, youth groups, choirs, preschools, and other services, suburban evangelical churches soon provided a cradle-to-grave subculture. This reflected the shift in emphasis from churches as sources of faith to churches as providers of spiritual and community resources for personal and family needs. As they embarked on their quest to claim the "crabgrass frontier," evangelicals were thus able to replicate the institution-building successes of Methodists and Baptists in the nineteenth-century West.[65]

Likewise, Christian shopping centers, supermarkets, and other "born-again businesses" created a baptized counterpart to secular suburban middle-class life that combined the embrace of the trappings of modernity with the rejection of secular liberalism. As Bethany Moreton has convincingly argued, "Christian corporations" such as Wal-Mart addressed many of the socioeconomic insecurities generated by changes in race and gender relations, the rise of a globalized postindustrial economy, and service-sector employment by promoting family-friendly, home-protecting, religious-values-oriented policies. While pursuing cut-throat business practices, engaging in fierce anti-unionism, and offering low wages, Wal-Mart successfully defined the corporation as a family in ways that compensated for benefits previously gained through union organizing. For example, it offered flexible scheduling that allowed a largely female workforce to attend to their "home duties" and glorified the role of women as mothers and wives.[66]

## Competitiveness

Researchers who emphasize the role of markets in sustaining religiosity have added to this mosaic of interpretations. In their view, the vigorous competition between sectarian groups in a liberal capitalist society, rather than their social function or accommodation to modernity, explained the vitality of religion in the United States. They attributed the rise in religious involvement and the resurgence of evangelicalism to the ability of sectarian suppliers to satisfy the demand for spiritual "goods." People separated from their denominational grounding and their traditional sociocultural contexts, Robert Ellwood has argued, often linked their identity to their ability to choose. Thus religion in the 1950s, more than during any previous decade, turned into a spiritual marketplace. "Ordinary people wanted products whose basic principles were easy to understand, user friendly and troublefree, whether in home appliances or faiths." In turn, the theological liberal Norman Vincent Peale, the Catholic Bishop Fulton Sheen, and the evangelical Billy Graham became the "big three" vendors of modern spirituality.[67]

Similarly, economic historian Robert Fogel has argued that the growing desire for spiritual resources, such as a sense of purpose, social inclusion, self-esteem, and a deeper meaning in life, was at the root of the appeal of evangelicalism. The postwar welfare state's successes in income transfer and the general growth in health and life expectancy, he maintained, had resulted in a decline in sociocultural inequality. In turn, as traditional bread-and-butter concerns receded in the competition for votes in the American religio-political landscape, "moral issues" became more important. Although the income gap once again started to increase dramatically in the 1980s, the moral and cultural agenda of religious conservatism in his view more fully addressed the modern need for more equality in the distribution of spiritual, rather than physical, resources.[68] This analysis also provided an explanation of the comparatively low levels of religious identification in Northern and Western Europe. Since these societies were less market-driven and more structurally stable and regulated, normative codes were reinforced via community relations and publicly funded social services. These provided social connections, meaning that the church was not required, to the same extent as in the United States, as a social space and a spiritual home for shared heritages and experiences. Instead, religious institutions, often in the form of established churches, were taken for granted as part of the cultural landscape.

## Cognitive Resilience

In contrast to studies that focused on the way conservative Protestantism adopted or adjusted to modernity, religious scholars such as Joel Carpenter and George Marsden have emphasized evangelicalism's protean and innovative elements as the key to understanding its enduring appeal. Although they accepted that evangelicalism was both subject to accommodationist pressures and often a willing executioner of capitalist market strategies, they contended that it remained grounded in an epistemological and institutional difference. In their view, theological beliefs and subcultural resources, rather than sociostructural dynamics, needed to be considered in order to understand the evangelical phenomenon. In effect, they raised Talcott Parsons's old question: Does modernization truly promote secularization, or does it simply force people to express their religiousness in different ways? In other words, why should we assume that modernity is working its way into evangelical affections, when it could also be that modern conceptions of self and society are defined by evangelical narratives?[69]

Carpenter, for example, has credited the buildup of an alternative church-based movement infrastructure in the 1930s with providing the institutional basis of postwar evangelicalism. Adaptive to the deprivations of the Great Depression, evangelicals successfully established new subcultural institutions, such as Bible institutes, day schools, seminaries, colleges, foreign mission societies, publishing houses, journals, and radio stations. These provided protective "shelter belts" for conservative Christians that could later be used to launch a new campaign for mass evangelization.[70] Similarly, George Marsden, Robert Wuthnow, and others regard the networks linking "positive fundamentalists" and conservatives within the mainline Protestant denominations as instrumental in bringing about the evangelical revival. While evangelicals distanced themselves from separatist fundamentalism, conservatives questioned the modernist and postmillennialist tendencies of liberal Protestantism. In turn, a remarkably high degree of consensus prevailed among Protestants after the Second World War. Although the new evangelicalism remained a religiously diverse movement, it finally shed the Menckenite image of religious backcountry bacchanalia and donned the stylish outfits and clean-cut looks of a Billy Graham, who offered a transdenominational, transracial, and transethnic alternative to traditional fundamentalism. In the same vein, the NAE exemplified the effectiveness of new links between separatist evangelicals and conservatives who had remained in mainline denominations.[71]

## Secularization

Finally, scholars at the other end of the interpretive spectrum have questioned the notion that the high levels of religiosity in the United States indicated that the country was indeed out of sync with the secularization trends characteristic of other modern industrialized nations. Pippa Norris and Ronald Inglehart, for example, have suggested that the global expansion of religion could be attributed largely to population growth. In their view, immigration rates from Latin America and extreme levels of socioeconomic inequality largely explain the high incidence of religiousness in the United States. If one controlled for these factors, they claim, the country would show significant movement toward secularization.[72]

Similarly, other researchers found that active rates of churchgoing have dropped and are nowadays far below rates of private faith. Although eight in ten Americans say they are Christians, only four in ten know that Jesus delivered the Sermon on the Mount, and only half could name the four gospels. This "cycle of biblical illiteracy" (as Gallup and Castelli call it) brings to mind Henry Steele Commager's old quip that in the United States religion prospered while theology went slowly bankrupt.[73] However, while belonging in the sense of church membership and attendance has clearly suffered, personal faith and levels of religious commitment have intensified. Though organized religion is on the wane, spiritual concerns are growing, and a rising percentage of the public throughout advanced industrial societies is apparently spending time thinking about the meaning and purpose of life.[74]

## Three Critiques

In contrast to the explanations of the political mobilization of evangelicals discussed earlier, the various interpretations of the organizational resurgence of the movement cast doubt on three staple elements of the culture war and backlash theses. First, they query the automatic link between theological and political conservatism and the depth of the evangelical alliance with the Republican party. Second, they note the lack of significant societal polarization along "culture war" lines at grassroots levels. And, third, they maintain that socioeconomic and sociodemographic factors remain more important in explaining partisan realignments than moral orientations.

## *Critique I: Political Diversity*

The close association between Protestant orthodoxy and political conservatism, James Davison Hunter has noted, "is perhaps the most reliable and enduring of all commonplaces concerning this subject."[75] By assuming an intrinsic affinity between conservative Protestantism and rightwing politics, however, most observers ignore the fact that in U.S. history the link between theological and socioeconomic conservatism remains tenuous at best. In the past, evangelicalism constituted a distinct cultural and intellectual tradition whose egalitarian and democratic impulses had fanned the flames of abolitionism, the women's suffrage movement, Populism, and American socialism. Despite the apparent trend toward political conservatism after the Second World War, evangelicalism continued to consist politically of numerous groups with distinct social and economic views.[76] Analyzing a *Christianity Today* poll conducted in 1956, evangelical theologian Carl Henry noted that "the turmoil of conflicting Protestant opinion on far-reaching social issues may provide little comfort to those who feel that the church should vote and act with one mind on the political scene." In his view, the diversity of opinion on leading social issues constituted a great risk for churches aiming to become lobbying groups for specific policies. "Division on social strategy runs as deep today as the theological cleavage in Protestantism," he concluded.[77] Even by the mid-1970s, roughly two-thirds of the critical studies of conservative religion failed to discover a clear link between theological conservatism and other forms of conservative beliefs. As one researcher put it, only when "orthodoxy is combined with . . . radically 'fundamentalist' views does it show frequent correlations with conservative secular attitudes."[78]

Although in overall terms evangelical political loyalties shifted to the Republican party, evangelicals remained politically divided. Crucially, evangelical dealignment from the Democrats did not automatically translate into Republican gains. Despite the racial and cultural liberalism embraced by the Democratic party in the 1960s and 1970s, which alienated the largely southern and white evangelicals, most of them either grudgingly stayed with the Democrats or became independents until the 1980s. The Baptists, for example, the second-largest religious group and one of the most religiously orthodox, were politically conservative yet remained mostly Democratic in their party affiliation.[79] Indeed, as noted earlier, what drove partisan realignment was often not theological identity as such, but the level of religious commitment and church attendance. Regularly attending evangelicals exhibited a strong Republican partisan identification, whereas the identification with the GOP among less observant evangelicals increased only marginally in the 1980s and 1990s. Republican gains were especially high among northern regular attenders and among southerners, and particularly spectacular among churchgoing evangelicals under the age of 35. However, Republicans were significantly less successful among pentecostals and independent fundamentalist denominations. Moreover, while there is evidence that traditionalist evangelicals are more Republican than mainline Protestants, modernist evangelicals are often more Democratic than religious traditionalists in the mainline and Catholic communities. In other words, the Republican party effectively mobilized the most devout and committed wing of evangelicalism, but did not equally reach into the broader evangelical spectrum.[80]

There were similar variations within other religious traditions. Among Catholics and mainline Protestants, for example, theologically orthodox parishioners, rather than those who were religiously committed, were more likely to vote for the Republican party. Not only did Catholics in general remain loyal to the Democratic coalition, but even the religiously more observant ones were more likely to identify with the Democrats. In summation, these discrepancies between orthodoxy and commitment as factors in partisanship suggest that the culture war model of a partisan divide, which sees secularists and religious modernists lined up on one side and the religiously orthodox on the other, has not fully come to pass. While there have been critical shifts in the religious bases of the party system, no general political alliance centered on religious orthodoxy has replaced partisan ties rooted in ethno-religious identities. As Layman concludes, "just as was the case thirty years ago, white Protestants constitute a majority of Republican identifiers, while Catholics, Jews, and black Protestants are much more likely to be Democrats." Rather than having undergone a realignment, the American party system since the 1960s has in fact been in a state of "dealignment."[81]

## Critique II: The Limitations of the Culture War

The diverse political identities of evangelicals and the continuing importance of ethno-religious loyalties also cast doubts on the notion of a general deepening of the cultural polarization of American society. A number of researchers have noted the lack of sufficient evidence of a hardening of the cultural divide at the grassroots level.[82] Waged mainly by small political elites, the culture war does not reflect a pervasive bunker mentality in the broader populace. In addition, analysts have found it difficult to identify a single organizing axis of conflict that defines the two ideological camps. "Actual public opinion is more a both/and than either/or," as many people "hold and understand the usefulness of two potentially contradictory positions, using them situationally in varying relevant contexts."[83]

Neither did religion prove divisive enough to produce two mutually exclusive moral-cultural camps. Overall, most studies confirmed the mildness and centrism of American religion.[84] For most Americans, the *Economist* pointed out in 2003, churchgoing was "a matter of personal belief, not conservative activism." The biggest change in American religious life in the past 40 years was that the number of survey respondents who maintained that the purpose of churches was to teach people to live better lives increased from half to almost three-quarters. Indeed, religious belief had a Volkswagen Beetle profile: "A bump of evangelical Protestants at the front, a bigger bulge of uncensorious congregations in the middle, and a stubby secular tail."[85]

These findings mirror conclusions about long-term trends in American religion since World War II. They indicate that the postwar spiritual boom was cultural, rather than theological, and that this "culture religion" frequently amounted to a shallow, self-congratulatory rationalization of the "American high." In his famous book on religion in the 1950s, Will Herberg maintained that religious commitment, despite its high levels, was superficial and largely a matter of vogue rather than conviction. He found that most self-proclaimed believers had little knowledge of the teachings of the Bible. To be a member of a mainline church, he argued, was more a matter of adhering to convention born of the desire for social belonging. Churches were functioning mainly as social and civic clubs.[86] As R. Stephen Warner put it more recently in a study of a congregation in California, "to be a 'Presbyterian' in Mendocino in those days was less a matter of affirming the teachings of John Calvin and John Knox than of testifying that one was decent, churched, and not Portuguese."[87] Likewise, Robert Ellwood concluded that 1950s religion was the spiritual equivalent of Heinz products: There were 57 varieties, but all came in familiar bottles. Indeed: "Fifties clergy tended to be conventional, well-organized, business-like men who knew the value of real estate and how to emcee a dinner."[88]

Many observers have welcomed this "end of ideology" among the mainstream denominations and regarded it as the rationalizing and civilizing of religious competition, similar to "the process of cartellization in the secular economy."[89] Others, however, were more scathing. Joseph Viteritti, for example, has denounced the "hollow middle" of a "passive, undecided, ambivalent sector of the American populace" whose putative faith shaped neither their lives nor their politics.[90] In any case, these findings raise doubts about whether the culture war truly unites evangelicals. On many social issues there is significant diversity among conservative Protestants. Nancy Davis and Robert Robinson have found that on gender divisions, race, and economic inequality, as well as on teaching about sex in school and making birth control available to teens, less than half of the orthodox were conservative.[91] While evangelicals have become more conservative on abortion and pornography, they have become more liberal on feminism. Even on abortion, one of the most polarizing issues, differences between denominations and between secularists and religionists tended to disappear when people were asked more detailed questions about specific circumstances in which it should or should not be legal.[92] As noted earlier, while white evangelical Protestants were the most conservative group on issues of sexuality, reproductive rights, and the traditional family, this did not always translate into a clear-cut conservative political stance.[93]

## Critique III: The Limited Political Salience of Moral Issues

Finally, the limited appeal of the culture war rhetoric raises the question whether moral orientations truly prevail over socioeconomic ones as the most important factors in determining partisan identity. Here the evidence shows once again that political attitudes and voting behavior continue to follow class, race, and gender indicators, rather than the polarized moral worldviews that define the religious cleavage. A study of the political scene after the 1984 presidential elections indicated that although voters moved away from the Democrats and toward the Republicans, New Deal issues had lost none of their potency. Indeed, voters' concern with the issues associated with the New Deal was stronger in 1984 than in 1952.[94] While cultural and moral issues have become more salient relative to socioeconomic factors, they "generally took a back seat to issues such as tax cuts, health care reform, and campaign finance reform in both parties' nomination battles."[95]

Moral issues were also rarely at the center of a party platform. Noting that public opinion does not cluster at the two contrarian ends of the political spectrum, some critics consider the culture war mindset to be at odds not only with mainstream attitudes, but also with the structure of the party system. In contrast to Layman's view of the partisan divide, Rhys Williams notes that political parties were means of "marginalizing uncompromising minorities." They "diffuse and defuse the passion necessary for war" and "put together logically inconsistent platforms in order to accommodate the specific, impassioned, but often limited visions of their major constituencies." In contrast to social movements, which were often extrainstitutional and uncompromising, the key tendency of parties was to "aggregate differences, force compromise, and facilitate cross-cutting cooperation," producing centrist solutions in their wake.[96]

These findings have two crucial implications. First, they indicate that the rightwing political turn of conservative Protestants might be rooted more in their socioeconomic background than in their moral worldview. The improvements many evangelicals experienced as a result of the postwar economic boom, relocation to the South and West, suburban lifestyles, and higher levels of education had predictable political consequences. Since socioeconomic improvement is generally accompanied by political conservatism, the evangelical electorate became markedly more Republican. This simply mirrored the general shift to the Republican party among postwar boomer, 1970s, and Reagan cohorts. Churchgoing white Christians, therefore, do not appear to be particularly distinctive in their partisan leanings and instead reflect a larger national trend.[97]

Second, the data suggest that in order for moral issues to be politically salient, they have to coalesce with traditional socioeconomic concerns. The problem for the Republicans in this regard was that on social and economic issues, the electorate frequently continued to show a Democratic bias. Despite a pervasive sense of the "moral failures" of 1960s-style social policy, broad-based popular support for the administrative state remained strong and continued to shape political opinion. Many polls in the mid-1970s recorded entrenched support for macroeconomic intervention and the expansion of the human services infrastructure. They showed that many Americans supported both redistribution of income and a tough stance on social issues. As Christopher Lasch has maintained, the tax revolt of the 1970s was not a mandate for supply-side economics, since it was directed against regressive property taxes, not the more progressive federal income tax.[98]

What had changed by the 1980s was not the attachment to the liberal state itself, but the partisan bias of voters in regard to issues such as Social Security, medical care, welfare, and education. Hence, Republicans were elected not because voters rejected New Deal–style socioeconomic concerns and programs, but because they had lost faith in the Democrats.[99] Indeed, many political scientists attribute the backlash of the 1970s and 1980s to a crisis of the Democratic party, rather than to a serious shift to the right in the ideological outlook of the electorate. As Mickey Kaus has surmised in the *New York Times*, Republicans discovered that "the voters never really hated government, they just hated welfare."[100] The evangelicals were no exception in this respect. Despite severing their linkage with the Democratic party, a significant percentage of evangelicals remained comfortable with Democratic economic policies and the New Deal/Great Society state. As George Gallup put it in the late 1980s, the future of the Democratic party lay in fact in crafting a platform that defended the party's traditional economic policies and promoted a moderate image on social issues, especially on crime.[101]

This suggests that the ability to define social and economic issues in moral terms, rather than the politics of morality itself, was the crucial component in mobilizing a broader working- and lower-middle-class electorate for the Republican party.[102] As Lasch has argued, for example, the conflict over abortion was first and foremost a class issue. Pro-choice advocates were generally better-educated professionals, unmarried, and for the most part without religion, while pro-lifers tended to be housewives, predominantly Catholic, and with large families. In his view, the abortion debates thus pitted an "ethic of competitive achievement" against the "petty-bourgeois or working-class ethic of limits."[103] Likewise, Moreton views the recourse to moral issues as a rational way of addressing specific socioeconomic concerns generated by changes in race and gender relations in the postindustrial economy. In her study of Wal-Mart, she argues that the corporation's family-oriented polices provided a kind of substitute for union-based benefits. They addressed the normative and socioeconomic upheaval caused by the transition from an industrial to a service-sector-dominated economy. This appealed to the social needs of a largely feminized and underpaid workforce. At the same time, the company's "servant leadership" management system reasserted male authority at a time when the masculine imagery embedded in industrial labor, which glorified the husband as breadwinner, had begun to unravel.[104]

Finally, despite the pervasive culture war rhetoric, Republican policies in the 1980s and again after 2000 failed to rigorously pursue a moralistic agenda. They also largely accepted or expanded upon the existing level of government activity and involvement. Ronald Reagan, for example, fused fiery rightwing rhetoric with a legacy of moderate policies based on the New Deal consensus, a combination that Alonzo Hamby has called "reactionary Keynesianism." In the social policy arena, Reagan attacked the welfare state, yet oversaw no wholesale dismantling of New Deal social provisions or net reduction in social spending. Though causing real suffering, most cuts in social programs were directed against the fiscally irrelevant welfare programs, rather than the large social insurance system.[105] As Rebecca Klatch has concluded, the Reagan legacy lay in the diminution and rejection of governmental authority to remedy social inequality, not in the reduction of government expenditure and power.[106]

## Toward an Interpretive Model

The critical review of these analyses of evangelicalism's postwar resurgence and political mobilization highlights the contested and conflictual dimensions of a diverse movement. As Carpenter has put it, evangelicalism was characterized by a "strange dance" between conflicting impulses.[107] On the one hand, it was marked by ecumenical consensus building, theological softening, cultural engagement, and postmillennial sociopolitical action. On the other hand, the postwar resurgence reaffirmed the lines of cognitive defense, biblical orthodoxy, culture warring, and subcultural isolation. The desire for ideological and institutional self-assertion in conjunction with the urge to adjust to the Cold War context formed the parameters of postwar evangelicalism. This suggests that evangelicalism's theological outlook, cultural resonance, and political alignments were defined by the dynamic tension between its integration into mainstream culture and its preservation of a militant identity. Evangelicals wanted to convey the message of being both uncompromising and contemporary.[108]

This attempt to square the circle calls to mind the findings of both social movement theorists and students of religious mobilization, who have identified the ability to calibrate between an insurgent message and institutional ties as a crucial factor in sustaining a resurgence. Carpenter, for example, regards the mixture of alienation and engagement as the key to understanding the cultural strength of fundamentalism.[109] Likewise, in his subcultural identity theory of religious strength, sociologist Christian Smith argues that evangelicalism's staying power was the "result of the combination of its socially constructed cultural distinction *vis-à-vis* and vigorous sociocultural engagement *with* pluralistic modernity." He notes that the evangelical movement opened up a "space" between religious orthodoxy and theological liberalism, with an agenda quite distinct from fundamentalism, yet a clear subcultural identity outside liberal secular society.[110]

By showing that the creative tension between accommodation and antagonism was at the center of the evangelical identity, these approaches suggest an interpretive model that pays close analytical attention to both internal movement conflicts and the contingency of the evangelical political positioning. They locate the substance of postwar evangelicalism less in objectively manifested markers, such as consolidated institutional structures, firm theological concepts, established sociocultural identities, and fixed ideological outlooks. Instead, they shift the spotlight onto the way in which evangelical beliefs, institutions, and ideologies were constituted in the context of the movement's engagement with socioeconomic change, the rise of consumer capitalism, sixties cultural insurgencies, and the conservative political resurgence since the 1970s. As Jon Stone has suggested, "boundary maintenance"—that is, the process by which evangelicals negotiate tensions and contradictions in their relationship with the state, society, and other denominations—was as much a constitutive principle of their political and cultural orientation as the theological axioms they subscribe to. In his view, evangelical identities were formed in the context of a continuous process of sociocultural negotiating and political coalition building driven by the structural dynamics of Cold War society.[111] Similarly, Williams interprets the culture war less in terms of a deep ideological divide than as an effective linguistic strategy to define "us" and "the other." In his eyes, the key to political positions is found not in pre-existing attitudes, but in social networks and institutional processes. "Political conflict *is* often between the orthodox and the progressive," he concedes, "but these are not as much descriptions of attitude clusters as they are symbolic markers of identity and difference." Belief in a transcendental source of moral authority, therefore, does not automatically result in a specific political ideology. Rather, these connections are constructed in particular social settings.[112] The dominance of a particular political group, such as the Christian Right, is therefore dependent upon the way in which it manages internal divisions and marginalizes dissident groups within a volatile movement.

The following three chapters examine more closely these internal movement dynamics and processes of negotiating ideological positions, which have received comparatively little attention in scholarship. They divide the resurgence of conservative Protestantism since World War II into periods of "mainstreamization" (early 1940s to mid-1960s), "mobilization" (mid-1960s to mid-1970s), and "militancy" (since the late 1970s). By paying particular attention to evangelicalism's interaction with Cold War society, its efforts to navigate between contradictory positions, and its internal power struggles, these chapters revise many of the conventional views about the movement's sociocultural presence, theological profile, and political alignments.

# 2

# The Postwar
# Neo-Evangelical Awakening

In their desire to reaffirm orthodox Protestantism as a significant cultural and political force in modern American society, a cadre of "progressive fundamentalists" (Joel Carpenter) or "post-fundamentalist evangelicals" (Donald Dayton) set out in the early 1940s to strip fundamentalism of its gloom and doom. Advancing a platform of "cooperation without compromise," they sought to reassert the spirit of revivalism, establish a broad interdenominational basis, and create a network of evangelical institutions. The main impetus behind the postwar neo-evangelical yearning for a revival was twofold. First, after years of self-imposed isolation a new generation desired to make fundamentalism relevant again within mainstream culture and theology. Many conservative Protestants felt that the divisive fundamentalist-modernist controversy that had marked the previous decades and had climaxed in the Scopes trial had faded into the background. The stark realities of Depression-era and wartime life made the theological squabbles look petty, the small number of separatist fundamentalists who had left the mainline denominations seemed irrelevant, and the great controversy had turned into a distant memory. Second, many evangelicals were dismayed at both the growing liberal influence within the mainline denominations and the wartime government's elevation of the mainline Protestant bodies to the status of official representatives of American Protestantism. Though not socially or economically dispossessed, they felt culturally marginal and powerless.[1]

A network of "neo-evangelicals," which included such luminaries as Billy Graham, Carl F. H. Henry, and Harold John Ockenga, became the driving force behind the postwar resurgence of conservative Protestantism. Institutionally, their move away from separatist fundamentalism led to the formation of the National Association of Evangelicals (NAE) in 1942, the establishment of Fuller

Theological Seminary in 1947, and the creation of the magazine *Christianity Today* in 1956. Theologically, the neo-evangelicals positioned themselves as a "third force" between fundamentalism and theological liberalism. They rejected fundamentalist exclusivism but affirmed its religious orthodoxy. By the same token, they denounced liberal theology but embraced its ecumenical impulses.[2] Using terms such as "positive fundamentalism" and "fundamentalism with a touch of class," the neo-evangelicals sought to move out of the sectarian ghetto, and by the end of the 1950s they had largely succeeded in this quest.[3] They had "shed the stigma of being a religious sect and had come to enjoy a central place within the mainstream of American culture." At the same time, they had drawn the "lines of cognitive defense" of postwar evangelicalism that proved crucial in establishing firm subcultural foundations.[4]

As indicated in the previous chapter, scholarship on the postwar evangelical resurgence is often divided between those for whom religious beliefs remain at the center of the evangelical phenomenon and those who regard evangelicalism as driven by structural dynamics in which theological issues are merely symbols demarcating social, cultural, and political boundaries. The former argue that evangelicalism "has an inner theological unity in the midst of external theological and cultural diversity."[5] The latter maintain that the movement's interaction with postwar society, its engagement in coalition building, and the pressure to negotiate between conflicting impulses shaped evangelical content to a larger extent than fixed theological concepts. Its ideological and political "coherence" thus mainly emanated from the need to differentiate itself from both fundamentalism and liberalism.[6] The following look at the theological origins and institutional challenges of the movement indicates that both aspects are crucial in understanding the resurgence of conservative Protestantism after the Second World War.

## Neo-Evangelicals, Fundamentalists, and Liberals

The evangelical distancing from prewar fundamentalism was central to the postwar resurgence of conservative Protestantism. Though often ignored in popular perception, the separation of evangelicals from fundamentalism was more than just a minor internecine conflict that diverted attention away from the main liberal-orthodox battle raging within the Protestant camp. As *Christianity Today* editorialized, evangelicals were turning away from the term fundamentalism "not because of any inclination to disavow traditional fundamentals of the Christian faith," but because of "its inadequate scriptural content and its current earned and unearned disrepute."[7] Indeed, by the 1960s evangelicals and fundamentalists had largely ceased to be part of the same movement.[8]

As explored in the previous chapter, evangelical revivalism continued to spring from different theological and political sources than separatist fundamentalism. As a result, even doctrinal positions that appeared to be a bedrock of conservative Protestantism were often deeply controversial.[9] According to Dayton, the label "evangelical" identifies those expressing the ethos of the awakenings and revivals, whereas, as Ernest Sandeen notes, adherence to "dispensationalist premillennialism" defines fundamentalism. The latter encompasses not only strict faith in the inerrancy of the Bible, but also the belief that Christ's imminent Second Coming will mark the end of a long period of worldly decline, and that the current age is characterized by the corruption of the large Christian churches. It informs the fundamentalist desire to separate from the mainstream churches and elevate individual piety over social witness.[10]

This matches Timothy Weber's understanding of the division within conservative Protestantism. In his view, the "theology of the word" denotes the adherence to literalism, legalism, and formal doctrine that tends to identify fundamentalists. In contrast, the "theology of the spirit" emphasizes the intuitive, mystical Christian experience that forms the core of evangelicalism.[11] In turn, simultaneously upholding the orthodoxies of the faith and promoting a type of "soft conversionism" became the hallmark of neo-evangelicalism. Noting that the "NAE has never undertaken to say how much a person must know in order to be born again or a 'true Christian' in that sense," NAE president Stephen Paine declared in 1956 that "a person might be 'born again' without having faced and resolved the implications of this doctrine," but a person "rejecting the virgin birth of Christ would not be acceptable for membership in any of the communions comprising the affiliation of the NAE."[12]

What ultimately distinguished the neo-evangelicals from the fundamentalists, however, was not so much doctrine as cultural sophistication, social status, and a desire for social and political involvement. Fundamentalists were more clearly allied with political and social conservatism, displayed a fortress mentality, cultivated an outcast image, and formed an "exclusivistic substratum" within the evangelical fold.[13] As pundit Garrison Keillor put it in a story about a tiny fundamentalist sect: "Jesus said, 'Where two or three are gathered together in my name, there am I in the midst of them,' and the Brethren believed that was enough."[14] In contrast, most evangelicals called for a positive message of social transformation and redemption. While the "salvation of lost men and women by the preaching of the Gospel" remained the "primary emphasis," Clyde W. Taylor, the NAE's secretary for public affairs, asserted in 1956, "this does not exclude the application of the Gospel to current social, economic or racial issues."[15] Neo-evangelicals thus combined an emphasis on Augustinian orthodoxy with a positive social program and the desire for renewed cultural and political involvement.[16]

Like the differences between evangelicals and fundamentalists, those between both groups and liberal Protestants involved matters of doctrinal substance as well as style and social status. Though softening their fundamentalist image, neo-evangelicals remained staunch opponents of theological liberalism. The liberals' modernist view of the Bible, which regarded the scripture as a culture-bound inspirational text expressing symbolic, rather than literal, truth, was anathema to conservatives. Liberals saw Christ mainly as an example of righteous living and a teacher to self-sufficient human beings. They promoted ecumenical openness and moral tolerance. They were committed to a social gospel that sought to address exploitation and socioeconomic inequality, was critical of the prerogatives of private property, and regarded the state as an important agent for bringing about structural change and income redistribution.[17]

On all these fronts liberals encountered evangelicals ready to engage in battle. Insisting that the Bible was the sole authority and the revealed word of God, evangelicals stressed the need for humans to acknowledge their sinfulness, experience God's intervention via individual conversion, embrace Jesus as a personal savior, and focus on moral living on the basis of biblically grounded absolute rules. "Even at best liberalism reflected the invasion of a secular spirit," Henry declared. "It exaggerated God's immanence, minimized man's sinfulness, concealed Christ's supernaturalness and the centrality of his redemptive work, attached utopian expectations to history and ignored the task of evangelism."[18] The recovery of the theological concepts of Jonathan Edwards, who regarded man as under sentence of condemnation by a wrathful God until rescued by the supernatural grace of Christ's intervention, was among the primary neo-evangelical objectives. Arguing that liberal Protestantism had evaded issues of human guilt and depravity by emphasizing "the forgiveness of sins, the new birth and sanctification," Henry concluded that it ignored "the corollary doctrines of justification and imputation."[19] As Frederick C. Fowler, Presbyterian minister and NAE president for a brief period, put it, the church's ministry until the time of the Second Coming was "for the gathering and perfecting of the saints." It was not "primarily a world improvement program."[20]

The neo-evangelical crusade, however, was not limited to restoring concepts of sin and salvation within the churches. It also extended to recovering the spiritual grounding of American culture that had been abandoned in the course of the rise of theism, transcendentalism, and the social gospel.[21] In the eyes of the neo-evangelicals, the theological pitfalls of liberalism could not be separated from its political shortcomings. Reducing liberalism to a naïve faith in progress, the milk of human kindness, and instrumental reasoning, Henry mingled belligerent polemics and perceptive criticism in his 1946 book *Remaking the Modern Mind*. In light of the totalitarian threats of Nazism and communism, he argued, the relativistic foundations of a moral order built on Kantian concepts of pure reason and moral autonomy had lost their plausibility. Stretching from Descartes to Dewey, "anthropocentric optimism" had falsely posited the natural goodness of man and the notion of automatic progress. Painting a vivid image of the desolation, spiritual emptiness, and cataclysmic doom of the period from 1914 to 1945, Henry concluded that "the controlling ideas of modern philosophy, supposedly gleaned from the touchstone of a sound rationalism or empiricism, are not nearly as relevant to the judgment hour of western civilization as were the revelational views of man."[22]

Yet Henry and other evangelical thinkers, such as Edward Carnell and Dirk Jellema, went beyond simply denouncing liberalism as philosophically ineffectual in countering twentieth-century ideologies. They also implicated liberalism in the rise of totalitarianism. Henry viewed Nazism as an outgrowth of Enlightenment liberalism because both asserted the ultimate reality of nature and the ultimate animality of man over supernatural revelation. Not mincing his words, he concluded that liberalism was an inner ideological disease because it elevated contingent goals, pragmatic experimentation, utilitarianism, and instrumentalist reasoning over fixed moral norms.[23] Likewise, Jellema maintained that the "modern and post-modern mind" had failed to sustain political freedom as more than a means to an end. And Cecil De Boer in *Christianity Today* called for the replacement of the instrumentalism and focus on problem solving embedded in liberal Deweyan educational thought with a focus on character building and universal morality rooted in Christian traditions of education.[24]

By merging their attack on theological liberalism with the denunciation of political liberalism, evangelical thinkers asserted their claim to political relevance in the wider Cold War order. In Henry's words, Christianity was "vibrant with social implications as a religion of redemptive transformation." In order to "express and continue the vitality of the gospel message," he declared, "marriage and the home, labor and economics, politics and the state, culture and the arts, in fact, every sphere of life, must evidence the lordship of Christ."[25] In a rousing stump speech at the second annual conference of the NAE in 1944, Claude A. Watson, presidential candidate for the Prohibition party, made it clear that the biblical call was for the righteous to govern and that "the purpose of administration in government is that [rulers] shall be ministers of God to the people for good and a terror to evil-doers." He admonished the Protestant clergy to speak out on politics and to live up to their role as "character-building people." Claiming that "nearly two-thirds of that Bible has to do with God's dealing with the nations, national programs and national affairs," Watson maintained that God wanted righteous people to "organize for political action to establish the ethics of the Christian religion in our administration of government."[26]

Encouraged by the convention to continue his speech, Watson urged evangelicals to unite for partisan political action. "Having charge of administration, having charge of the legislation, having charge of the judiciary," he declared, could destroy "every immoral and anti-social and debauching force." Using New Deal power politics as a model, he called on evangelicals to fight for Christian legislation. If America could send millions of men "to lick Japan and lick Germany and put Italy down," it should have enough power "to take a fellow with a quart of whiskey and to keep him from slipping it to the lips of some other fellow." Concluding that the "Christian citizen's most powerful weapon is his vote" and that prayer alone was insufficient, he pleaded with his audience to disregard the split political loyalties of evangelicals and unite "under a great Christian philosophy for political action" that "could elect the next President of these United States." "I am liable to say 'Amen' to myself—I get so in the habit of it," he mused, before closing his speech with the obligatory story of conversion.[27]

Despite these forays into partisan mobilization, however, many postwar evangelicals remained leery of the political realm. Although Henry noted that "more liberal churchmen . . . today acknowledge the fallacy of socialism, and appear ready to combine the theological left with the economic right," he predicted that conservative politics as a way of engineering theological unity would fail. Instead, he insisted that a focus on biblical belief, spiritual regeneration, and the gospel of personal salvation was the only way forward.[28] Hence, the neo-evangelicals of the 1940s and 1950s embraced first and foremost what one might call an evangelical popular front approach that focused on creating a broad interdenominational base. In this process they tapped into the existing organizational infrastructure of fundamentalist and liberal Protestantism alike. Although at pains to separate themselves from the dour premillennialism and fortress mentality of fundamentalism, the neo-evangelicals benefited greatly from the thriving fundamentalist institution building that had throughout the 1930s provided protective "shelter belts" for conservative Christians. For example, fundamentalist businessman Herbert J. Taylor played a key role in establishing the Inter-Varsity Christian Fellowship in 1941. This provided new tools for mass evangelization that could be used to propel an evangelical coalition in postwar

America.[29] Likewise, Billy Graham's efforts to take evangelicalism's message to the world were a way of bringing together a wide variety of conservative doctrinal positions, religious sentiments, and denominational traditions.[30]

The fledgling networks between neo-evangelicals and conservatives within the mainline denominations were equally instrumental in bringing about the evangelical revival. Despite their vocal rejection of theological liberalism, neo-evangelicals were theologically and institutionally geared toward a spirit of ecumenical bridge building with mainline Protestantism. Their goal was to make evangelicalism respectable again within the Protestant fold and to present themselves as the solution to the fundamentalist-modernist divide that had torn American Protestantism apart. Their willingness to cooperate with mainline Protestants, Catholics, and Jews marked a significant shift from their previous fundamentalist stance.[31] Meanwhile, a new spirit of ecumenism prevailed among mainline Protestants after World War II, characterized by new efforts to overcome the vitriolic and acrimonious infighting after the traumas of war and totalitarianism. In an age of conformity and consensus, many valued the neo-evangelicals' rejection of fundamentalist extremism. As a result, the evangelical Youth for Christ movement, for example, received vital financial and logistical support from the Christian Business Men's Committees, which had begun organizing businessmen from mainline churches and the Protestant establishment.[32]

Conservative Christians who had remained inside the larger mainline denominations during and after the divisive theological battles of the 1920s also spearheaded a new interest in conservative doctrine and evangelism. Spiritually prodded by the neo-orthodox theology of Karl Barth, Emil Brunner, and Dietrich Bonhoeffer, a new emphasis on the sinfulness of man, as well as on the transcendence of God and on Christ as supreme authority, entered mainline debates. Shaken in their faith in progress by the terrors of the twentieth century, many mainline Protestants questioned modernism and its postmillennial identification of the Kingdom of God with worldly social programs. They embraced instead Reinhold Niebuhr's neo-Calvinist skepticism about human nature and his view that the love and kindness present in interpersonal relations were impossible to achieve on a societal level.[33]

## Institutionalizing the Protestant Divide

By the early 1940s, the tripartite rift between liberalism, fundamentalism, and evangelicalism had been institutionalized in competing umbrella organizations that both embodied diverse theological positions and were characterized by different organizational styles. The mainline Federal Council of the Churches of Christ in America (FCCCA) embraced the social gospel, political engagement, and a liberal theological position. By 1950 it had moved to a more ecumenical and conciliar structure in the shape of the National Council of the Churches of Christ (NCCC).[34] Separatist fundamentalists, led by Carl McIntire, had left the FCCCA in 1941 to found the American Council of Christian Churches (ACCC). Strictly fundamentalist in theology and opposed to involvement in social causes, the ACCC was hierarchical and exclusionary in its organization. It demanded strict separation from liberal apostasy, and its member organizations were not allowed to affiliate with the NCCC. Displaying a similar mentality and remaining steadfastly loyal to dispensationalist premillennialism, numerous fundamentalist churches and organizations, including Billy James Hargis's Christian Crusade, Edgar C. Bundy's Church League of America, Verne P. Kaub's American Council of Christian Laymen, and Fred Schwarz's Christian Anti-Communist Crusade equally thrived in the postwar period.[35]

Meanwhile, the neo-evangelicals formed the NAE in 1942 and elected as president the renowned pastor of Boston's Park Street Church, Harold John Ockenga. The grounds for disagreement between the NAE and the ACCC were threefold: the question of separation from liberal organizations, the conflict between a centralized council of churches and a fellowship of believers, and "the issue of a polemical and negative approach as against a constructive program."[36] Although the neo-evangelicals retained fundamentalist Biblicism, premillennialism, and antiliberalism, they did not demand separation, dropped dispensationalism, and emphasized broad interdenominational revivalism. As NAE president Billy Melvin explained in 1982, "on traditional fundamental doctrines, NAE and the fundamentalists are in agreement, except that not all of us hold their view of ecclesiastical separation."[37]

By the same token, the neo-evangelicals, while "doctrinally fundamental," were "not organizationally fundamentalist."[38] The NAE linked diverse sectarian traditions together in a decentralized, democratic, and loosely organized body. In its desire to see "a movement, rather than a hierarchical organization," it kept membership open to denominations, congregations, mission boards, Bible colleges, parachurch organizations, and individuals. Though expressing a willingness to cooperate with liberal churches, however, the NAE denounced the alleged tendency of the NCCC to create a "superchurch" as prophesied in the Bible. The NAE's reliance on spiritual affinity, rather than bureaucratic organization, was expressed in its broad Statement of Faith, whose acceptance NAE Secretary of Public Affairs Clyde W. Taylor regarded as nothing short of "miraculous," considering the mix of Calvinists, pentecostals, and adherents of Wesleyan-Holiness traditions in the organization.[39]

By the late 1950s the separation of evangelicals from fundamentalism was almost complete. *Christianity Today* identified a three-way split among Protestant ministers, asserting in a survey that 39 percent saw themselves as conservative, 35 percent as fundamentalist, and 26 percent as either liberal or neo-orthodox.[40] The definitive break with hardline fundamentalism came in 1957 when Billy Graham's New York crusade accepted sponsorship by the city's Council of Churches. In turn, his supporters had to defend Graham against accusations that his cooperation with liberal churches undermined his evangelical credentials and spiritual solidity. By the early 1960s NAE staff retreat minutes showed that "contact with the ACC is much less than previously . . . they denounce NAE on compromise; they are not at all related to us."[41]

Building upon the institutional framework of fundamentalism on the one hand, and theological doubts among mainstream churches on the other, the neo-evangelicals thrived on the basis of their distinctive organizational and ideological identity. Institutionally, they staked out a claim in contrast to both separatist fundamentalism and liberalism, yet they also sought to remain organizationally inclusive. Theologically, they desired to restore orthodoxy to societal relevance, yet rejected rigid dispensationalist theology in favor of a broad-based revivalism. Culturally, they nurtured a sense of alienation and a way of life centered on absolute moral codes, biblical literalism, and spiritual purity. At the same time, they were adept at modern managerial, organizational, and advertising techniques, innovative in their religious practices, and veritably postmodern in their emphasis on mobility, individual faith experience, institutional flexibility, and opposition to traditional authority.[42]

Crucially, this merger of ecumenism and orthodoxy, and the ability to combine a traditional message with a modern image, formed the backdrop for evangelicalism's success in the context of the large-scale socioeconomic and demographic changes during and after the Second World War. As noted in the previous chapter, under the impact of the postwar economic boom and the politics of growth in the evangelical strongholds in the South and the West, evangelicals had moved out of the socioeconomic margins of society. By the same token, evangelical churches were more successful in adapting to the migration patterns of the postwar period than many of the mainline denominations. In the quintessentially modern setting of the suburban South and West, conservative forms of religion thrived because of their institutional adaptability and resource provision. They often supplied the social and community services missing in the fluid and unstable suburban environments.[43] The increase in wealth, newfound cultural self-confidence, and influx of new members found expression in a surge of evangelical institution building. A wide variety of new national and local associations, lobbying groups, social agencies, hospitals, child care centers, old-age homes, Bible institutes, seminaries, colleges, think tanks, relief agencies, and foreign missions came into being. What is more, evangelicals engaged in new ventures in publishing, journalism, and radio and television programming. As the careers of Charles Finney, Dwight Moody, Billy Sunday, Carl McIntire, Charles Fuller, and Billy Graham indicate, evangelicals had traditionally been masters of the rationalized techniques of modern advertising and promotion. Skillful in the use of the air waves and television, they successfully conveyed their traditional message via the most modern of media. Likewise, they embraced modern expressive styles and presentational modes. Graham, Jack Wyrtzen, Percy Crawford, and others used split-second timing, fast-paced gospel music, quick-fire announcements, and current events lead-ins ("D-Day at Bethlehem") in their revivalist ministry.[44] There was no need to disclaim modern science or technology, Carl Henry concluded. The former simply had to be freed from the prejudices of the modern mind, while the latter might also be used to serve the glory of God.[45]

Billy Graham's ministry, Fuller Seminary, and the magazine *Christianity Today* best exemplified the neo-evangelical style and aspiration in the heady days of postwar expansion. The towering figure in postwar evangelicalism was Graham. From the Wheaton College revival in 1950, which gave broad-based exposure to the neo-evangelical message, to the Madison Square Garden revival in 1957, which marked the break with separatist fundamentalism, Graham succeeded not only in "saving souls" but also in popularizing the evangelical worldview within mainstream American culture. According to Robert Ellwood, the winning formula of Graham's style consisted of combining a "countercultural message" with "cultural conformity." He utilized the latest communications technology and up-to-date personnel mobilization, and he directed his rhetoric to the individual. Whereas mainline theologians talked about "man," Ellwood noted, Graham talked about "you."[46]

Media tycoons such as William Randolph Hearst and Henry Luce actively supported Graham's quest through large-scale coverage. Hearst had become aware of the neo-evangelicals in the 1940s and gave clear instructions to the editors of his newspapers to "puff Graham." Luce, owner of *Time* and *Life*, had encountered Graham in 1950 at a meeting arranged by North Carolina governor Strom Thurmond and subsequently made sure that appealing images of the evangelist would feature in his publications.[47] "Our greatest weapon . . . is the press," the NAE's Clyde Taylor mused; "slowly the American press is showing its willingness to print the news. Then public opinion becomes our best weapon."[48]

A less lofty but equally important place in the movement was occupied by Carl F. H. Henry. While Graham furnished the mass appeal, Henry and others provided the movement with ideological leadership, straddled the built-in contradictions of evangelicalism, and gave it the necessary vision for its cultural assertion. Dubbed "the thinking man's Billy Graham" by the press, Henry knew that evangelizing was not sufficient to produce stable institutional patterns and that evangelical think tanks were needed to provide intellectual legitimacy, guidance, and continuity. He was instrumental in the founding of Fuller Theological Seminary, which was designed to become the "Cal-Tech of modern evangelicalism" in its cosmopolitan and upscale setting in Pasadena, California.[49] "It seemed imperative to me that in the cultured context of Pasadena evangelical Christianity be seen as an intellectually viable and vibrant faith and not as a suspect cult," Henry later recalled.[50]

Founded with the support of radio evangelist Charles E. Fuller, the venture coincided with the emergence of a new generation of evangelical leaders who had been trained at elite universities rather than at fundamentalist Bible schools. In an example of postwar government subsidies promoting neo-evangelicalism, the expansion of funding for education and the GI Bill allowed many conservative Protestants training for the ministry to enter such bastions of theological liberalism as Harvard Divinity School. Neo-evangelical thinkers like Henry, Edward Carnell, Everett Harrison, Paul K. Jewett, George Ladd, and Gleason Archer earned doctorates from leading liberal institutions, bringing both status and sophistication to evangelicalism. They formed crucial networks that provided ideological and organizational leadership to the evangelical resurgence by straddling highbrow interest in existentialism and neo-orthodoxy and lowbrow interest in revivalism. Fuller Seminary was able to recruit many of them, including Carnell, Archer, Wilbur Smith, Harold Lindsell, and Dirk Jellema. Although squabbles and administrative problems wracked the fledgling seminary, it eventually became one of the leading centers of evangelical ministerial training and later on, ironically, a stronghold of liberal evangelicalism.[51]

The fortnightly magazine *Christianity Today*, edited by Henry, was built upon premises similar to those behind Fuller Seminary. Funded by oil magnate J. Howard Pew and other donors with close ties to corporate America, it was designed to give the liberal *Christian Century* "a run for its biases."[52] With its modern look, up-to-date printing technology, and effective distribution network, *Christianity Today* confidently set up headquarters in Washington, D.C., to mark "the place of the evangelical witness in the life of the republic." From its offices, Henry proudly pointed out, editors "daily look down Pennsylvania Avenue and glimpse the White House, Blair House, and other strategic centers of national life." After some controversies over editorial control, Henry was able to assert his claim, leading the magazine from a rocky start to unexpected success. Under his editorship it featured articles ranging from Jellema's philosophical musing on the postmodern mind to J. Edgar Hoover's exhortations about the evils of communism. Its self-declared mission was to show the relevance of the "total Gospel message for every area of life" and to be the "salt and light in a decaying and darkening world." Interpreting national and international news through the lens of scriptural revelation, *Christianity Today* asserted that "the historical evangelical faith is vital for the life of the Church and of the nations." Not only did biblical teachings offer answers to contemporary social crises, Henry declared, but Christian laymen were "becoming increasingly aware that the answer to the many problems of political, industrial and social life is a theological one."[53]

The magazine also engaged with the main theological debates of the postwar years and printed many essays by formerly modernist or neo-orthodox clergy who had veered toward evangelicalism. As Billy Graham wrote in a letter to his father-in-law, L. Nelson Bell, the "prime objective would be not to reach or please American fundamentalists but to lead confused and bewildered liberals to accept the authority of Scripture."[54] In turn, Henry declared both Karl Barth and Billy Graham symbols of "a religious springtime after the long, cold winter of Liberalism."[55] These efforts paid off handsomely and brought Henry and the neo-evangelicals the respect and recognition they had longed for. *Christianity Today* soon surpassed *Christian Century*, its liberal competitor, in circulation, and some say in influence.[56]

One of the telltale signs of the neo-evangelical makeover of traditional fundamentalism was the fact that Ockenga, Henry, Fuller, and other leading lights sought to disentangle themselves from the more xenophobic and bigoted aspects of fundamentalism. While prewar fundamentalism had been fervently anti-Semitic, the postwar era ushered in a profound reversal of attitudes. Evangelicals interpreted the founding of the state of Israel as a sign of the impending return of the Messiah and the fulfillment of biblical prophesies. Their embrace of a pro-Israel foreign policy plank was part of a desire to show that conservative Christianity had moved with the times. Moreover, anti-Semitism had become socially unacceptable in the aftermath of the Holocaust.[57] Even in regard to race, arguably one of the most intractable issues, especially in the South, evangelicals began to disown their dubious legacy. As Steven P. Miller has convincingly argued, leading public figures such as Billy Graham accepted the new racial norms with relative ease, in spite of their past ambivalence about an expanding, rights-based liberal state. Similarly, theologian Francis Schaeffer was a key figure in pioneering racial reconciliation among evangelicals. Effectively, evangelical leaders took race off the agenda, thus creating space for the seemingly new morality-based social concerns that rose to prominence in the 1970s.[58] Finally, neo-evangelicals were also comparatively moderate when it came to anticommunist witch-hunts. While separatist fundamentalists such as Carl McIntire and Billy James Hargis gleefully published McCarthy-style exposés on the alleged ties of liberal church leaders to communism, the neo-evangelicals kept their distance.[59] Presenting the "Communism Report" at the 1961 NAE staff retreat, Ron Arnold emphasized that the NAE's answer to communism was "not to stage investigations or expose Reds as such, but to have a spiritual ministry to be related to churches."[60]

Nonetheless, tensions over these issues continued to surface between rank-and-file communicants and denominational leaders.[61] Anti-Semitism, for example, continued to raise its ugly head. At the 1961 NAE conference on church-state relations, leading figures in the organization insisted that evangelicals should push for a "Christian Amendment" to the Constitution and that "care is needed that we do not move into a position of simply tolerating such minority groups as atheists and Jews."[62] Neither did neo-evangelicals relinquish their efforts to convert Jews. They also continued to harbor the notion that the Holocaust was God's punishment for the waywardness of the Jews.[63] Likewise, although evangelicals sought to tone down indiscriminate red-baiting, their rabid anticommunism justified some of the worst excesses of McCarthyism. In its most extreme form, this church militant mindset provided spiritual legitimacy not only for J. Edgar Hoover's surveillance and intimidation apparatus, but also for the use of extreme military force. Ockenga, for example, demanded an "aggressive diplomacy" that "will maintain access to Berlin whatever come even if this means using atomic weapons."[64]

It was anti-Catholicism, however, that proved most resistant to the postwar efforts to domesticate evangelicalism. Evangelicals in the 1950s and 1960s were often more virulently anti-Catholic than anticommunist, and they rarely acknowledged that any differences existed between Moscow and the Vatican. In fact, they often put their anticommunism in the service of fighting their much older enemy by conflating communism and Catholicism.[65] "The largest strength of the Communist party, next to Russia and China, is in Italy, home of Vatican City," Carl Henry warned in 1956. "Only European lands on which the Reformation made a strong theological impact are today virile in their resistance to Communism."[66] Likewise, Clyde Taylor noted a few years earlier that American Catholics "have been just as guilty of falsifying facts and in publishing them as have the Communists from the Kremlin."[67] This reached a fever pitch in 1960 when the prospect of the first Catholic president sent evangelicals into a tailspin. However, even after the fears and emotions generated by the Kennedy election had subsided, anti-Catholicism remained a tie that bound together the disparate evangelical ranks. Reporting in October 1963 on the Kennedy administration's landmark Civil Rights Bill, Taylor strongly criticized the involvement of Catholics in political action and stressed that many lawyers had denounced the legislative proposal "as a handover to the government of the basic rights and freedom of the individual. . . . They are convinced that a President who wanted to be a dictator could use this legislation to destroy a very large percentage of the individual freedom in America."[68] Likewise, the NAE campaign to prevent diplomatic relations with the Vatican continued well beyond the 1960 election. Indeed, the muting of anti-Catholicism did not begin until the 1980s.[69] Instead, in many ways it remained a constitutive element of neo-evangelicalism that enabled a movement deeply divided by theological controversy to submerge members' differences by focusing on common enemies.[70]

## Close-Up: The National Association of Evangelicals

The body that best illustrated both the possibilities and the pitfalls of the postwar evangelical journey back into the cultural and political limelight was the National Association of Evangelicals. Its history between the 1940s and the 1980s reflected the remarkable institutional growth of evangelicalism, but also its struggles and failures. Representative of the sprawling movement, the NAE embodied not only the desire for institutional consolidation and organizational effectiveness but also the reality of fragmentation and volatility. While seeking to develop a broad-based appeal and pursuing integration into mainstream culture, it was also shaped by the constituency's longing to preserve a militant and subcultural identity.

In 1941 the Temporary Committee for United Action among Evangelicals urged conservative Protestants in the United States to develop the "corporate means of making their wishes known" via a loose association. It sought to counter the influence of mainline Protestantism in the media and mission work, to organize social services, and to provide evangelicals with a voice in church-state matters. "Relations with Government" headed the list of areas envisaged by the committee as "fields of cooperative endeavor." This was followed by radio broadcasting, public relations, evangelism, preservation of the separation of church and state, freedom for home and foreign missions, local cooperation, and Christian education. An exploratory meeting in Chicago in 1941 was followed by a gathering of 147 evangelical leaders in Saint Louis in 1942 to found the NAE. A constitutional convention in Chicago in 1943 subsequently brought together around a thousand participants representing 15 million conservative Protestants. Most were organized into denominations, mission boards, Christian educational institutions, and single churches, but some simply came as individuals. The meeting thus reflected both the diverse and fragmented nature of American evangelicalism and the organizational trend away from denominational patterns.[71]

In part because of the decision to disallow dual membership in the FCCCA, however, only about twenty denominations and around a hundred churches and other organizations, representing roughly one million evangelicals, had affiliated with the NAE by 1945. Although the organization had succeeded in embracing a broader denominational and geographical sweep than the ACCC by including pentecostals and members of the Holiness and Anabaptist traditions, NAE membership consisted mainly of smaller denominations. The largest ones were the Assemblies of God and the National Association of Free Will Baptists, with approximately 400,000 members each. Moreover, the NAE had to straddle a wide variety of backgrounds within its constituency, which consisted of entire denominations, independent congregations, and conservative factions within mainline denominations. While membership gradually increased, by the mid-1950s it still had not broken through the 2 million mark. Not only did the organization remain hampered by Carl McIntire's tactics of dissuasion, but the jewel in the crown, the membership of the Southern Baptist Convention (SBC) and the Lutheran Church–Missouri Synod, also kept eluding the NAE.[72]

Despite tremendous efforts, the NAE did not achieve its goal of uniting evangelicals and remained beset by a plethora of financial, organizational, and personnel problems. Slow membership growth hampered its effectiveness as many evangelicals remained in old-line denominations and independent congregations.[73] It also lost potential members to competing organizations, such as the National Black Evangelical Association, founded in 1963. Some groups left the fold, among them the National Association of Free Will Baptists in 1972. By 1990 membership still stood at 4.5 million out of a potential constituency of 50 to 60 million evangelicals.

These membership figures, however, hide the actual impact of the NAE as a "small but broad" organization.[74] Its influence "came not so much from formal membership as from the networks into which it was connecting." Although many larger denominations did not join, their members were often part of the NAE's various committees, making the organization a "convener, catalyst, and confidence-builder."[75] Counting membership in commissions and affiliated agencies, NAE executive director George L. Ford therefore could boast of a "service constituency . . . in excess of 10 million."[76] Moreover, the NAE paved the way for overcoming the North-South divide in American evangelicalism in ways that resonated particularly with future SBC leaders such as Richard Land and Albert Mohler. As Barry Hankins has argued, neo-evangelicalism "became attractive to Southern Baptist conservatives at precisely the point where it differentiated itself from fundamentalism—that is at the point of engagement with culture. This was made possible largely as a result of the influence of Francis Schaeffer and Carl Henry."[77]

What the NAE lacked in membership it therefore made up for in administrative activism and coordinating. The association's formation was followed in rapid succession by the creation of a number of influential affiliates, such as National Religious Broadcasters (1944), the Evangelical Foreign Missions Association (1945), the National Sunday School Association (1945), and the National Association of Christian Schools (1947). Likewise, the NAE created a range of commissions and agencies, such as the Commission on Evangelism (1942), the Office of Public Affairs (1943), the War Relief Commission (1944), the Commission on Chaplaincy and Service to Military Personnel (1943), and the Commission on Social Action (1951). In addition, *United Evangelical Action*, the fortnightly NAE magazine, was launched by J. Elwin Wright in 1943, and by 1945 the NAE had established offices with full-time staff in nine cities across the United States, including Detroit, Minneapolis, Portland, and Los Angeles.

National Religious Broadcasters (NRB) and the Evangelical Foreign Missions Association (EFMA) gradually emerged as the most important and successful affiliates. NRB, which acted "on behalf of the NAE in all matters pertaining to broadcasting," included major evangelical broadcasters such as Charles Fuller, M. R. DeHaan, and William Ward Ayer. It was formed in reaction to the decision by the Mutual Broadcasting Company to limit Protestant religious broadcasting to mainline churches. Led by Ayer as its first president, NRB established links with the Federal Communications Commission (FCC) and the National Association of Broadcasters (NAB). It eventually succeeded in opening up network broadcasting time for evangelicals. Moreover, NRB "set the pattern for other similar structures in the NAE orbit" by becoming an affiliate with its own statement of faith, constitution, by-laws, and officers approved and ratified by the NAE. It was also instrumental in streamlining and professionalizing the operations of evangelical broadcasters by establishing an NRB Code of Ethics, which included rules on content and fund solicitation. By the early 1970s Clyde Taylor could boast that "NRB represents 86 percent of all Gospel broadcasts in the U.S. and three-fourths in the world. . . . Its conventions bring together the broadcasting interests . . . representing 17 million church members."[78] By 1980 NRB executive director Ben Armstrong reported that "90 percent of the total religious broadcasting in the U.S. are [*sic*] by evangelicals and 75 percent of the total religious broadcasting is by NRB members."[79]

Starting out as a commission of the NAE in 1943, EFMA was incorporated in 1945 under the auspices of the Office of Public Affairs in response to war-time restrictions on foreign missions.[80] It was the first association of missions "limited in membership to those subscribing to an evangelical statement of faith."[81] As exporting equipment, acquiring passports, and obtaining visas were posing growing logistical problems for mission leaders, EFMA, led by A. C. Snead of the Christian and Missionary Alliance and Clyde Taylor, the NAE's secretary of public affairs, became the main liaison between missionary agencies and the government. Its services included representation in Washington and providing mission executives with information from State Department briefings and consultations. EFMA services also encompassed a purchasing department, a visa and travel bureau, a missionary news service, and retreats for executives.[82]

Growing rapidly in the decades after its inception, EFMA had by 1961 reached a purchasing volume of $800,000 and a membership of 49 boards with approximately 5,000 missionaries.[83] These numbers increased steadily, reaching 64 mission agencies with almost 7,500 missionaries in 125 countries by 1974, and 81 agencies with more than 10,000 missionaries in over 130 countries by 1982.[84] EFMA established close ties with international bodies such as the Interdenominational Foreign Missions Association. Renamed Evangelical Fellowship of Mission Agencies in 1992, it became the largest missionary association in the world. Although evangelical mission work has received little scholarly attention, it became one of most prominent areas of evangelical success. Similarly, organizations such as the Inter-Varsity Christian Fellowship (IVCF) became effective recruiters of missionaries on university campuses during the height of the postwar student enrollment wave and paved the way for the rise of parachurch organizations within the conservative Protestant fold. Whereas the number of missionaries among mainline Protestant denominations declined from 7,000 to 3,000 between 1935 and 1980, evangelicals recorded an increase from around 5,000 to a staggering 32,000 in the same time period, with the most dramatic growth taking place after World War II.[85]

The most prominent NAE agency and the organizational hub for many of its political activities was the Office of Public Affairs (OPA), set up in 1943. Led by Clyde W. Taylor, its main role in the 1950s and 1960s was to provide services for mission agencies and chaplaincy commissions, liaise between the Pentagon and the clergy, and serve as "watchman" on church-state issues. Viewing the Washington office as "a service agency before government," Taylor worked with the FCC to retain equal evangelical access to the airwaves, kept "the doors open for evangelical missions through relations with both the U.S. and foreign governments," and promoted a biblical thrust in Christian education.[86] As a clearinghouse for Beltway-related matters, the OPA engaged in activities ranging from securing visas for missionaries to participating in congressional hearings. By organizing training seminars, facilitating political contacts, and promoting specific appointees, it became the main coordinating body for the NAE's efforts to place evangelicals in government and push for legislation. Taylor, for example, campaigned against President Truman's appointment of a personal representative to the Vatican, and against the U.S. ratification of the United Nations Declaration of Human Rights. He also helped the NAE establish representation at a variety of White House Conferences. Nearing retirement in 1972, he proudly noted that "government officials have an appreciation of agencies that esteem the government worthy of easy contact through a Washington representative."[87]

By the mid-1970s the NAE, desiring a more visible evangelical presence in the nation's capital and a more active part in the political process, expanded the OPA's staff and functions. Under the leadership of Robert P. Dugan Jr., the OPA became a key facilitator of closer ties to both the Republican establishment and the resurgent neo-fundamentalist Christian Right. (This process is discussed in detail in chapter 4.) Dugan expanded the political range of the OPA by bringing in a constitutional lawyer and a legislative researcher "to provide the legal analysis and political research necessary to maintain credibility." He also began publishing political newsletters such as *NAE Washington Insight* (1979). Dugan defined the public remit of the NAE more broadly as encompassing "religious freedom, the sanctity of human life, justice for the poor and oppressed, peacemaking, stewardship of natural resources, and the proper role of church, family, and government," noting that "such biblical principles are translated into political action consistent with NAE resolutions, such as one condemning abortion on demand."[88]

In addition to the OPA, a wide range of task-specific commissions set up by the NAE as permanent working groups for planning, research, and policy recommendations indicated the main areas of neo-evangelical interest and organizational activism. The Industrial Chaplaincy Commission sought to place evangelical clerics in plants and factories; the Commission on Chaplaincy and Service to Military Personnel assisted evangelical ministers in the armed forces; the Commission on Evangelism organized conferences and city-wide campaigns and sponsored cooperative efforts by churches, such as the World Day of

Prayer; and the Evangelical Home Missions Association focused attention on urban problems, inner-city needs, hospitals, and correctional institutions. Various other commissions, some quite short-lived, were concerned with higher education, social action, theology, and women's fellowship.[89] Moreover, the NAE established the Evangelical Action Committee, whose remit as a "policy defining body in the field of social matters" included religious education in schools, welfare, and family relations. It also stretched to "care for all matters in connection with church-State separation," the implementation of NAE resolutions relating to government and outside agencies, and testimony before congressional committees.[90]

The NAE's most successful task-specific commission, however, was the War Relief Commission (WRC). As the NAE's international aid agency, WRC was initially concerned mainly with sending clothing and medicine to refugee camps in Germany, Italy, and other European countries. Renamed World Relief Commission after the war, it was incorporated as a nonprofit subsidiary corporation of the NAE in the 1960s and gradually expanded its field of action, especially in emergency relief (Biafra, Bangladesh), long-term self-help programs (Korea), and refugee programs (Vietnam). Its remit also included agricultural rehabilitation and development, the creation of farming cooperatives, reclamation, refugee settlement, literacy programs, and children's clinics. The commission was "rather unique in its policy of always endeavoring to present the Gospel in every relief program it establishes." Later renamed World Relief, it became one of the most influential foreign aid organizations.[91]

As the cases of EFMA, NRB, and World Relief show, the NAE spawned some of the most powerful and effective parachurch and single-interest groups in the evangelical fold. At the same time, the mother organization continued to struggle. Indeed, not only did political involvement more often than not emanate from the agency level, but NAE affiliates were also significantly more successful in securing funding. In 1968 World Relief had a budget of $275,000, the National Sunday School Association $150,000, and the National Association of Christian Schools close to $72,000.[92] Meanwhile, the NAE's finances remained on shaky ground because of the organization's small budget and recurrent crises. By 1948 it had a budget of $68,000 and a deficit of $8,000 (excluding commissions and affiliated agencies). Though a political and organizational boon, the OPA continued to be a financial liability. It had a deficit of over $11,000 by 1948 and continued to cause the NAE financial headaches throughout the ensuing decades.[93] By 1953, with obligations in excess of $75,000, the financial problems were compounded by a leadership crisis when R. L. Decker and Harold Taylor resigned and a number of regional offices were without leaders.[94]

Though finances stabilized in later years, problems with operational costs continued to plague the organization.[95] One of the problems was that the NAE relied mostly on regional and national contributions, rallies, subscriptions, and the sale of materials. It did not receive major income from charitable agencies or corporate sponsors. By the early 1960s, when "deficit spending of regional and national bodies" began to mount again, the Board of Administration issued an urgent call for reorganization and for "creative thinking being given to a possible change of policy as far as fundraising was concerned."[96] Subsequent attempts to gain outside funding, however, encountered a number of obstacles. When the NAE asked J. Howard Pew for $150,000 in 1968, for example, the man whose funds had been crucial in setting up *Christianity Today* instead accused the organization of accepting the "Darwinian theory," which he claimed he could "prove mathematically" to have been "a fraud." He also admonished evangelicals to refrain from getting involved in economic, social, and political affairs.[97]

Not until the 1980s did the NAE engage in more active fundraising among business and political leaders. By then its budget stood at just below $1 million. Under the NAE Washington Associates program set up by Robert Dugan, politicians, businessmen, and church leaders, each pledging $1,000, were brought together primarily to provide the OPA with funding.[98] Nonetheless, a frustrated Dugan wrote in 1982 that the "perpetual financial struggle" continued to beset the office and suggested that it be made an affiliate of the NAE, "like World Relief, with its own board and its own responsibility for raising its funds."[99] Similarly, asked in a 1982 interview what was his biggest problem as executive director of the NAE, Billy Melvin answered: "Money! It's a constant challenge and battle."[100]

What is more, the NAE suffered from both organizational weaknesses and from being the victim of its own success. On the one hand, it was hampered throughout its history by its unbureaucratic and ad hoc administrative setup. This manifested itself in high staff turnover, frequent changes in executive leadership, and extended periods of theological conflict and political upheaval. Since many dynamic impulses within postwar evangelicalism emanated from outside the NAE, it had to compete with the efforts of existing denominations and parachurch organizations. Moreover, the meeting minutes of many of the NAE's commissions reveal that members spent a lot of their time trying to define their areas of work. They often lacked knowledge about what was happening on church levels, and were preoccupied with concerns about ministers who claimed to represent the NAE. In addition, the pressure to differentiate themselves from liberal and fundamentalist tendencies turned fears of infiltration and dissent into a dominant mindset. Reporting on the progress of ecumenicity, for example, the minutes of the 1961 staff retreat noted that "the problem is that the NCC [National Council of Churches] is seeking to infiltrate and neutralize the NAE." In reaction to this "deliberate plan," the meeting suggested sending a letter of warning to regional representatives, issued a request "to send in all evidence or documents available relating to this matter," and recommended talking to individuals personally.[101]

The organization's soul-searching in the aftermath of the 1953 leadership crisis provides a good snapshot of these built-in organizational problems. In his address to the Board of Administration, NAE president Paul S. Rees warned that "we have lost something of the sense of 'movement'; we have allowed a film to form over some of our 'positive goals'; we have come perilously close to financial insolvency; and, unhappy as is the truth, we have not realized in full the promise of that 'influence and power' which Dr. Ockenga envisaged in his message to us in 1944." Concerned that "our days of grace from making serious mistakes are running out on us," Rees located the causes of the NAE's weakness in a variety of centrifugal tendencies that had resulted in a lack of commitment on the part of member denominations. While independents and denominational dissenters urged the NAE to engage in projects as a "church," well-organized doctrinal groupings, such as the pentecostals, saw the NAE mainly as a "service organization" for their own cooperative endeavors and for other successful coordinating bodies, such as the purchasing arm of EFMA. Rees recognized that "some of the services which no cooperative evangelical agency was supplying when NAE was formed are now available through other agencies" and that "weakening at the center has been simultaneous with strength at the circumference—where NAE commissions or organizations have become conspicuously successful." As pentecostals and members of the Wesleyan-Holiness traditions formed their own national bodies, namely the World Fellowship and the National Holiness Association, he feared that the NAE would end up a rump organization of dissenters and independents from mainly Calvinistic churches. Worried that the NAE might break apart, Rees urged a more business-like approach, efficiency savings, financial reorganization, and strengthening either the regional offices or the commissions and affiliated organizations.[102]

Though the NAE implemented some changes, controversies continued over issues of unity, a clear doctrinal statement, and social and political involvement.[103] In October 1962 NAE executive director George L. Ford told the Board of Administration that the "development of a stronger national organization and the changing conditions we face including financial pressures, public opinion and world affairs" necessitated a thorough review of the NAE's organizational structure, particularly its commissions, affiliates, and regional programs. Indicating the controversial nature of this, Clyde Taylor scribbled "centralization of power corrupts" on the margins of his copy of the report.[104] Ten years later, similar issues still dominated the internal debates. Offering "criticism and hope about the future of NAE," leading evangelicals called for the professionalization of the organization. They decried the lack of coordination and communication, and criticized the duplication of effort. They also wanted to see a younger leadership that could develop new strategies for uniting the vast variety of evangelical groups and bring lay movements into the organization's orbit.[105]

## Conclusion

By the late 1950s, white evangelical Protestants had attained a measure of sociocultural legitimacy, theological authority, internal unity, and political influence that they had not experienced since the nineteenth century. Dominated by moderate neo-evangelicals from its Puritan-Reformed wing, the postwar movement had established itself as a "third force" in American Protestantism. While denouncing liberal Protestantism, with its modernist theology and social gospel tradition, evangelicals had also distanced themselves from the culturally isolated and largely apolitical fundamentalism. They had largely abandoned traditional fundamentalist anti-Semitism, toned down their racism, and were more moderate in their anticommunism than the fundamentalist hardliners. The growing gulf between fundamentalism and evangelicalism culminated in the formation of two competing organizations. The ACCC (1941) demanded strict separatism and doctrinal purity. The NAE (1942) focused on evangelism and on creating a broad interdenominational evangelical basis. While the NAE provided the organizational focus, Billy Graham's evangelism became the public face of the movement, and the magazine *Christianity Today*, Wheaton College, and Fuller Theological Seminary provided intellectual leadership.

Not only had evangelicals emancipated themselves from separatist fundamentalism; they had also found crucial support among conservatives within the mainline churches. The war years had made the modernist-fundamentalist rift feel rather remote. They had revived interest in conservative doctrine and raised doubts about the wisdom of liberal modernism and postmillennialism within mainline denominations. The evangelicals' desire to overcome the squabbling of the previous periods, soften the hard edges of prewar fundamentalism, and build bridges across denominational divides was appreciated in the postwar age of consensus and helped them gain new theological authority, social relevance, and political access.

The neo-evangelical position, however, was characterized by the tension between two sets of conflicting objectives. While its advocates sought ecumenical inclusiveness, intellectual legitimacy, mass appeal, and integration into mainstream culture, they simultaneously desired to preserve a subcultural identity and a clear theological demarcation from the liberal and orthodox camps. Evangelicalism's rabid anti-Catholicism, especially, continued to mark the movement's distance from the liberal currents of American culture. By the same token, evangelicals strove toward organizational consolidation, yet continued to display diversity and fragmentation. This dual institutional and ideological provenance of neo-evangelicalism shaped its particular political and sociocultural appearance in the postwar period. It also suggests that the movement's identity as a "third force" within American Protestantism was based less on fixed theological concepts than on continuous coalition building and negotiating in the context of the dynamics of Cold War society.

The NAE in particular came to reflect these contradictory impulses. Under its auspices, evangelicals organized lobbying efforts in Washington, set up a clearinghouse for legislative campaigns, coordinated relief and missionary work, spawned powerful parachurch agencies, and fostered the training of conservative Christians for positions in government. To an extent the NAE managed to bring together the divided field of conservative Protestantism. At the same time, however, its attempts at forging evangelical unity continued to be stymied by doctrinal fragmentation, the association's loose organizational features, its financial shortfalls, and its failure to draw in some of the larger denominations. Moreover, conservative Protestantism remained characterized by raucous theological debates and a wide range of political identities. The NAE's records reveal the often arduous attempt to mobilize evangelicals and to find a consensus on theological, social, and political issues across a diversity of sectarian traditions linked together in a decentralized body. By the early 1960s it had become clear that the organization had failed to provide an institutional umbrella and a unified voice for moderate evangelicalism. As the next chapter shows, it soon began to show the problems typical of a movement aspiring to "cooperation without compromise."

In April 1942, around 150 evangelical leaders met in the Coronado Hotel in St. Louis to found the National Association of Evangelicals (NAE). Although membership consisted mainly of smaller denominations and grew only gradually in the postwar decades, the NAE emerged as the key umbrella organization of American neo-evangelicalism. (property of the National Association of Evangelicals)

The NAE elected Boston pastor Harold John Ockenga as its first president. Ockenga represented a new generation of evangelical leaders who had been trained at elite universities, rather than at fundamentalist Bible schools. He added the coveted "touch of class" to the new organization that sought to distance itself from the more xenophobic and bigoted aspects of prewar fundamentalism. (Wheaton College Archives)

The organizational hub for many of the NAE's political activities was the Office of Public Affairs, led for more than three decades by Clyde W. Taylor. In his role as OPA Secretary and later as NAE General Director, Taylor was the main liaison between the organization and the federal government, as well as a key figure in setting up a range of NAE affiliates and agencies, including World Relief, National Religious Broadcasters, and the Evangelical Foreign Missions Association. (property of the National Association of Evangelicals)

*Bottom left*: Carl F. H. Henry was one of a group of neo-evangelical thinkers who brought intellectual sophistication to postwar evangelicalism. Straddling highbrow interest in theology and lowbrow interest in revivalism, Henry remained an influential figure in the movement throughout his long life. He was instrumental in the founding of Fuller Theological Seminary and the creation of *Christianity Today*, which he edited until the late 1960s. (Billy Graham Center Archives, Wheaton College)

Founded in 1947, Fuller Theological Seminary was the jewel in the crown of new evangelical educational institutions. Although squabbles and administrative problems wracked the fledgling seminary, it eventually became one of the leading centers of evangelical ministerial training. In the 1960s and 1970s it turned into a stronghold of liberal and left evangelicalism. (Archives and Special Collections, David Allan Hubbard Library, Fuller Theological Seminary)

Although often cooperating closely with the NAE, many parachurch organizations, such as Youth for Christ (YfC), remained outside the organizational framework of the association. Inspired by the youth work of Jack Wyrtzen and others, YfC rallies included entertainment, singing, and vigorous preaching, and provided a platform from which Billy Graham was able to launch his career as full-time evangelist. (National Association of Evangelicals Records (SC-113), Wheaton College Special Collections)

# 3

# The Evangelical Left and the 1960s

If the 1940s and 1950s provided ample opportunities for the institutional and theological assertion of conservative Protestantism, the insurgent movements of the 1960s and 1970s challenged neo-evangelicals to add a social and cultural dimension to their quest. Inspired by Carl Henry, Francis Schaeffer, and other neo-evangelical thinkers, and influenced by their own participation in the civil rights and antiwar movements, a younger generation of liberal and leftwing evangelicals explored new ways of reconciling theological orthodoxy with cultural relevance, sociopolitical influence, and organizational effectiveness. Throughout the tectonic shifts of the 1960s, they engaged in a spate of grassroots institution building. Indeed, they thrived through their engagement with issues such as racial segregation, economic exploitation, anticolonialism, and the revolution in morals and manners, rather than on the basis of their opposition to the insurgencies and countercultural impulses of the period.

The resurgence of evangelical social concern constitutes one of the least studied aspects of the postwar religious upsurge, mainly because the assumption of the "great reversal" of evangelicalism has dominated scholarship. This refers to the alleged switch from the nineteenth-century emphasis on the social gospel to a twentieth-century focus on personal piety and evangelism.[1] In addition, the singular focus on the rise of the Christian Right and its staunch support for free-market policies, spiritualization of liberal capitalism, and advocacy of "morality politics" has obscured the diversity of evangelical social and political attitudes. In contrast to the common image of its uncritical embrace of the American way of life, however, evangelical social thought has traditionally contained some uneasiness about unfettered capitalism, which found expression in, for example, campaigns against Sunday work and money lending. It has viewed both socialism and capitalism not as Christian frameworks, but as secular dogmas.[2] Indeed, as late as the 1990s capitalism was one of the more divisive issues within American evangelicalism. While evangelicals at one point may have been unified as defenders of capitalism, "a vociferous evangelical left . . . has become increasingly influential over the last twenty years," and even the evangelical mainstream "has become troubled by the issue of capitalism."[3]

As the sixties turned into a period of unmistakable renaissance in social concern comparable only to the time before the Civil War, vigorous evangelical institution building and a new popular openness to spirituality came together to allow conservative Protestantism to reach into new constituencies. This set the stage for one of the most remarkable feats of the resurgence: Evangelical and fundamentalist churches, rather than being swept away by the waves of antitraditionalism and iconoclasm in the sixties, emerged victorious from the upheaval. Unlike mainstream churches, conservative denominations experienced continuous and sustained growth in a period of declining levels of religious involvement. Evangelicalism also enjoyed a new surge of popular and media interest, culminating in *Time* magazine's declaring 1976 the "year of the evangelical."[4]

While the 1960s re-energized evangelicalism and gave it a new public presence and popularity, however, the decade also exposed the movement's fault lines. As had been the case with the social gospel earlier in the century, the issue of social and political action turned into the Achilles' heel of the movement. In the words of George Marsden, in the 1960s "evangelical social-political involvement, which neo-evangelical leaders had called for in the 1940s and 50s, now indeed emerged, but as a prime source of division." For a time the evangelical Left's political liberalism, in combination with its strong dedication to the biblical tradition, appeared to be able to bridge the gap between religious progressives and conservatives. As the decade unfolded, however, left evangelicalism's renewed commitment to social action in the context of the insurgencies of the period polarized the movement, which had never been unified in the first place and had "at best maintained a tenuous antiliberal theological unity."[5] Acrimonious debates about social involvement, political participation, and race issues, as well as battles over inerrancy and other theological quarrels, left the movement both divided and adrift. By the late 1960s the evangelical coalition was hopelessly split.[6] This ushered in a period of soul-searching and internal purges during which liberal and left-leaning groups were effectively marginalized.

Nonetheless, the way in which left-leaning evangelical groups accommodated sixties impulses and transported a countercultural identity ironically ended up providing the success formula of the resurgent New Christian Right. Although many observers locate the rise of the Right primarily in its opposition to liberal tendencies within the movement and its efforts to undo the 1960s, the growing supremacy of this wing of conservative Protestantism is rather more effectively explained by its ability to build upon the ideological, institutional, and cultural trailblazing of its adversaries. The New Christian Right retained the Left's impetus for social action in its campaign for political mobilization. It combined ecumenical inclusiveness with a renewed insistence on the absolutes of biblical faith, and it appropriated countercultural styles and cultivated an insurgent image while embracing consumer capitalism and traditional morality. In the end, the particular way in which conservative Protestantism selectively integrated sixties impulses was at the center of its socioeconomic appeal and cultural resonance.[7]

In placing the rise of the New Christian Right since the 1970s in the broader context of postwar evangelicalism, one might be tempted to substitute an exaggerated notion of the impact of the evangelical Left for the excessive emphasis on the Right in established scholarship. The evangelical Left, however, was neither large nor deeply entrenched in the broader movement. Nonetheless, it posed a clear challenge to the evangelical establishment. While small in number, leftwing advocates were highly educated, motivated, outspoken, and ready to shape the movement during a time of organizational and ideological upheaval. Although it was ultimately not that difficult for the Right to sideline its internal opponents, the conservatives' own sense that they needed to rein in liberal and leftwing tendencies in order to assert themselves meant that they were profoundly shaped by their engagement with their adversaries. The latter were thus crucial for New Right mobilizing and ideology formation. Furthermore, the limited resurgence of leftwing evangelicalism in the early twenty-first century continues to highlight the breadth of political sentiment within evangelicalism. It also shows that the Right became dominant on the basis of internal movement struggles, rather than simply on the basis of the natural proclivity of evangelicals for rightwing politics.

## Evangelicals and Social Concern in the 1950s

By the late 1950s the neo-evangelicals were riding high. Carl Henry had achieved three of his four goals for the movement. First was the creation of a neo-evangelical revivalist ministry, which Billy Graham had pulled off. Second came the foundation of new educational institutions, of which Fuller Theological Seminary was the crown. Third was a magazine of evangelical thought, embodied in *Christianity Today*. Yet all was not well. As evangelicals gained public recognition, established a media presence, lobbied in Washington, converted souls, and sent new missionaries to the farthest corners of the earth, Henry's fourth goal—a breakthrough in evangelical social action—kept eluding them. "It would be simple to name northern fundamentalists who drink hard liquor, southern fundamentalists who are Nazis on race questions, eastern fundamental- ists who are blind on labor rights, and western fundamentalists who glory in war," Harold John Ockenga noted with dismay. "Too many fundamentalists are on the wrong side of ethical questions."[8]

Theological uneasiness exacerbated this sense of social failure. By the late 1950s it exceeded the normal levels of cultivated gloom prevalent in a religion obsessed with sin, depravity, worldly corruption, and the expectation of cata- clysmic collapse. In particular, evangelical leaders were deeply disturbed by the flock's lack of knowledge about theology and religious texts and feared that religion did not change people's lives to the degree one would expect from the level of professed faith. This indicated that religion served as a collective cultural and psychological affirmation of established lifestyles and the institutional status quo, rather than as a source of transcendence. The yearning for relevance, acceptance, and respect had driven evangelicals toward the embrace of consumer capitalism, popular culture, and the norms and values of middle-class white America.[9]

Reflecting a fear that evangelicalism could turn into a "culture religion," evangelical theologian Francis Schaeffer warned his fellow believers that "it will not do . . . to carry on Christian work with the means or techniques of the world (which so admirably sell cornflakes, cars, and strange sects), and then expect men to be convinced that God exists and that He is personal." Empha- sizing that biblical grounding was an antidote to the subjectivism of modernity, he exhorted evangelicals to witness the living spirit.[10] Similarly, a 1956 survey of the 50 editors of *Christianity Today* revealed growing concerns about the worldliness of evangelicalism. Many saw the current revival as superficial and lacking biblical emphasis. They feared that secular aspects had crept into the religious resurgence, and that the rising prestige and wealth of churches undermined the sense of dependence on God. "Alongside the hopeful signs of spiritual renewal, we must set the continuing materialism and moral softness of much of American life," evangelical educator Frank E. Gaebelein warned. Reminding readers that "the divine plan is not world conversion but world evangelization," he counseled that "so long as our way of life shows little of self denial, we must ask whether the current revival is deep as well as widespread."[11]

In turn, many neo-evangelical leaders regarded renewed social involvement as a way of reviving the transformational spirit of the movement. Once again they demarcated the evangelical approach in contrast to both fundamentalism and liberalism.[12] According to Henry, Ockenga, and other leading evangelical lights, fundamentalists had made a great mistake in abandoning the field of social problems. Instead of advancing a social program steeped in redemptive supernaturalism, they had reacted against the social gospel and thus allowed secularists and liberals to capture the field. The judgment of two world wars, however, had revealed the shallowness of the modernist insistence on inevitable progress based on man's essential goodness, as well as the narrowness of the fundamentalist focus on individual sins and its exhortations about the moral dangers of dancing, drinking, and mixed swimming.[13] Henry in particular argued that these deficiencies offered the opportunity for a new generation of evangelicals to reclaim their rightful leadership in the field of social reform with a program of redemptive regeneration. Invoking the great tradition of the antislavery campaign, the British crusade for child-labor laws and prison reforms, and the evangelical origins of the British labor movement, he exhorted his fellow believers to get involved in social and political affairs.[14] By working with both non-evangelical liberals and fundamentalists with a social conscience, he argued, evangelicals could furnish the moral dynamics of social reform and show that conservative Christianity could "compete as a vital world ideology."[15]

For this purpose, the social action agenda of the neo-evangelicals was carefully calibrated. On the one hand, Henry, Schaeffer, Graham, and others urged evangelicals to develop a new attitude to economic issues. They arranged meetings on social issues such as "aggressive warfare, racial hatred and intolerance, the liquor traffic, and the exploitation of labor or management, whichever it may be."[16] Henry's renowned 1947 book *The Uneasy Conscience of Modern Fundamentalism*, while generally suggesting a conservative direction, urged the formulation of alternatives to both secular socialism and secular capitalism. Convinced that American capitalism was not beyond Christian criticism, he chided management for its excesses and acknowledged the need for workplace democracy, even as he rebuked the labor movement for its lack of spiritual roots and focus on materialistic goals. Although he saw trade unions as at times "illicitly organized," he recognized that they constituted the largest social movement next to the churches and were here to stay.[17] Similarly, Schaeffer voiced a limited critique of materialism and capitalism. Arguing for the "compassionate use of accumulated wealth," he revived notions of Christian "revolution" and communal life, and presciently urged his fellow believers to reflect upon environmentalism, alienation, and sensitivity to nature.[18] Likewise, Graham at times promoted a liberal approach to social problems. Though he made no specific policy recommendations, he endorsed Lyndon Johnson's War on Poverty. By the late 1960s,

Graham was guardedly progressive on issues such as poverty and the arms race, and increasingly urged involvement in social ministries. While an opponent of women's liberation, he supported equal pay.[19]

In the same vein, Henry, Schaeffer, and Graham urged evangelicals to address the race problem. They warned that liberals were stealing the evangelicals' thunder in the struggle for racial equality, even though evangelicals had spearheaded abolitionism. Henry in particular complained that "the Negro's plight became for some liberal reformers an opportunity for promoting social revolution, and for some conservative reactionaries an occasion for perpetuating segregation and discrimination."[20] Sharing Henry's view that evangelical Christianity "has a burden for social renewal but no penchant for revolution or reaction," Graham was cautiously progressive on civil rights. A pioneer in racial integration, he led the first integrated crusade in Chattanooga, Tennessee, in 1953, and supported Lyndon Johnson's Civil Rights Act in 1964.[21]

Despite regarding social action as crucial for establishing cultural relevance and political influence, however, the neo-evangelicals continued to define evangelical social witness as different from the aspirations of liberal social gospellers. Henry insisted that social change had to start with individual conversion and with a realistic assessment of human nature as sinful, but not lost. Charging that liberals were dissolving "righteousness into love" and diluting "social justice into compassion," he located the origins of spiritual decline and the rise of secularism in the modernist attack on historical Christian theology.[22] Since the good society and a republican order could only be based on individuals driven by an inner conformity to moral commands, the emphasis on evangelism and soul-winning had to be the basis for recapturing social concern.[23] In the same vein, Graham continued to call for spiritually based social action to help the poor. Seeing sin as the root of all evil, he did not regard social action as a substitute for evangelism. Hence, conversion remained the "conceptual core" of neo-evangelicalism.[24]

Henry's 1965 essay "Evangelicals in the Social Struggle" illustrated the neo-evangelical vacillation between a desire to engage in social action, worries about its divisive potential, faith in salvationist theology, and concerns over growing worldliness. Henry declared that "surely evangelical Christianity has more to offer mankind than its unique message of salvation, even if that is its highest and holiest mission," and that evangelicals needed to "articulate mobilization on their own account." Nonetheless, he wavered between a focus on saving souls that "restores men to moral earnestness" and a desire to get evangelicals politically involved in an unregenerate world. While critical of the liberal identification with a specific political and legislative program, he wanted redeemed men to be concerned about "relations between nations and about minority rights" and to "use every political opportunity to support and promote just laws, to protest social injustice, and to serve their fellow men."[25]

Postwar attempts by Henry and his wayfarers to place social action at the center of the NAE were equally ambivalent. On the one hand the movement clearly experienced an upsurge of social involvement and institution building that stretched beyond the foreign aid field, where four major evangelical relief agencies had been created in the 1950s.[26] The Greater Minneapolis Association of Evangelicals, for example, successfully organized social welfare efforts, pooling the resources of more than 200 churches and supporting prison chaplaincies, halfway houses, coffee houses, and involvement in urban politics and moral affairs.[27] Similarly, the NAE's Evangelical Child Welfare Agency grew out of the "new concept" of social consciousness among evangelicals. Primarily involved in family counseling and placing babies given up for adoption, it "put NAE on the map and opened the door to acceptance by many."[28] Other successful individual evangelical welfare agencies included those in Chicago, Los Angeles, and Syracuse, New York.[29] Moreover, the NAE became increasingly involved in moves to establish evangelical retirement homes.[30] Evangelicals outside the NAE likewise sought to recover the social action tradition of the faith. By the middle of the twentieth century, the Southern Baptists, for example, had created two full-time agencies devoted to social issues.[31]

Despite these efforts, however, many evangelicals on the other hand remained reluctant to elevate social action to a central objective of the NAE's national mission, and in the end the NAE failed to become an effective coordinating body for the movement's social impulses. Intellectually, social concern remained the Cinderella of neo-evangelicalism throughout the 1950s and early 1960s. While the efforts of Henry and others had put social action back on the movement's agenda, their views hardly caught on before the mid- to late 1960s. A survey conducted by *United Evangelical Action* indicated that the period between 1945 and 1960 was, in fact, marked by diminishing interest in social concern among the rank and file.[32] Preferring to see social action confined to local efforts, participants in the 1961 NAE staff retreat voiced the view that the NAE "should only perform what cannot be done by churches," and that "it is not the job of regional director to run a welfare agency." Office of Public Affairs staff member Don Gill reported that "a pilot study of Maine churches showed that evangelical churches were not interested in community life."[33] As Jon Stone has noted, "all the grandiloquent pronouncements to the contrary, evangelicals were not, in the main, at the forefront of social issues."[34]

The reluctance on the part of the pioneers of neo-evangelical social concern to embrace a specific program contributed to this lack of a clear strategy. Though Henry pleaded for social action, embraced racial equality, and called for adequate health care and economic sustenance, he did not outline a detailed plan. In part his recognition of the deep divisions on political and social issues and the disruptive potential of obscure theological debates within evangelicalism strengthened his conviction that the gospel of personal salvation and spiritual regeneration formed the only basis for engineering evangelical unity on political goals.[35] Refraining from social action in this way, however, amounted to a spiritual sanctioning of American-style liberal capitalism and gradualism in race relations. Although Henry saw substantive social change in the form of racial equality and the elimination of poverty as highly desirable, he asserted evangelical support for private property rights, anti-unionism, the profit motive, and patriotic nationalism. He adhered to an atomistic view of the individual and a contractual concept of society, preached a limited concept of government, favored management over labor, and taught loyalty to the free enterprise system.[36] In turn, *Christianity Today* featured diatribes against socialism and the labor movement as well as adulatory tracts about the virtues of liberal capitalism.[37] Economist Norman C. Hunt, for example, argued that capitalism was consistent with Christianity, while "collectivism" was not.[38] Likewise, Irving E. Howard discarded "collectivism" and its "idealistic" philosophical origins as automatically leading to a police state, whereas the "materialistic" theory of free enterprise merely lacked moral depth. Regarding capitalism, voluntarism, and limited government as biblical, he justified economic inequality and limits on labor unions.[39]

In the eyes of many critics, this dismissal of social concerns constituted the failure of the evangelical conscience. Whereas evangelicals had once played "a more progressive innovative role socially and culturally," neo-evangelicalism, dominated since World War II by the NAE, Billy Graham, and the Evangelical Theological Society, remained predominantly white, middle-class, Calvinist, and politically conservative.[40] This set the stage for a revolt instigated by a group of young evangelical leaders who had grown up during the morally charged Cold War era and were keenly aware of its profound contradictions.

## The Rise of the Evangelical Left

Radicalized by the civil rights movement, the nuclear threat, the youth rebellion, and the Vietnam War, a new generation of restless, articulate, college-educated evangelicals chided the NAE for having failed to develop a coherent social action agenda or to address the social shortcomings of American society. While adhering to the orthodox Christian faith, they rejected the social and political conservatism of established evangelicalism. Attacking blatant racism, sexism, militarism, and indifference to economic injustice on the part of the white churches, these insurgent evangelicals, such as Jim Wallis, John Howard Yoder, Clark Pinnock, Dale Brown, and Art Gish, challenged the cozy relations that prevailed between Graham and the political establishment, and made social action the distinguishing mark of their religious commitment. Their concept of "social holiness" emphasized once again the transformation not only of sinful individuals, but also of a sinful social order. While conservative W. T. Miller regarded the "use of profanity" as the greatest evil, evangelical activist and later historian Richard Pierard declared that "for me, . . . the napalming of Vietnamese children, the bugging of Democratic Party headquarters, and the widely publicized corrupt milk and grain deals are far more serious sins."[41]

Linking radical social thought to a renewed emphasis on strict evangelical piety in ways that recalled the social gospel, leftwing evangelicals regarded capitalism as a system of oppression and exploitation by powerful corporate elites that placed profit over the social good. Capitalism undermined democracy, they argued, because it promoted consumerism, manipulative advertising, greed, envy, fear, and selfishness as the engines of the economy. It commodified life, led to the breakup of communities and families, and destroyed the environment. In the eyes of many leftwing evangelicals, the church had become part of this "collective sin." It had bought into the idols of the age by marketing the gospel, worshipping church growth, and selling Jesus as a spiritual commodity.[42]

Stressing the traditional Christian notion of the "epistemological privilege of the poor," evangelical radicals reminded their fellow believers that poverty was essential to Christian discipleship, that private accumulation of wealth was prohibited by the Bible, and that wealthy Christians who refused to identify with the poor were incapable of understanding the biblical message. They called both for a return to a simple and communal lifestyle and for economic redistribution to redress the imbalance of power in society. In seeking to recover a holistic understanding of the faith, left evangelicals understood conversion as a social renewal, rather than as an ahistorical transaction between God and individual sinners. Although they did not deny personal evil, left evangelicals viewed conversion in part as the repentance for the sin of involvement in structural evils. It was part of a quest to unmask the idolatrous claims to sacredness made by existing "principalities and powers" on their own behalf. Conversion was thus not only the basis for individual spiritual change; it also generated impulses for social action leading to the transformation of capitalism and the assertion of a moral Christian will over allegedly uncontrollable economic laws.[43]

In many ways the rise of the evangelical Left was a sign of the success of postwar evangelicalism's emphasis on education, intellectual stature, theological leadership, and cultural engagement. It mirrored many of the sociodemographic trends that fed into the broader political and cultural upheaval of the 1960s, such as growing affluence, college education, desire for individual fulfillment, and involvement in new organizational forms. By the late 1960s the number of evangelicals with college degrees had increased substantially, and campuses and religious seminaries had become places where leftwing evangelicals gained influence and visibility by appealing to zealous students organized in the Inter-Varsity Christian Fellowship and similar groups. Trained as pastors, youth ministers, missionaries, or clinical psychologists at evangelical powerhouses such as Fuller and Wheaton, left evangelicals were at the core of the social ferment within the evangelical churches of the 1960s.[44] Having been raised in the belief in America's beneficent global role while witnessing the country's slide into corruption, they combined an anti-establishment mood with social engagement through their work among the poor and underprivileged.[45] By the 1960s only a little more than half of Fuller students thought social justice less important than evangelism—as compared with the 1950s, when consistently more than 90 percent thought the latter more important.[46]

The resurgent evangelical Left was instrumental in inspiring the kind of social activism and grassroots organizing that had failed to materialize under neo-evangelical auspices. Pierard, Ron Sider, Lewis Smedes, David Moberg, John Alexander, Robert Webber, Stephen Monsma, and others involved in Evangelicals for McGovern called for an end to "the outdated stereotype that evangelical automatically means a politics unconcerned about the poor, minorities, and unnecessary military expenditures."[47] Groups such as the People's Christian Coalition (Sojourner Community) championed women's rights, pacifism, progressive social justice, and civil rights. With the support of many older evangelicals, the resurgent Left formed Evangelicals Concerned, the National Black Evangelical Association (NBEA), the Evangelical Women's Caucus, Evangelicals for Social Action, and other organizations.[48]

Sixties evangelicals were also instrumental in adding a strong religious strain to the "community populism" (to use Peter Carroll's term) of the 1970s. In turn, the mushrooming evangelical social service sector expanded, became more formalized, and attained a more prominent position in evangelical rhetoric.[49] Among crucial evangelical organizations of the period were The Bridge, an alliance of a dozen Phoenix-area churches providing rent for homeless families; the Lutheran Church–Missouri Synod Church Extension Fund; the Interfaith Hunger Coalition in Houston, Texas; Citizens for Community Development in Waterloo, Iowa; Sand Mountain Parish, which operated a cannery and offered employment and low-cost housing in rural Alabama; and the well-known Habitat for Humanity, which, though not specifically evangelical, received strong support from conservative Protestants. Other examples include the Christian Rehabilitation Center in Charlotte, North Carolina, the Emmanuel Gospel Center in Boston, and Voice of Calvary Ministries in Jackson, Mississippi. The last-named was the brainchild of John Perkins, an African American minister who was a member of both Evangelicals for Social Action and the NAE's Social Action Commission. Voice of Calvary primarily sought to strengthen black communities via medical help, cooperative stores, low-cost housing, education, and civil rights advocacy.[50]

The renewed involvement of evangelical churches in inner-urban relief after a long period of downtown flight led to similar expansions in social service efforts. The traditional concerns with health care, immigrant aid, youth ministry, and treatment for alcoholism were enhanced by organizations that addressed systemic issues such as economic development, job training, housing, and legal aid. Examples include the Church of the Saviour in Washington, D.C., La Salle Street Church in Chicago, and the Church of the Nazarene in New York.[51] Moreover, established evangelical social relief agencies, such as World Relief, World Vision, and Medical Assistance Program, experienced significant growth in the 1970s.[52] Most apparent, however, was the upsurge in social concern among African American evangelical churches, which ventured far into the area of medical aid, housing corporations, and credit unions.[53]

The decentralized and personal approach of evangelicalism fit the spirit of community organizing in the early 1970s. Geared toward addressing problems emerging from a spiritual crisis, reliant upon an existing network of social service institutions, and skilled in modern promotion and organization, evangelical agencies thrived in the aftermath of widespread post-1960s frustration with government. In light of this, the commonplace assumption that the religious revival of the 1970s was marked by a retreat from social activism and a concentration on personal spirituality needs to be revised. Beneath the media hype and the florid conversion stories of Black Panther Eldridge Cleaver, *Hustler* magazine's Larry Flynt, and musician Eric Clapton, a more lasting legacy of renewed social activism was established during this time.[54]

Closely linked to the renewed call for social action by the evangelical Left was its challenge to traditional doctrinal positions. Sharing the sense of unease about "civil religion" voiced by establishment evangelicals like Henry and Schaeffer, many left-leaning activists sought to recapture the movement's radical promise from its co-optation and corruption by a materialistic culture. And, in turn, many questioned the orthodoxies of the faith. Challenges ranged from Paul K. Jewett's critique of the subordination of women to Daniel P. Fuller's attack on the doctrine of inerrancy. As a highly educated and zealous elite, left evangelicals engaged with both biblical criticism and social science scholarship. They wrote about evolutionary theories and expressed support for feminism and Marxism. Likewise, as the number of left evangelicals with academic credentials increased significantly in the 1970s, they became more liberal in their attitudes toward alcohol, tobacco, sexuality, divorce, social dancing, and civil liberties. They discarded old taboos and became more culturally sophisticated and socially mobile. Theologically speaking, the left evangelicals rejected the theology of the word in favor of the theology of the spirit. With Karl Barth, Dietrich Bonhoeffer, and Reinhold Niebuhr as their theological heroes, their focus was on the transforming power of the Bible, not on scripture as the retainer for divine truth. As sixties evangelicalism came into its own, it became less insistent on exclusivism, more tolerant of differences in belief, more insistent on social witness, and less dogmatic about inerrancy and the historical-critical method.[55]

## Social Concern as a Source of Movement Conflict

In combining theological challenges with social concerns, many left evangelicals sought to bridge the gap between liberals, who denied the need for conversion to Christ, and evangelicals, who had in the past rejected social action. For a time the Left's combination of progressive political engagement with a strong commitment to the biblical tradition appeared to offer a unifying vision. Combining political participation and separatist institution building, these efforts had the potential to unite the evangelical fold and to reach out across denominational boundaries by adding to the movement the social dimension that had so far failed to materialize. Leading figures in the evangelical establishment lent their support to this cause. The 1969 Congress on Evangelism, for example, put the emphasis on social action. Billy Graham's brother-in-law Leighton Ford criticized the postwar evangelicals' anticommunist stance and their failure to address racism. He supported the War on Poverty, denounced racial inequality, and raised the issue of housing discrimination, unequal distribution of property, and international inequality. Likewise, Carl Henry became a signatory of the 1973 Chicago Declaration of Evangelical Social Concern, which confessed evangelical complicity in racism, sexism, materialism, militarism, and economic injustice.[56]

Yet, as Henry had feared back in the mid-1950s, the upsurge of social action ultimately fragmented and polarized the movement. The "division on social strategy runs as deep today as the theological cleavage in Protestantism," he had concluded, cautioning that "to compensate for a disunity which grows out of a basic departure from biblical norms by a unity which is man made is to jump out of confusion into caprice."[57] His warnings were prescient. Conflicts over race issues and over levels of political involvement tore the Left apart; many traditionalist evangelicals remained suspicious of social action and rejected the Left's theological innovations; and while evangelical subgroups, churches, and NAE affiliates thrived, the central organization remained weak and adrift. By the late 1970s Henry worried that the controversies over inerrancy and social involvement, and the weakness of the evangelical center, might overshadow the evangelical successes achieved since the 1940s in public recognition, evangelism, and mission work. His assessment of the evangelical condition in the waning days of the Carter presidency was blunt: Evangelicals were "out of the closet but going nowhere."[58]

The history of the interaction between the NAE's various social action commissions and the left-liberal organization Evangelicals for Social Action (ESA) illustrates the divisive potential of infusing social concerns into the national organization. The NAE's first Commission on Social Action (CSA) was founded in 1951. Chaired by S. Richie Kamm, head of the social science division at Wheaton College, the new body was intended to speak out on social, economic, governmental, and related issues. It sponsored forums at NAE conventions on sociopolitical topics, such as race and labor-management conflicts. It also engaged in fact-finding and awareness-raising, sought to channel students into social work, and urged the creation of evangelical schools of social work.[59]

Throughout the 1950s and 1960s, however, the commission lacked a clear definition of its mission, experienced a high turnover in membership, and remained largely ineffectual. Many early discussions about its remit revolved around the question whether the NAE should sponsor welfare agencies or simply act as a coordinating body and clearinghouse for Christian welfare groups.[60] By the fall of 1956 the commission had decided to focus on the latter, less ambitious goal and "make available advisory and consulting services in its field of social work."[61] A year later the commission "departmentalized" into divisions concerned with governmental work, welfare work, and civil defense. It also joined the Office of Public Affairs in sponsoring the Washington Seminars on Federal Service, which trained evangelicals for public office.[62] Designed to prepare a fledgling evangelical political elite from Christian colleges for federal employment, "where they will have an opportunity to witness for Christ and to serve their nation," the seminar series, which had begun in 1957, grew in popularity over the years. Its programs typically included training on government organization as well as visits to departments, the White House, and Capitol

Hill.[63] In effect, evangelicals defined government service as a mission field. The seminars, historian Earle Cairns declared at the NAE's 1961 conference on church-state relations, were part of a larger "strategy of infiltration of well-trained, devout Evangelicals into all branches of government." Indeed, Cairns compared them to the antislavery campaigners of the nineteenth century.[64]

Although it sought to counteract the tendency among conservative churches to abandon social programs, the commission ultimately failed to transcend the emphasis on traditional moral issues. Indeed, its main concerns throughout the 1950s and early 1960s were film censorship and liquor.[65] This did not change much in the ensuing years. In 1961 the CSA focused on pornography, in 1962 on juvenile delinquency, and in 1963 on premarital counseling. Although Kamm suggested in 1963 that the commission deal "with questions which will help the local church implement means for a peaceful solution to racial problems such as real estate (housing) and educational encouragement," his efforts came to naught, and the planned conference on race did not materialize.[66] In 1965 the CSA changed its name to Commission on Social Concern (CSC) to reflect its limited function: "to highlight concerns and give help to the local pastors rather than to bring action or to make pronouncements."[67] Although "Race and the Evangelical" was eventually chosen as the seminar theme for the 1966 NAE convention, the commission's work remained hampered by a lack of knowledge about the social activities of NAE denominations, and its annual budget remained well below $1,000.[68]

A new sense of activism briefly engulfed the commission in the mid-1960s, when Peter Pascoe became the new chairman. By 1966 the commission anticipated a budget of over $2,000, and a "buzz session" for the 1967 program included a report on "the Evangelical and his responsibility to state programs, war on poverty, head start, and international conflict."[69] Pascoe sought to put the CSC on a more solid footing by writing by-laws, compiling a resource paper documenting evangelical social activities, and urging chairs of local, regional, and state committees and denominations to become commission members.[70] His efforts to create a more secure financial structure and to improve the effectiveness of the CSC, however, were often frustrated.[71] After Pascoe's resignation in 1969, Chairman Theodore E. Gannon's report showed ongoing organizational and financial problems, as well as a return to the commission's traditional limited remit. It called for a "Statement of Purpose," effective by-laws, and adequate funds, and it reiterated that the CSC was not in a position to lead a crusade but could only "develop tools" and "provide motivation."[72]

Traditional moral themes such as pornography, sex education in schools, and the "inner-city challenge" once again dominated the commission's agenda.[73]

The only difference was that by 1971 drugs and abortion had been added to the list.[74] A questionnaire sent out by Gannon to members of the NAE Board of Administration informed the commission's thematic priorities. Twenty-eight of the 45 respondents requested "inner-city evangelism" as the primary theme. This was followed by premarital counseling (27), abortion (26), drug abuse (23), homosexuality (21), gambling (20), the evils of alcohol (13), crime (12), pollution (9), and "social disease" (9). Conversely, political issues, such as "more just distribution of goods and services," "women's liberation from a Biblical viewpoint," the "growing power of industrial-military complex," and "peace and war" received only one vote each.[75]

In 1973 the CSC merged with the Evangelical Action Commission to form the Evangelical Social Action Commission (ESAC), which set out to meet with representatives of black evangelical churches and become involved in outreach to the "unevangelized black population."[76] By this time, however, advocates of renewed social concern, frustrated by the inaction of the NAE, had already moved toward establishing their own alternative structures. Suggesting a national congress of evangelical social activists, Ron Sider, a historian at Messiah College's satellite campus in Philadelphia and a driving force behind Evangelicals for McGovern in 1972, hoped to marry conservative theology and progressive politics.[77] Sider, who had recently joined ESAC, not only saw a religious tide sweeping the country, but linked the "massive, widespread concern for social justice" to the evangelicals becoming "the dominant religious influence in the 1970s."[78]

Sider's efforts culminated in the Chicago Declaration and the creation of Evangelicals for Social Action (ESA) in 1973. Over Thanksgiving, 50 evangelical leaders met in Chicago in a workshop to address pressing social issues. Seeing biblical faith and social concern as inseparable, the workshop participants focused on the need to "overcome a purely white outlook" in evangelicalism and denounced "social sins and institutionalized evils as vigorously as personal sins." They "confessed their involvement as evangelicals in individual and institutional racism," insisted that biblical repentance was "inseparable from a Christian discipleship that confronts the social and political injustice of America," and "pledged to rethink their lifestyles and work for a more just distribution of the world's resources."[79]

The Chicago Declaration of Evangelical Social Concern did not just attack the church's complicity in injustice, oppression, racism, sexism, militarism, and international exploitation. Criticizing the "materialism of our culture and the maldistribution of the nation's wealth and services," the signatories also called on institutionalized religion to work actively toward overcoming the racial divide, the inequitable distribution of resources, and gender inequality. In particular, they denounced the "misplaced trust of the nation in economic and military might," which promoted "a national pathology of war." They called on evangelicals to repudiate civil religion and militarism and to "resist the temptation to make the nation and its institutions objects of near-religious loyalty." Many establishment evangelicals, however, remained predictably skeptical of these ambitious aspirations. "I hope they don't suggest dismantling the Armed Forces," an unidentified author wrote on the margins of the copy of the declaration in the NAE records.[80]

The Chicago Declaration, which was "hammered out in three days of careful and sometimes heated discussion," meant a break with established ways of doing things within the evangelical fold. Those assembled "in the stuffy squalor of the Wabash YMCA on the seamy underside of Chicago's Loop" went beyond the old-line evangelical focus on moral issues that didn't challenge the status quo.[81] They "restored a social dimension to the faith that had been missing in conservative Christianity for many years."[82] The declaration also appealed for action beyond the traditional Anabaptist focus on pacifism and relief work. It called on Southern Baptists and Missouri-Synod Lutherans to pursue their causes as part of the larger evangelical family rather than just within their own churches. Moreover, it sought to overcome the isolation of black churches, for whom, in the words of Chicago pastor Clarence Hilliard, "social action is . . . not an option but a way of life."[83]

The declaration attracted support not only from liberal and leftist evangelicals, such as Hilliard, Perkins, John Alexander, Mark Hatfield, Paul Henry, Jim Wallis, Theodore Gannon, World Vision's Paul Rees, and the Southern Baptist Convention's Foy Valentine, but also from such staunch evangelical traditionalists as Carl F. H. Henry and Rufus Jones, the director general of the Conservative Baptist Home Mission Society.[84] Indeed, a 1975 survey of original signatories showed that a majority came from establishment evangelical backgrounds and that many were Democrats or Independents. It also showed that their sociopolitical perspective had "changed mostly from right to left." This change included not only "a more sensitive social conscience," but also "a more socially inclusive definition of sin and salvation." In fact, the survey showed that involvement in a movement or subculture had been the most important influence on their social awareness.[85]

As the don of establishment evangelicalism, Carl Henry had long fretted over the lack of social concern in the postwar movement. In signing the Chicago Declaration, he expressed the hope that it would balance calls for individual conversion with demands for change in social structures, and that it would help transcend the evangelical division in a specifically biblical way. In his view, the manifesto did "not leap from a vision of social utopia to legislative specifics, but concentrated first on biblical priorities for social change," seeking to overcome the polarization of "right" and "left." Commending the initiators for taking the "evangelical initiative in social action at a time when the secular and ecumenical social thrust is sputtering for lack of steam," Henry likened their efforts to eighteenth- and nineteenth-century evangelical campaigns "in such matters as slavery, factory working conditions, child-labor laws, illiteracy, prison conditions, unemployment, poverty, education for the underprivileged, and much else." Finally, he saw the new movement as indicative of the need for political involvement. Though not inclined to launch an evangelical political party, he saw "mounting concern for open evangelical engagement in the political arena."[86]

Crucially, theological quibbles were largely absent at the Chicago workshop. This helped unify activists across traditions and denominations. As the *Reformed Journal*'s Marlin Van Elderen noted, "Those who came to Chicago . . . were given no saliva tests." The declaration's theological content was intentionally toned down so as not to burden a statement of social concern with "doctrinal niceties." Theologically, the meeting brought together "old line evangelicals" (such as Henry, Gaebelein, and Vernon C. Grounds, the dean of Denver Conservative Baptist Seminary), "traditional anabaptists" (Alexander, Wallis), black evangelicals (Perkins, Hilliard, William E. Pannell), nonaligned evangelicals (Donald Dayton, Rufus Jones, Foy Valentine), and Calvinists (Paul Henry, Richard Mouw, Smedes, Pierard, Van Elderen). As Van Elderen noted, "The notion, then, that the common foe—the oppressive social structures that give birth to racism and racist wars—is powerful enough to warrant overlooking some of our differences was the spirit of the 1973 Chicago workshop."[87]

When it came to concrete proposals for action, however, the issues that subsequently divided the movement began to surface. In keeping with evangelical tradition, many participants, including liberals like Paul Henry, Sider, Moberg, and Leighton Ford, eschewed general calls for social and political change. They favored working through churches and changing individual consciences. In the words of Paul Henry, "rather than calling for support of a national minimum income program, we should call on Christians to be concerned about the problem of income distribution."[88] Fact-finding, soul-searching, awareness-raising, the creation of grassroots networks, and organizing evangelical caucuses at national party conventions were at the center of their strategy. Although they deplored the corruption of the Nixon administration, they made few references to government social policy, the welfare state, and church-state relations.[89] Fearing that political quarrels would divert attention from applying conservative theology to social and economic problems, Rufus Jones cautioned that "any political activity should be carried on outside of the framework of whatever structure we adopt."[90]

Others, however, were more forceful in emphasizing insurgent political activism. Joseph Bayly, president of the David C. Cook Publishing Company, went as far as suggesting that "all this is too privatistic" and that "we should be telling the gov't how to run the welfare institutions we support w/ our taxes."[91] John Alexander, editor of *The Other Side*, criticized the lack of emphasis on sin, forgiveness, Holy Spirit, prayer, and identification with the weak in the original draft. He pushed for a more specific, biblical, and forceful declaration.[92] Noting that African American evangelical activists John Perkins and Clarence Hilliard had already pledged to submit articles, he announced that his journal would make the examination of social issues and recommendations for practical action its main focus.[93]

This tension between advocates of participatory and separatist models of social action, already present in 1973, subsequently evolved into a full-blown conflict. Although the 1974 ESA gathering saw the number of participants almost double to 117, Van Elderen decried the "perceptible loss of the sense of common purpose that had characterized the 1973 meeting."[94] Instead, the "marked differences" between Calvinist and Anabaptist theological models had found expression in the tension between "political reformers and counter-cultural communitarian styles of action." Issues of economic lifestyle, race, and gender proved the most controversial.[95] Among the action proposals adopted by the second meeting were the development of affirmative action programs, the involvement of black representatives in national and international church bodies, the promotion of women's studies programs in seminaries, and the encouragement of a lifestyle of "joyful simplicity and ecological responsibility."[96] In a letter to all participants in the 1974 workshop, however, Ron Sider expressed his concern that the group was trying to do too much and had lost sight of the biblical groundings of its actions.[97] Likewise, Rufus Jones denounced the pressure to rubberstamp resolutions and the lack of time for discussion reminiscent of "what fundamentalists have usually done in the past."[98]

These debates revealed the extent to which the evangelical Left had splintered by the mid-1970s. On the one hand Jim Wallis, Wes Michaelson, Arthur Gish, John Howard Yoder, and others emphasized the need to form alternative communities for living, worship, and care for the poor. Calling for the total separation of the church from the majority culture, suspicious of compromise with the system, and keenly aware of the evils of many social structures, they challenged both the liberal confidence in governmental power to create a fairer society and the conservative reliance on converted individuals. Seeking to combine the pacifist, communitarian, and nonmaterialistic lifestyles of their sixteenth-century Anabaptist and Mennonite forebears with modern-day political and social activism, they expressed faith in the efficacy of Christian communities to embody a new way of living.[99] As Dale Brown put it during the 1975 ESA workshop, "the Christian who enters politics to transform society likely ends up being changed to conform to the norms of society."[100] Among the most prominent manifestations of these communalist impulse were groups such as Sojourners, or People's Christian Coalition, in Washington, D.C., which included Wallis, Yoder, Lucille Sider Dayton, Clark Pinnock, and Bill Pannell; the radical evangelical community in a middle-class section of Philadelphia that published *The Other Side*; and the Berkeley Christian Coalition, which started out as Christian World Liberation Front and aimed to Christianize counter-cultural students and street people.[101]

On the other hand were those who strove for constructive participation in the political process. As Van Elderen noted, with tongue in cheek, the neo-Anabaptists regarded "as a critical facet of their spiritual heritage" not only disillusionment with the American way of life, but also "disillusionment with their initial response to their disillusionment with the status quo." This drove them either into the "violent alternative of the SDS [Students for a Democratic Society]" or "the placid legalism of Campus Crusade."[102] In contrast, Paul Henry, Richard Pierard, Mark Hatfield, John Anderson, and others, influenced by reformed traditions and neo-orthodoxy, accepted that political possibilities in a society permeated by human sin were limited, but nonetheless sought to work for justice within its structures as the social expression of Christian love.[103] As David Moberg put it, "it is more effective to 'infiltrate' than to 'come out from among other groups.'"[104]

Even more divisive than the conflict between participatory and communitarian approaches was another issue that dominated evangelical debates in this period—namely, race. The inaugural 1973 ESA meeting provided early indications of the volatility of this issue. As Van Elderen noted, Ron Sider's "tone of evangelical triumphalism" in his opening address was shot down by "assiduous reminders by the black representatives that white evangelicals' record in racial matters is little different from that of any other group of whites—and a good deal worse than some."[105] This conflict between black and white evangelicals began to tear ESA apart during the 1975 workshop. When the group met to engage in a serene and scholarly discussion of various biblical models for social concern, William Bentley, president of the NBEA, "rose to shatter the calm, analytical atmosphere." "I question whether you people can even *see* us blacks," he declared. Shouting matches erupted, and the open hostility made it "painfully clear" that the issue to be dealt with was the racism embodied "in the individuals, the structure, and the methodology of the entire weekend."[106]

The focus on long-term strategy and theological consensus was subsequently pushed aside. During a "rip-roaring business session," the existing ESA planning committee was dissolved and a new one established with four white males, four white females, and eight African Americans.[107] The group also voted to make racism the focus of a meeting in 1976, feeling that the emphasis on theologically grounded strategies was too legalistic and theoretical. Critical observers like Bonnie Greene, however, saw ominous signs of the group's ignorance of "both the problems and the strategies" involved in "taking the highly political steps demanded by the racism crisis." She rebuked ESA for failing to extend support to organizations already involved in fighting racism, notably John Perkins's Voice of Calvary Ministries in Mississippi and the campaign by Evangelical Christian Urban Ministries of Boston (ECUMB) to get blacks elected to white-controlled school boards.[108] Similarly, Judy Brown Hull described the workshop in an open letter as "a hard time. . . . Our black brothers and sisters raised a painful voice of protest over our insensitivity to them; our white sisters lamented our continued sexism in language and thought patterns." She left Chicago unsure of what the future would hold "for this now fragmented group of people."[109] Meanwhile, Jim Wallis declared that he was leaving ESA, and others predicted the group's demise.[110]

While conflicts over social activism and race relations tore ESA apart, forces within the NAE's Evangelical Social Action Commission (ESAC) sought to co-opt the left evangelicals and to infuse issues of social injustice, racial discrimination, and civil religion into the association. At the 1975 ESAC meeting, participants decided to hold a colloquium on the Chicago Declaration and urged the NAE Board of Administration to involve NBEA representatives in its annual conventions.[111] ESAC chairman Clarence Hilliard was asked to appoint a committee to "edit and revise as necessary the Chicago Declaration toward the end of its acceptance by E.S.A.C. and its recommendation for adoption by N.A.E.," so that it could be included in the NAE Statement of Faith in 1976.[112] Drafted by ESAC secretary Martin Schrag, "The Biblical Basis for Social Action" noted that "in our dealings with evils, we must deal both with evil hearts and evil social structures." It listed materialism, economic and racial injustice, and militarism alongside abortion, tobacco, liquor, and drugs as major issues of evangelical concern.[113]

This attempt to break through the conservative mold of the NAE met with some success. Participating in ESA's Evangelical Women's Caucus, conservative

Rufus Jones, for example, confessed that he had not been "emotionally prepared to have women serve as pastors of a church" because he had been "conditioned by the culture to the extent that I am biased at this point."[114] Although his new-found progressive stance caused unease among his fellow Baptists, who forced him to insist that he was opposed to abortion and lesbianism, Jones noted the muted nature of many reactions. "I have not had as much reaction of a negative nature that we might expect from a conservative fellowship such as ours. When I preach on the subject, as I often do, I have had a good response."[115]

Despite these efforts to find common ground, however, relations between left evangelicals and the NAE continued to be characterized by suspicion and even outright hostility. Asked whether she would accept the nomination for ESAC, Lucille Sider Dayton refused, stating that she would not want to be "identified with an organization that embraces civil religion the way N.A.E. apparently does. Our national sins, e.g. racism, classism, and sexism are too rampant for me to align myself with an organization that does not repent of these, but rather seems to promote them." She also refused to sign the NAE Confession of Faith "because I am unable to use words such as 'infallible.'" For NAE executive director Billy Melvin, this was a "clear indication of where some 'evangelicals' stand on Scripture," as he noted on the margins of Dayton's letter.[116] Similarly, as a delegate at the World Congress of Evangelization in 1975, Clarence Hilliard objected to signing the meeting's Lausanne Declaration because of its alleged failure to face up to the historical guilt and complicity of evangelicals in racial exploitation and oppression. He complained that "the control over the selection of black participants would undoubtedly be considered by most blacks to be a classic example of 'plantation politics.'" In his view, people like Perkins and Fuller Theological Seminary's William Pannell should have been present. Instead, the few black delegates from the United States were "staunch supporters of Billy Graham," whose message was to "get man properly related to God and pay little or no attention to his relationships to his fellowman."[117]

Conservatives gleefully observed the self-destruction of the evangelical Left. Predicting the failure of ESA in the aftermath of the divisive 1976 meeting on race, *Christianity Today* pointed out that many architects of the movement had gone off in different directions. This had deprived ESA of effective leadership and exposed its ramshackle planning, ideological divisions, and lack of theological substance.[118] This assessment, reflecting the traditional conservative suspicion of social action, bore the signature of Harold Lindsell, who had succeeded Carl Henry as the magazine's editor. To Henry's chagrin, Lindsell, who had taken over in 1968, had steered the magazine firmly back into conservative waters and kept it away from participation in the various social concern workshops.[119] The magazine, Paul Henry noted angrily, was "still so deadset against meaningful social involvement" that it "will be hard to work with."[120]

The dual failure to overcome the social action divide within the evangelical fold and to heal the rifts within left evangelicalism also nurtured a sense of disillusionment among those less hostile to ESA. Responding to a request to join ESA, Ira Gallaway, pastor at First Methodist Church in Peoria, Illinois, replied that he thought there was too much middle-class guilt in the organization for effective political action. "Quite frankly, I became disenchanted because I saw them making the same mistake that our church has been making in almost being masochistic in their attitude toward minority and women participation," he remarked.[121] In the wake of such conflict and tension, ESA largely withdrew from the public arena. By the late 1970s, its focus had shifted to the development of college courses on social concern, racism, sexism, inner-city ministry, human rights, and poverty.[122] Under Sider's leadership, and with Perkins, Hilliard, Rufus Jones, and Stephen Monsma still among its supporters, ESA became a national membership organization. It sought to implement the Chicago Declaration via education, networking sessions, publications, and consultations. "In essence, E.S.A. will attempt to be an educational resource and 'think tank' with a desire to serve a growing evangelical church-at-large," board member Michael Cromartie concluded.[123] Some observers, however, put it more bluntly: ESA had simply outlived its usefulness.[124]

## The Crisis of the NAE

The flag-carrier of establishment evangelicalism fared little better after a decade of internal tension and division over issues of sociopolitical involvement and scriptural authority. Neither the NAE nor *Christianity Today* had much to offer in the way of guidance for a robust social action platform. After a flurry of promising NAE resolutions on law and order (1968), relations with government (1968), the moral crisis in America (1969), ecology (1970), and Vietnam (1971), subsequent resolution themes in 1971 reflected the abandonment of substantive political activity and the focus on renewing the spiritual mission: abortion, homosexuality, "Jesus Christ, Lord of All," and "God's Word—Our Infallible Guide."

Minutes and correspondence from the period after 1973 in particular reveal a sense of drift and an inward-looking focus on administrative matters, funding crises, personnel issues, theological quibbles, and a desire for organizational renewal. In a letter to David McKenna, who was briefly considered for the NAE presidency, Robert Dugan, who later headed the Office of Public Affairs, expressed a desire "to see the organization take on a younger, more vital, contemporary image."[125] In his reply, McKenna suggested that "the N.A.E. needs to capitalize on the national interest in Jesus Christ and the national image of Billy Graham in order to be acknowledged as a significant 'third force' in the moral climate and in social concern."[126] However, major problems continued to beset the organization. They ranged from trouble financing the Washington office to the embarrassing rejection of G. Aiken Taylor, editor of the *Presbyterian Journal* and a key figure in the founding of the conservative Presbyterian Church in America (PCA), as NAE president. Administrative headaches over finding a successor for Clyde Taylor after his retirement as OPA director exacerbated these difficulties.[127]

With his usual acuity, Carl Henry diagnosed correctly the evangelical malaise. His assessment provides a good summary of the quandaries evangelicals faced by 1980. At the same time, it shows that Henry, while accurately describing evangelical successes and predicaments alike, was at a loss when it came to choosing the direction in which to take the movement. Homing in on the controversies over inerrancy and social involvement, Henry identified division, complacency, and withdrawal as the key ingredients in the evangelical "identity crisis." He especially lamented the absence "of powerful intellectual analysis" by those "who hold the reins of evangelical power." This had left the field to "a restless vanguard" that "tends to divide and subdivide into conflicting camps prone to question each other's biblical adequacy and even authenticity." Since "many institutions firmly committed at midcentury to consistent evangelical faith now have theologically divided faculties and accommodated destructive critical views," he feared a "massive revolt against biblical inerrancy." At the same time, however, he was concerned that many young evangelicals, "critical of secular capitalism or of mounting militarism, have been alienated by a swift branding of their views as communist or socialist." He warned that they were "turning for support outside the evangelical arena to avowed ecumenical leftists whose theological deficiencies they reject but whose social protest they share."[128]

Although he was pleased with the growing evangelical presence in the upper echelons of business, the media, higher education, and the White House, he regarded many of these advances as more apparent than real because they had not led to a "wide-scale penetration of our society by evangelicals." Voicing fears about a watered-down evangelicalism that had adjusted to an increasingly secular and morally lax society, he pointed out that listeners to evangelical radio stations were "confused by the proffered prospect of constant miracle and by the erroneous impression that tongues-speaking validates an authentic Christian experience." Moreover, despite the movement's successes in higher education, evangelicals had not shaped a nationally recognized university or infused comprehensive liberal arts learning.[129]

Finally, Henry was alarmed about the "broken confidence in divine providence" that accompanied traditional evangelical expectations of decline, rejection of the social gospel, and emphasis on the corrupting influences of power. This had the effect of limiting evangelical interest in politics to "little more than pulpit exhortation and support of single issues and personalities." Stemming this tide, he concluded, required more than just "devotional vitality." It meant that evangelicals had to "place worldly culture on the defensive" on the basis of clear evangelical goals and an "elaboration of strategy and tactics for moving beyond principles to policies and programs that enlist the move-ment's resources."[130]

Henry's candid assessment also threw into stark relief the organizational weakness of the NAE. Whereas peripheral organizations like EFMA, NRB, and World Relief thrived, the core was mired in theological and political division. At the end of his long service as general director of the OPA in 1974, Clyde Taylor concluded that the "strength of NAE services is far greater than its numerical strength warrants," but warned that "if we do not offer adequate service to our people in such fields as missions, evangelism, church growth, stewardship, education, etc., para-church organizations which usually are dominated by one or two strong personages, will substitute their services." He admonished his fellow believers that "we must keep the action in the family or become superfluous."[131] A member survey conducted in 1980 by the NAE Task Force on Long-Range Planning "on the present effectiveness and future priorities of the association" came back with equally sobering results. Not only did less than 10 percent of NAE members—and only 30 percent of its functionaries— even bother to return the questionnaires; their replies also highlighted the weak-ness of the central organization in comparison to affiliates and commissions.[132]

In his report on the survey, David McKenna noted that the OPA and the World Relief Corporation stood out in terms of perceived effectiveness and future importance. Likewise, NRB and EFMA received high marks, while moderately high marks were given to the Evangelical Purchasing Service. The NAE commissions, however, were rated only moderately effective, and many respondents indicated that they felt unqualified to answer questions about their future importance. Interpreting the findings, McKenna concluded that NAE members wanted to see the association "assume leadership, visibility and voice for evangelical Christianity" in the way that World Relief and the OPA had. "Evidently there is a leadership vacuum yet to be filled" after years of "benign neglect," he noted. In his view, this indicated a "major shift in attitudes" since the last survey (1976), when the association was mainly identified with services to local pastoral needs. This time around, a national and international presence was as coveted as grassroots service, he observed, and should thus be made the basis for rewriting the mission statement and sharpening NAE's focus.[133]

Henry's article and the 1980 NAE survey illustrate the dilemmas the association faced in its search for organizational strength, political influence, and ideological coherence. The confusion and drift in matters of social action clashed with the constituency's desire for a unified political and theological voice, and the weakness of the central organization was counterbalanced by the effectiveness of subagencies. "Evangelical Christianity in our generation has come out of the closet," Henry declared, but "it has yet to discover what it means to come confrontationally and creatively into the culture." In raising the question "Where do we go from here?," however, both Henry and McKenna sketched out a direction that diverged from their original approach. Despite his earlier concerns that the lack of effective social action on the part of the neo-evangelicals had provided opportunities for rightwingers to occupy the arena, Henry's call for an "orderly vision and coordinated strategy" amounted to an adoption of their agenda. Declaring that "the Lord of nations holds society accountable and offers hope in public affairs," he singled out the right-to-life movement as the most promising "one-issue banner under which to learn the public use of political power for registering moral conviction."[134] As chapter 4 shows, with the failure of the evangelical Left to provide a unifying vision, this combination of single-issue orientation with broad ecumenical engagement, theological orthodoxy, and conservative politics came to characterize the approach and appeal of the New Christian Right.

## Evangelicals and the Counterculture

In addition to social-consciousness-raising and theological iconoclasm, another aspect of the sixties that shook postwar evangelicalism to the core was the revolution in manners and morals that culminated in the rise of the counterculture. Conservative Protestants, however, confronted this challenge in much more imaginative and complex ways than the rhetoric of "culture war" and "backlash" would indicate. Rather than constituting the nemesis of countercultural impulses, evangelicalism kept alive countercultural ways of thinking and feeling while at the same time relegitimizing established core myths and institutions of

American society. Resurgent evangelicalism established itself as a distinct cultural form in postindustrial society that reconciled biblical religion and countercultural modes, and did so in ways that domesticated insurgent passions and resocialized former hippies without forcing them to relinquish their sub-cultural identity. In many ways the evangelical engagement with the counter-culture was more important for the political salience and cultural resonance of conservative Protestantism than the tortured history of its postwar social engagement. Indeed, the success of evangelicalism was ultimately located in its ability to interact with, adapt to, and appropriate sixties approaches, and to combine a traditional moral message with a contemporary appearance. In the end, this merger of evangelical Christianity and countercultural styles turned out to be one of the more stable legacies of the sixties.[135]

Conservative Protestantism has a lot more in common with the 1960s movements it despises than is generally assumed, and the boundaries between evangelicalism and the insurgent movements of the 1960s are rather more fluid. Although evangelicals and fundamentalists opposed the excesses and moral relativism of the period, scholars such as Steven Tipton, Doug Rossinow, Maurice Isserman, Robert Wuthnow, Leo Ribuffo, and George Marsden have noted that both displayed numerous similarities with the spirit of the sixties, particularly in regard to epistemological assumptions, expressive styles, and organizational modes.[136] As historian David Swartz put it, evangelical "engage-ment with 'the world' came not in a reactionary rejection of the dramatic cultural shifts of the sixties, but rather in resonance with elements of the counterculture." According to journalist John Leland, anyone looking for the spirit of American counterculture today "need look no further than the nearest evangelical bookstore, youth ministry or clothing line."[137]

Epistemologically, evangelical revivalism, with its reliance on the immediacy of the divine, faith in intuitive knowledge, pursuit of self-purification and holy living, and desire for a profound personal conversion experience, resembled closely the spiritual aspirations of the sixties movements. Rooted in transcen-dentalist and romantic conceptions of knowledge, countercultural thinking regarded truth as the result of intense, unmediated, and pre-rational experiences that dissolved the rationally constructed dualism of subject and object and revealed the unity behind fragmented existence.[138] Likewise, countercultural ethics were situational and expressive. They rested on an intuited moral sense, not on pragmatically calculated outcomes. While this ethical code could be described as utilitarian because of its focus on good consequences and the satisfac-tion of human needs, its ends differed from those of mainstream technological rationality. Not wealth, power, and technical control, but love, awareness, and "good vibes" were in focus. The ethical rule was that individuals should act in a given situation by giving full expression to their inner feelings. An act was right if it felt right. "The counterculture assumes that all persons can know with certainty what is good by means of direct experience and intuition. They can simply look at and see their own feelings, whether on drugs, making love, or sitting alone in an empty room."[139]

Direct inspiration, intuited knowledge, ecstasy, and authentic human relations were thus at the center of countercultural systems of meaning. Once authentic feelings were established and social role-playing (such as "power tripping" and "head tripping") was overcome, people could relate to each other as ends in themselves. The true needs for love, self-awareness, intimacy, understanding, and friendship were revealed as a result of intuitively shared moral standards.[140] Although the counterculture challenged not only the calculated rationality of utilitarian individualism but also the traditional moral authority of biblical religion as the basis for social norms, it still displayed similarities with revivalistic religion. The beliefs that knowledge and truth were gained through mystical experiences, and that emotional purification and self-revelation held the key to authentic links between true believers, were shared by hippies and evangelicals. In both movements the experience of profound personal conversion and the unmediated spiritual experience formed the epistemological center and the primary way of constructing meaning.[141]

Similarly, the deliberate air of spontaneity, emotionalism, penchant for public confession, and ascription of spiritual insight to ecstasy were characteristic of the expressive styles of both the counterculture and revivalist religion. Pentecostal and charismatic practices, in particular, had equivalents in the mysticism of hippie culture. The confessional mode of evangelical gatherings, where individuals openly discussed personal problems, publicly repented their sins, humbled themselves before God, and shared stories of salvation, resembled the shift from "external sources of authority toward internal, subjectivist insights" that characterized the journey of self-discovery in the counterculture, as well as its emphasis on "letting it all hang out" and "doing your own thing."[142] Thus, evangelical meetings often resembled sixties happenings, and some charged that evangelical services looked more like rock concerts than religious gatherings. Indeed, evangelical organizations of the 1960s and 1970s, such as the Christian World Liberation Front, explicitly aped the rhetoric of the insurgent movements. There were religious sit-ins, pray-ins, sing-ins, and be-ins.[143] Though the moral message was strict, church structures were casual. Particularly in the 1970s one could see people with long hair wearing jeans or bib-overalls, carrying fur-covered Bibles, and talking about Jesus.[144] It was, as one book title suggested, the "Old-Time Religion in the Age of Aquarius."[145]

Finally, for all their differences conservative Protestantism and the counter-culture shared a disdain for liberalism, rational-legal authority, large-scale bureaucracies, and technological rationality. Both embraced decentralized, unstructured communities, and favored a small-groups culture. Seeking indi-vidual spiritual revelation and authentic personal relationships, the counter-culture was characterized by egalitarian traditions, critiques of established hierarchies, an emphasis on mobility, a voluntaristic spirit, and self-supporting communes.[146] Likewise, evangelical revivalism traditionally juxtaposed a personal, loving, forgiving God with the "impersonal, uncaring, frustrating, bureaucratic authority that controls our lives through science, medicine, and government."[147] Jim Wallis, leader of the radical evangelical Sojourners com-munity, for example, was an ex-SDS organizer and a neo-Anabaptist who saw America as "the Great Harlot, the Beast of Revelation." Rejecting the "mealy-mouthed pieties of liberal Protestantism," he viewed the state as "under the sway of the demonic," and urged Christians to "radically and prophetically dissent from its values." Wallis and his supporters also staged a small but noisy antiwar protest on the fringes of the 1972 Campus Crusade for Christ "until Dallas' finest persuaded them to stop."[148] Loose associationalism and spontaneous, spirit-led communalism were expressions of a temper that crossed the normative divide. As evangelical Art Gish put it, the New Left was Anabaptist without knowing it.[149]

The counterculture and evangelicalism thus resembled each other in their rhetorical styles, organizational patterns, and expressive modes. In turn, these similarities formed the basis for the development of movement linkages, in-filtrations, and crossovers that helped elevate evangelical revivalism to new prominence. In the post-sixties era, conservative Protestant groups were sur-prisingly successful in converting hippies and offering them sustainable com-munity structures built on biblical teachings. Spiritually, the revival of the 1970s was in many ways a "Jesus trip" that grew out of the experiential culture of the 1960s.[150] While regarding countercultural communalism as a "caricature of Christian society," a number of evangelicals recognized "real affinities between this American type of existentialism and the Christian faith," and acknowledged that hippies and beatniks were involved in a spiritual quest.[151]

The scope and impact of evangelical incursions into the counterculture remain subject to debate and await further scholarly analysis. While Steven Tipton, Doug Rossinow, R. Stephen Warner, Lisa McGirr, and others have provided evidence for linkages between evangelicalism and the counterculture, Robert Wuthnow found in a study of new religious movements in the San Francisco Bay Area that hippie conversions were an altogether limited phenomenon. Although religious experimentation was a characteristic feature of the counterculture, he noted that the primary focus of hippies was on Eastern traditions and other non-Christian philosophies. In addition, the key development was not the emergence of new religions, but the rise in the number of people who abandoned the established churches and became essentially nonreligious.[152]

However, Wuthnow left unanswered the question of fundamentalism's later ability to tap into this reservoir of unchurched post-hippies. Plenty of anecdotal evidence indicates that the rigid line of division drawn in public debates between the counterculture and Christian fundamentalism does not do justice to their complex interaction, and that these links offer a rich field of primary sources waiting to be researched.[153] Although the anti-establishment mood prevalent among students was also directed at the institutionalized church, levels of religious belief among young people continued to be high and frequently found expression in revivalist evangelicalism.[154] This applied in particular to the Jesus Movement, which encompassed both established groups, such as Bill Bright's Campus Crusade for Christ, the Fellowship of Christian Athletes, Inter-Varsity Christian Fellowship, and Youth for Christ, and new groups, such as Jack Sparks's Christian World Liberation Front. Here evangelicals could build upon their skills in modern promotion, organization, and communication, their highly sophisticated network of institutions, and their strong tradition of youth ministry.[155] According to the "Remembering the Jesus Movement" survey, close to 40 percent of Jesus People followers considered themselves to have been hippies prior to their involvement with evangelical groups.[156]

Evangelicals particularly benefited from the spiritual crisis among hippies and the desire for moral certainty in the face of the moral burnout and structural fragility of the counterculture. From the drug-fuelled derangement of Haight-Ashbury kids to the violence at the Altamount Raceway, from the Chicago Democratic Convention riots to the Kent State killings, from the assassinations of Malcolm X and Martin Luther King to the explosion of the ghettoes, and from My Lai to Watergate, the deflowering of the symbols of the counterculture, the collapse of the Democratic party, the growing militancy of the civil rights movement, and the mounting hostility toward the federal government nurtured a sense of disillusionment and a retreat from activism toward a concentration on personal spirituality.[157] Moreover, sex, drugs, and rock 'n' roll turned out to be unreliable foundations for authentic human relations based on inner moral codes. As hard drug use, drifting, prostitution, and doping itinerancy ravaged flower power communities, bad trips, betrayals, and emotional indifference showed that drugs lacked intrinsic moral value. The cut-throat economy of dope-peddling often mirrored the worst excesses of market capitalism. Situational ethics all too frequently collapsed into the instrumental pursuit of individual satisfaction.[158]

Evangelical religion thus addressed both the spreading post-Vietnam disillusionment with the liberal-scientific-secular establishment and the social disintegration resulting from failed marriages, drug addiction, and other personal crises. At the same time, however, evangelicalism appealed to hippies not simply because it provided clear moral direction and emphasis on discipline, but also because it condoned the expressive styles and anti-establishment message of the counterculture.[159] Strict normative guidance based on biblical authority, in combination with validating ecstatic experience, intuited knowledge, and communal relationships, appealed to hippies who were on a spirit quest but morally adrift. It offered carefree ecstasy in a stable communal context. "Membership in alternative religious movements has meant moral survival and a sense of meaning and purpose recovered through recombining expressive ideals with moralities of authority, rules, and utility," Steven Tipton maintained. While these movements "adapted and reconciled their youthful adherents to the traditional order," they at the same time "meant moral survival precisely by sustaining countercultural themes."[160] However, as Peter Berger warned, this also raises the question whether the Jesus trip didn't simply mirror the attitude of a religious consumer "who shops around the denominational supermarket for just the right combination of spiritual kicks to meet his particular psychological needs."[161]

These patterns repeated themselves over and over again, most prominently in the Jesus People, a fundamentalist grouping that spread from California to college campuses all around the country. "They are young. They are zealous. They look like hippies. They have turned on to Jesus. They are as fanatic for the gospel as they once were for drugs and sex," Lowell Streiker wrote of the "Jesus Freaks" phenomenon. In his judgment, they were "part converted hippie, part redeemed drug scene, part the strange world of today's youth, part anti-establishment." They felt comfortable in places where they could go in Levi's jeans, shorts, tennis shoes, or with bare feet to sit and listen to someone teaching the Word of God. The Jesus Movement developed not only its own language, regalia, and symbols, such as the Jesus Cheer, the One-Way sign, and Jesus Teach-ins, but also its own newspapers and radio shows. Its adherents were "willing to abandon the sins of their former lives but not their youth-culture life-style." Many of the young, unkempt Jesus Freaks who often overwhelmed evangelical churches were former street people, dope-peddlers, and pot heads disillusioned with the counterculture.[162]

Flamboyant radical evangelicals formed a crucial cadre of leaders in the Jesus Movement of the late 1960s and early 1970s. Jack Sparks, former professor at Penn State University, founded the Christian World Liberation Front, which sought to Christianize countercultural students and street people, adopting their dress, language, and lifestyle. He also established an underground Jesus Movement paper called *Right On*.[163] Chuck Smith of Calvary Chapel baptized hippies en masse in the waves of the Pacific Ocean.[164] Pentecostalist Bobbi Morris set up the Living Word Fellowship in a suburb of San Francisco, a "born-again, spirit-filled revival church" that initially attracted hippies because of its alleged "weirdness." She had come from a "fallen" background and had been through a near-death experience and a miraculous recovery. This biography appealed to a broad-based hippie clientele that had been involved in taking or dealing drugs and came from families marred by alcoholism, chronic unemployment, abuse, and divorce.[165] Some Jesus Movement offshoots set up sectarian colonies across the country, forcing newcomers to turn over their worldly belongings. One of the most notorious was the Children of God. Led by David Berg, it made its followers engage in prostitution to win converts and gain funds.[166]

Reconceptualizing drug experiences in terms of religious conversion became a key component in the process of re-establishing biblical authority via the appropriation of countercultural images. Hippie converts often talked about "getting high on Jesus," and compared the "religious be-in" to a permanent good drug trip. "You don't have to pop pills to get loaded. Just drop a little Matthew, Mark, Luke, or John," flashy Southern Baptist Arthur Blessitt advised in his psychedelic nightclub, His Place, on Hollywood's Sunset Strip, an establishment whose logo combined a cross and a peace sign.[167] "You always come down when you're on drugs. But if you're keeping your life right in the Lord, and confessing your faults and forsaking them, then you don't ever come down," one convert told Steven Tipton. And another added: "When I did drugs, I had a carefree feeling. I didn't worry about anything. It's the same way with God." Drug ideology also counseled letting oneself go, which matched the Christian concept of self-surrender: "Acid enabled you to sit down and stop reacting to things and just perceive where you are and what you are doing." This notion of perception without reaction, observation without evaluation, seeing without thinking, knowing without words, was similar to the evangelical reliance upon the authentic, unmediated, emotional experience of the divine. Religious imagery could thus be grafted onto the countercultural notion of drugs as a means of self-transcendence and self-revelation.[168]

More important than this, however, was that evangelical narratives could make sense of the self-destructive aspects of drug use by integrating them into the religious drama of death and rebirth in which facing and expunging one's inner demons was crucial for the emergence of a converted individual. Bad trips and near-fatal overdoses had confronted many hippies with vicarious death experiences, their own inner dark side, and the judgment of the world as evil and doomed. One described the feeling of "a knife going into my stomach and coming out, and pulling all my insides out. I began experiencing fears and bad things from all my life up to then. And I became convinced that I had to work on all the bad things, the weak spots, in my life." Another recalled "feeling something coming up through my body from my stomach with a cork, and every time the cork moves, you can feel a tug. It was a horrible thing. After a while the demon actually used my voice. It came all the way from the bottom of my gut, this terrible voice." In turn, the ritual cleansing from the unnatural and "plastic" drug habit, the purification of motives via a "circumcision of the heart," and the preservation of the sense of authentic self-awareness and inner peace associated with drug taking became part of the process of recovery via religious conversion.[169] Arthur Blessitt, for example, was known for his "toilet ceremonies," in which new converts would gather around a toilet bowl and flush down their drugs, pills, powders, and paraphernalia—to the chagrin of city utility engineers, one might add.[170]

It is no coincidence that pentecostal and charismatic traditions within evangelicalism were particularly successful in attracting converts from the counterculture. Rather than just stressing doctrinal purity and literalism, pentecostals and charismatics emphasized the personal and therapeutic as well as the experiential and emotional dimensions of the faith. This proved attractive to individuals who had spent their formative years experimenting with new lifestyles, seeking inspiration in religious traditions other than the Judeo-Christian ones, and finding outlets for their moral fervor in the civil rights and other social movements. Experience-oriented members of the counterculture found meaning not only in conversion, but particularly in the practices gleaned from primitive Christianity, such as faith healing, laying on of hands, speaking in tongues, and getting filled with the Holy Spirit.[171] "It wasn't a head trip," one convert recalled. "It was a thing that really happened to me. My tongue began making these sounds without my mind telling it to. I had this wonderful light, warm feeling in my body." Pentecostal ritual validated ecstasy and made it controllable in a way that could not be achieved by psychedelic drugs.[172] Nonetheless, this symmetry of drug experience and religious fervor was sometimes difficult to maintain. There were a number of reports of burned-out cases for whom the Jesus trip had proven futile: "I'm back on acid," one former Jesus Freak said. "I used to be tripped out on Jesus. I was really zapped by the spirit. . . . But it was a bummer."[173]

As it turned out, however, over 94 percent of participants in the Jesus Movement in the 1960s and 1970s still considered themselves Christian in 2004, and although the number of those who believed that speaking in tongues was initial evidence of baptism of the Holy Spirit dropped from 52 percent to 24 percent, two-thirds of respondents retained their belief in the Rapture.[174] Thus, while evangelical forms of belief and worship maintained the ecstatic experiences and communal relationships at the center of countercultural identities, they at the same time re-established traditional biblical authority. The evangelical focus on individual sinfulness, the physical presence of God and the devil, public acts of repentance, complete self-surrender to God, emotional experience of divine love, deliverance, and resurrection in Jesus via a new baptism — all these resonated with recovering hippies and opened them up to the Christian conversion experience. By the same token, the validation of hippie precepts and experiences in the shape of evangelical styles facilitated the reassertion of traditional moral codes. The contradiction between fundamentalist absolutes and countercultural permissiveness was thus resolved in the merger of spiritual fervor and moral strictness. Jesus Freaks, while subscribing to intensely personal and individualistic pentecostal subjectivism, went along with the unambiguously authoritarian modes of fundamentalist moral objectivism. They led sober, disciplined lives and submitted to the restrictive rules and regimented existence of the many Christian communes. This adherence to strict moral codes, traditional gender roles, and a regulated sexual and courtship environment was a matter not of external enforcement, but of choice. The self-surrender of the conversion experience yielded a sense of agency, liberty, and individual self-actualization based on the recovery of moral self-control. As one former hippie put it: "I smoke as much dope as I want right now, which is absolutely none."[175]

In a larger sociocultural and political sense, these evangelical inroads into the counterculture were part of the domestication and transformation of the sixties legacy. They translated into the resocialization of former hippies as bourgeois individuals who subscribed to an ethic of self-control, sobriety, and individual responsibility. On the one hand the Jesus Movement was a phenomenon grounded firmly in the generation gap and countercultural thinking that did "not bind itself to middle class, middle American, pre-1960 morals and manners."[176] Via evangelicalism, on the other hand, the movement reaffirmed core values and institutions of American society, while preserving the insurgent spirit of the counterculture. It was on this basis that individuals who had subscribed to a "live-and-let-live" attitude were attracted to the rigid moral codes of fundamentalism, exchanging the celebration of nakedness and free love for monogamous marriages and strict sexual limits. Likewise, counter-cultural emotionalism was both contained and retained as men were encouraged to assume their traditional role as providers in the familial hierarchy while also being offered openly expressed emotional and spiritual support.[177]

As Warner concluded in his analysis of the evangelical revivalism surging through hippie communities in California in the 1970s, for evangelical veterans of the counterculture, Christian life was an exciting challenge and offered an opportunity to continue the exhilaration of the "nascent stage" of religious movements. At the same time, the evangelical turn was "a period of relief from overwrought times," where comfort was found in the assurance that God was still in His place after all the turmoil.[178] Hippie expressive ethics were thus stabilized by their alignment with specific biblical commands and examples. In turn, "former hip hedonists who once defined as right whatever act they antici-pated would give them pleasure" now reported that they found "pleasure in doing the right act, that is, the act commanded by God."[179]

The story of the relationship between the counterculture and resurgent evangelicalism, however, is not simply one of containing insurgent impulses and channeling them into culturally acceptable forms. It is also the story of the transformation of evangelicalism itself. Evangelical engagement with the counter-culture continued the trend toward the growing domestication and even secu-larization of the conversion experience since the 1940s. As explored in chapter 1, this process was characterized by a shift from an emphasis on theological dogma toward the experiential and therapeutic aspects of Christianity. Phrased in the language of psychology, sinfulness was discussed in terms of therapeutic maladjustment, rather than as the transgression of divine commands. In particu-lar, the growth of pentecostal and charismatic groups within the evangelical family, to the detriment of Calvinist and reformist denominations, was a clear indication of this shift from a liturgical and legal-rational emphasis to the emotional and experiential aspects of Christianity.[180] The focus on a sense of closeness to Jesus through an indwelling spirit, getting filled with the Holy Spirit, laying on of hands, and glossolalia was often more appealing to a generation reared in "situation ethics" and "make love, not war" rhetoric than the theologi-cal sophistication sought by Carl Henry and other postwar evangelicals.

## Conclusion

The postwar period not only gained evangelicalism a measure of cultural respect-ability, intellectual legitimacy, and access to mainstream churches, politics, and the media. It also awakened the movement's social reform impulses, which had been relegated to the sidelines during the long years of self-imposed isolation. Despite the efforts of leading evangelical thinkers such as Carl Henry, however, social concerns did not attain the significance he and others had envisioned for the newly confident evangelicals. In fact, Henry himself did not venture beyond an analysis of the failures of both liberalism and fundamentalism, and a vague outline for social action.

The tectonic shifts of the 1960s changed all this. As evangelicals struggled to come to terms with desegregation, the civil rights movement, the War on Poverty, anti–Vietnam War protests, and the revolution in morals and manners, a newly assertive evangelical Left challenged the dominance of the predominantly white, Calvinist, and politically conservative leadership represented by the NAE. Spawned by postwar evangelical inroads into higher education and the middle class, this energetic new generation of conservative Protestants established organizational, personal, and intellectual links with the insurgent movements of the period.

The renewed focus on social issues both energized evangelicalism and exposed the movement's internal fault lines. On the one hand, the reawakened social action impulses, the groundswell of grassroots institution building, lively theological debates, and evangelical inroads into the sixties insurgencies added a powerful social plank to the postwar evangelical platform. On the other hand, the wave of radical activism engendered acrimonious debates and painful political rifts that tore at the movement's seams. Pairing a critique of civil religion with a demand for structural socioeconomic change, radical evangelicals challenged conservative orthodoxies particularly regarding race, gender, warfare, anti-communism, and capitalism. They also increasingly questioned conservative tenets on biblical inerrancy and moral traditionalism, which at times brought them close to neo-orthodoxy and liberal theology. At the same time, however, the evangelical Left failed to develop broad resonance and to unite organizationally. It got bogged down in divisions over race issues and political strategy. Likewise, hopes for institutional unity under the mainstream neo-evangelical leadership had been dashed by the mid-1970s. The NAE thrived at the periphery, but not at the core. Its decentralized and centrifugal organizational structures failed to bring together an increasingly diverse clientele. In turn, a sense of drift and confusion engulfed the organization.

Nonetheless, the leftwing evangelicals and their social activism in the 1960s and 1970s created a legacy that continued to shape the evangelical resurgence in the ensuing decade. Crucially, the evangelical Left became a key means of reintegrating the insurgent spirit of the sixties into culturally acceptable forms of expression on the basis of the epistemological, expressive, and institutional compatibility between evangelicalism and the counterculture. Recognizing that hippies and beatniks were involved in a spiritual quest, conservative Protestants were often surprisingly successful in infiltrating countercultural groups. Egalitarian habits, the absence of strong institutional ties, the critique of established hierarchies, the epistemological reliance on intuitive knowledge, and the spontaneous spiritual experience were as much a part of leftwing cultural protest movements as of evangelicalism. Valuing personal choice, self-purification, holy living, and a decisive break with a former life, both conservative Protestantism and the counterculture scorned liberalism and its faith in technocratic social engineering.

By the same token, many aspects of the counterculture, while challenging the norms and practices of the established social order, revived older traditions of American cultural expression. The experience of a profound inner change and the language of a spiritual high and mystical unity were part of a revivalistic "temper," "climate of opinion," or "structure of feeling" that traditionally suffused American culture. William McLoughlin, for example, interprets American history as a series of revivals. Similarly, Michael Lienesch views the redemptive campaigns that occur with regularity on the American political scene as stemming from a revivalist undercurrent that desires to confess sins, seek conversion, and pursue a spiritual revolution. As Bob Dylan's 1965 song "It's Alright, Ma (I'm Only Bleeding)" put it, "He not busy being born is busy dying."[181]

The resonance and popularity of evangelicalism in the post-sixties era can to a large extent be attributed to the ability to combine traditional revivalism and countercultural appearance. While rejecting the counterculture's "tune in, turn on, drop out" attitude, left evangelicals validated its experiential and epistemological foundations. They denounced the secularity and moral relativism of the counterculture, yet thrived upon the appropriation of its organizational techniques, expressive modes, and anti-establishment language. While presenting a message of moral strictness, evangelical church structures were often nonhierarchical and loosely organized. Though asserting biblical orthodoxy, evangelicals offered a softened conversionism for the theologically challenged. In contrast to the backlash argument and the culture war thesis, post-sixties evangelicalism was less an expression of the rejection of the counterculture than an effective way of preserving its subcultural meaning while reaffirming established social norms.

This confluence of evangelical Christianity and countercultural styles allowed evangelicals to expand upon the cultural appeal and organizational growth that had developed in the context of their resurgence in the 1940s and 1950s. Merging "the myths of the hippie commune, the all-American small town, and Winthrop's godly 'City upon a Hill,'" evangelicalism eased sociocultural tensions after a decade of conflict and ushered in the domestication of the sixties.[182] It "came to function as a primary carrier of affirmations for an American culture otherwise in disarray."[183] As Carl Henry noted, "the wave of interest in Asian cults . . . has lent to evangelical Christianity a new aura of acceptability among parents who prefer that their teen-agers take up with the Jesus Movement or with the charismatics rather than join the Moonies, because these evangelical movements promote love of family rather than alienation, and at least reflect the American religious heritage."[184]

With the conversion experience becoming socially acceptable and desirable, postwar evangelicalism, riding a wave of popularity, had apparently succeeded in repositioning conservative Protestantism as a broad-based cultural under-current. In reflecting upon the previous decade, Henry claimed that "evangelical vocabulary has gained public acceptance and intelligibility."[185] This was an understatement. *Time* magazine declared 1976 to be the "year of the evangelical"; Southern Baptist Jimmy Carter was elected to the presidency; pollster George Gallup discovered that fully one-third of all American adults considered them-selves "born-again"; and a sequence of colorful conversions, ranging from *Hustler*'s Larry Flynt to Watergate villain Charles Colson, made frontpage news and established what pundit George Wills called "evangelical chic."[186] By the 1970s the composition of the movement had changed as a growing number of evangelicals were recruited from the ranks of political liberals, intellectuals, minority groups, Catholics, and hippies.[187] Separated from fundamentalist militancy on the one hand, and cleansed of the abominations of sex, drugs, and rock 'n' roll on the other, evangelicalism projected an upbeat and benign image.

Although the political and cultural dynamics of the 1960s and early 1970s thus helped to soften evangelicalism's public image and enabled the movement to extend its influence, they at the same time left a volatile legacy of internal rifts and conflicts. These deep divisions, nurtured during a decade of internal tension over sociopolitical involvement and scriptural authority, were about to erupt into a full-fledged battle for control. In this unfolding drama, a new push for institutional effectiveness and ideological unity originated with the neo-fundamentalist Right—a component of the movement from which many evangelicals had for decades been eager to disassociate themselves, but which had gained new stature throughout the period of cultural fragmentation. In its quest for dominance, the New Christian Right not only denounced and marginal-ized left-leaning and liberal evangelicals, but also continued the patterns of social action established by the postwar neo-evangelicals and the engagement with the counterculture pioneered by the left evangelicals of the 1960s. As the next chapter shows, the evangelical center and Left ultimately provided the template for the successes of the Christian Right.

Jim Wallis personified a restless younger generation of liberal and leftwing evangelicals eager to abandon both the social inertia and conservative dress codes of postwar evangelicalism. Pictured here in a photograph dating from the early 1970s, Wallis remains one of the most prominent "left evangelicals" to this day. (used with permission from Sojourners)

While liberal politicians and evangelical activists these days rarely mingle for happy group photos, efforts to join conservative theology and progressive politics were common in the early 1970s. Ron Sider (*fifth from left*), for example, organized evangelicals and other religious leaders in support of the 1972 presidential campaign of George McGovern (*seventh from left*). The photo also includes Walden ("Wally") Howard (*left*), editor of *Faith at Work* magazine; Tom Skinner (*sixth from left*), a leading African American evangelist; and Alan Geyer (*eighth from left*), editor of *Christian Century* magazine. (Evangelicals for Social Action, with kind permission of Ronald J. Sider)

*Bottom left*: In the 1960s and 1970s conservative Protestants were able to reach new constituencies as both established organizations, such as Bill Bright's Campus Crusade for Christ, and fledgling groups, such as Jack Sparks's Christian World Liberation Front, added new radiance to the cause. This photograph, taken on September 16, 1970, at the Congress on Evangelism in Kansas City, features (*from left*) Bright, Sparks, Billy Graham, and host pastor John Williams, holding up Jesus Movement "One Way" T-shirts. (with permission of Billy Graham Evangelistic Association, Charlotte, NC)

The evangelical revival of the 1970s was in many ways a "Jesus trip" that grew out of the experiential culture of the 1960s. One of the most prominent examples was the Jesus People, a fundamentalist group that spread from California to colleges all around the country. Pictured here are Jesus People at the Sacramento Spiritual Revolution Day, February 13, 1971. (Archives and Special Collections, David Allan Hubbard Library, Fuller Theological Seminary)

The potent mix of countercultural styles and traditional moralism offered by the Jesus Movement illustrates that the boundaries between evangelicalism and the insurgencies of the 1960s were rather more fluid than is commonly assumed. The prospect of being "High on Jesus" was attractive to many hippies disillusioned with the hard drugs that had ravaged flower power communities. Conservative Protestant groups were often surprisingly successful in converting hippies, as this image of Jesus People at the Sacramento Spiritual Revolution Day, February 13, 1971, shows. (Archives and Special Collections, David Allan Hubbard Library, Fuller Theological Seminary)

While the Spirit was guiding them, the direction of travel was not always clear, and for some it ended in a spiritual burnout. Nonetheless, evangelical and fundamentalist churches, rather than being swept away by the waves of anti-traditionalism and iconoclasm in the 1960s, were often surprisingly successful in getting disillusioned hippies started on the road to recovery. The image shows Jesus People followers attending to a broken-down car at the Sacramento Spiritual Revolution Day, February 13, 1971. (Archives and Special Collections, David Allan Hubbard Library, Fuller Theological Seminary)

Spontaneity and emotionalism were characteristic of both the counterculture and revivalist religion. Evangelicalism appropriated countercultural ways of thinking and feeling while at the same time relegitimizing core myths and institutions of American society. The image shows Jesus Festival concertgoers at the Hollywood Palladium in the 1970s making the One-way sign. (Archives and Special Collections, David Allan Hubbard Library, Fuller Theological Seminary)

Voice of Calvary Ministries in Jackson, Mississippi, embodied the evangelical grassroots activism of the 1960s and 1970s. Led by John Perkins, it sought to strengthen black communities through medical help, cooperative stores, low-cost housing, and education. A member of both Evangelicals for Social Action and the NAE's Social Action Commission, Perkins sought to straddle the divide between establishment and leftwing evangelicalism. The image shows the construction of a VoC thrift store in 1977. (Billy Graham Center Archives, Wheaton College)

# 4

# The Rise
# of the Christian Right

Observers in the mid-1970s could hardly be faulted for thinking that a type of liberal or at least middle-of-the road evangelicalism, rather than a vociferous and militant Christian Right, had emerged triumphant. Merging traditional moral norms, social tolerance, and soft conversionism, evangelicals appeared to have shed their fundamentalist image. Jimmy Carter embodied the moderate, Niebuhrian, neo-evangelical orientation of 1970s conservative Protestantism. While his presidential campaign appealed to the ideals of America's past and traditional values, he publicly expressed doubts about laissez-faire capitalism, was ready to abandon Anglo-Saxon imperialism, displayed a neo-Calvinist awareness of human limitations, and called out against pride after a decade of war, racial conflict, cultural questioning, and economic crisis. He was a born-again Christian and a nuclear engineer, a southerner and a champion of black equality, a businessman and a reformer. Despite the growing rifts within the evangelical fold, Carter was popular among the born-again, both white and black. Even at the time of the 1980 election, he still had the support of leading televangelists, such as Oral Roberts and Jim Bakker, in a three-way race that also featured John Anderson, who had solid left-liberal evangelical credentials.[1]

In this fluid setting the rightwing political swing of evangelicals was not a foregone conclusion. Peter Carroll even talked about the "crossroads of possibility" of the period, juxtaposing ascendant conservatives who "forecast a world of endless opportunity and growth" with the rise of community populists who "predicted an era of roots and limits."[2] Indeed, some observers noted that as recently as 1976 "it appeared that the gap between religious liberals and conservatives might be bridged by a significant segment of the evangelical community." Many of its leaders "had come to hold liberal views on many political issues" as a result of their exposure to higher education and their involvement with the period's insurgent movements.[3]

Underneath this centrist trend, however, an altogether different story unfolded. Internally, the movement was characterized by confusion, drift, and divisions on the one hand, and the desire for political involvement, social action, and a unified theological voice on the other. As the sense of despair reached its apex, it was the newly resurgent Christian Right, rather than the conflict-ridden and confused evangelical center, that emerged triumphant. As Carl Henry had presciently warned in 1974, the failure on the part of postwar neo-evangelicals to provide effective leadership for the new social action impulse opened up opportunities for rightwingers to occupy the arena.[4] In turn, in the 1970s and 1980s the large-scale political mobilization of evangelicals, which had been a key aspiration of the NAE but had also generated mixed feelings within the organization, finally came to pass under the auspices of neo-fundamentalists, who built a militant, broadly Christian, antisecularist political movement.[5] By 1982 theologian and *Christianity Today* editor Kenneth Kantzer had to acknowledge that although he "sometimes cringe[s] at Falwell (but 15 yrs ago a redneck)," the strongest leadership now came from fundamentalists.[6]

Contrary to many journalistic and scholarly depictions, however, the rise of the Right was not the result of "episodic eruptions of mindless anger and pain" in reaction to the iniquities of the 1960s. Neither, however, was it solely the result of a "systematic, rational effort to mobilize people and resources toward a political goal."[7] Indeed, ascribing coherence and goal-orientation to the New Christian Right can be equally misleading. Instead, rather than being located in fixed theological concepts, this "coherence" needs to be understood as the result of the particular way in which the New Christian Right positioned itself within the institutions and ideologies that had been forged by postwar and sixties evangelicalism.[8]

Three main features characterized this process. First, the Right sought to sideline the ideologically fractured and organizationally weakened evangelical center and Left as part of an "internal backlash." Having prevailed in a series of often fierce battles over social action, biblical inerrancy, and capitalism, the conservatives provided a new political and cultural vision for post-sixties evangelicalism. While the evangelical establishment and the Left were paralyzed by internal divisions, Jerry Falwell and others "took over the program of its right wing and mobilized many Americans with fundamentalist decisiveness."[9] Although radical and liberal evangelicals continued to vie with conservatives for political influence, by the late 1970s left-liberal positions had become a rarity. Their voice was "drowned out by the more strident voices of the religious right" as many evangelicals voted for Ronald Reagan in the wake of popular disenchantment with the Carter presidency.[10]

The second feature was the Right's ability to balance biblical rigidity, pietism, and separatism with the desire for transdenominational inclusiveness, social involvement, and accommodation to modernity. Indeed, the Right's strength derived less from presenting itself as the standard-bearer of moral absolutism, doctrinal purity, and antiliberalism than from its ability to blend a subcultural identity with cultural and institutional integration. Despite its divisive image, the Christian Right thus needs to be seen as in part an integrative force that mediated between conflicting trajectories. It offered a reasonably cohesive ideology that addressed the tension between evangelical identity and civil religion, traditional morality and the norms of consumer capitalism, and countercultural impulses and cultural affirmation. By combining radical promises with the assimilation of insurgent sentiments, it legitimized the American way of life in a post-sixties age in ways that proved attractive not only to evangelicals, but also to a broader populace. As the Cato Institute's Brink Lindsey aptly put it, conservatism's curious accomplishment was that "marching under the banner of old-time religion, it made the world safe for the secular, hedonistic values of Aquarius."[11]

Third, the Right thrived as a result of its effectiveness in constructing links with other religious groups, secular conservatism, and, ironically, the counter-culture. Office of Public Affairs director Robert P. Dugan, for example, firmly believed that the NAE needed to jump on the conservative bandwagon.[12] He and other conservatives in the movement built political networks across a broad spectrum of religious denominations by stressing inclusive moral issues, rather than doctrinal differences. Likewise, conservatives reinforced established ties with rightwing and business groups dating back to the 1950s and 1960s. These frequently provided the requisite financial and organizational resources for resurgent conservatism.[13] Finally, conservatives benefited from the linkages with the counterculture developed by left evangelicals in the 1970s. Militant neo-fundamentalists were often more successful in recruiting hippies than the left evangelicals who had formed the initial cadre of leaders in the Jesus Movement. In the end, the Christian Right sidelined the socially transformative dimensions of the insurgent movements but preserved their countercultural identities.

In short, "marginalizing," "calibrating" and "networking" were the operative modes in neo-fundamentalism's successes in solidifying its position within the broader evangelical movement. On this basis it was able to exploit internal divisions within the NAE, push out competing groups, and fill a leadership vacuum; to give direction to the movement's sociocultural, political, and theological aspirations based on a message that combined militancy and moderation; and to create both a functioning organizational substructure and lasting ties with external groups. In short, the interaction between these three strategies accounted for the Right's political effectiveness, ideological appeal, and cultural resonance.

## Marginalizing: The "Internal Backlash"

Intramovement dynamics play a much larger role in evangelicalism's partisan political affiliations than is commonly acknowledged. Indeed, the political orientations of conservative Protestants were frequently the result of power struggles and coalition building. Likewise, the New Christian Right had its beginnings in an "internal backlash" against the liberalizing tendencies within the evangelical fold. This intra-evangelical conflict coalesced mainly around three issues that had been the cause of many raucous debates over the past few decades: social action, biblical inerrancy, and capitalism.

The social gospel tendencies of leftwing evangelicalism had long been a cause of concern among conservative keepers of the faith. Mark Hatfield's opposition to the Vietnam War, Jim Wallis's attack on the sins of America's military power, even Billy Graham's outspoken denunciation of racism, incited the ire of conservatives. The evangelical Left's support for liberation theology, and its efforts to push social concern toward the center of the evangelical agenda, further polarized the movement. While the Left condemned establishment evangelicalism for promoting civil religion and denounced the complicity of the church in oppression and exploitation, the Right deplored the progressives' failure to focus on the gospel and individual conversion. By the mid-1970s, its vilification of evangelical liberals had become a common occurrence.[14]

Conservative evangelicals not only objected to the Left's social activism. They were even more worried about the questioning of theological absolutes in places such as Fuller Theological Seminary, which had emerged by the late 1960s as the stronghold of liberal and progressive evangelicals. The theological iconoclasm of Paul Jewett and other young evangelicals caused conservatives within the movement to rally around the flag of biblical orthodoxy. Challenged by a plethora of liberalizing tendencies, the Right was itching to assert control. Since theological apostasy was never far removed from social liberalism in the eyes of the conservatives, their efforts to impose doctrinal uniformity within the NAE were clearly designed to curb left and liberal forces within the movement.[15]

The inerrancy crisis in particular gave ideological shape to resurgent neo-fundamentalism. The 1976 publication of *Christianity Today* editor Harold Lindsell's *Battle for the Bible* was a catalyst for the impending showdown, and by the mid-1970s a raucous debate over the inspiration and authority of the scripture was in full swing. Led by *Christianity Today* and Trinity Evangelical Divinity School in Chicago, the inerrancy controversy went beyond theological nitpicking. By making inerrancy the benchmark for unadulterated evangelicalism, Lindsell and other conservatives crusaded openly against evangelical progressives and effectively split the movement.[16] Crucially, Lindsell had in the run-up to this confrontation not only sworn *Christianity Today* to theological orthodoxy, but had also taken the magazine in a more politically conservative direction, reinforcing the link between the two agendas. Likewise, as the NAE's Office of Public Affairs was making a hard turn to the right politically under the leadership of Robert Dugan, it moved to the forefront of the inerrancy debate. For example, it was involved in the ten-year program of the International Council on Biblical Inerrancy (ICBI). After the ICBI closed itself down in September 1987, it passed "the torch for applying the Word of God to society to NAE, and specifically to the Office of Public Affairs."[17]

The inerrancy controversy ended more than a decade after it had begun with conservatism triumphant, leaving behind a legacy of rancor and division. This was most apparent in the case of the Southern Baptist Convention. In a development paralleling the NAE story, the fundamentalist party that objected to "liberal infiltration" gained a majority voice within the SBC in the 1970s and 1980s. This resulted in one of the most bruising and divisive inerrancy conflicts among American evangelicals.[18] Hailing the appointment of Judge Paul Pressler as head of the Office of Government Ethics, OPA director Robert Dugan, for example, noted in a 1989 letter to White House Chief of Staff John Sununu that Pressler "has shown marvelous political skills in organizing a movement in the Southern Baptist convention to recapture the convention's major institutions for a conservative theology and ideology," but warned that "because of his effectiveness in that role, it may be that some Southern Baptists will be critical of his potential appointment."[19]

Finally, the internal backlash relied heavily on a theological defense of capitalism, which, as noted in the previous chapter, had by then become one of the most divisive issues within American evangelicalism. Conservatives had long regarded the free enterprise system as part of God's design, its universal validity comparable to the laws of physics. This adulation of capitalism permeated *The Fundamentals*, Carl McIntire's *The Rise of the Tyrant*, and his *Controlled Economy vs. Private Enterprise*, and it also reverberated across the neo-evangelical spectrum, especially after Lindsell took over the editorship of *Christianity Today*. By the early 1970s the defense of idealized market capitalism as a biblically based system had attained axiomatic status.

The conservatives combined their embrace of private property and the free market with a rejection of the traditional Protestant suspicion of wealth. Countering skepticism about the greed and selfishness that underlay the profit motive, they acknowledged that capitalism needed to be tied to an awareness of sin, but saw the pursuit of self-interest as a means toward a positive social end as long as it was wedded to a religiously inspired code of self-discipline, honesty, fairness, and charity. Rather than condemning material riches and property, the Right decried only their improper acquisition and immoral use. Neo-fundamentalists viewed investment as a "social service" and financial success as a reward for moral and spiritual vitality and a sign of godliness. Veering away from concepts of distributive justice, they extolled the virtues of the American consumer economy, regarded politically enforced equality as unjust, and located the answer to poverty in making the economic pie bigger. Despite its biblical grounding, the Right's position was thus largely indistinguishable from secular conservative attacks on the welfare state. Mesmerized by an atomistic view of individuals and a contractual concept of society, conservative evangelicals zealously denounced "collectivism" as automatically leading to a police state. Depicting America as engaged in a moral and spiritual war between capitalism and socialism, they called for biblically mandated limits on the power of the state. They also regarded redistributive taxation as theft, prohibited by the eighth commandment, denounced social welfare schemes as ungodly perversions based on the politics of resentment, and declared efforts to even out socio-economic injustices undesirable.[20]

An illustrative example of the attempts by conservatives to marginalize liberal tendencies, as well as of the divisions within leftwing evangelicalism, is the fate of the NAE's Evangelical Social Action Commission (ESAC), mentioned in the previous chapter. By the mid-1970s ESAC had formed a bridgehead of the evangelical Left within the NAE and had become the main forum for its social action agenda. After soliciting suggestions from ESAC members-at-large and NAE denominations, secretary Martin Schrag found in 1976 that issues such as involvement in elections, dealing with employer-employee relations, and "securing more health and welfare programs for employees of corporations," as well as hunger, junk food, and race, ranked as the highest priorities for evangelical action.[21] ESAC also sent a resolution to the NAE committee in 1976 urging fellow Christians to refuse to cooperate with CIA covert intelligence gathering. Likewise, it supported legislation forbidding the U.S. government to use Christian agencies, missionaries, and other church workers for this purpose.[22] In 1977 the commission submitted the manifesto "Biblical-Theological Basis for Social Action" to the Board of Administration, with the goal of making it part of the by-laws for ESAC. The rambling statement emphasized individual conversion, but also the need to address the structural causes of poverty. Social action "must engage the fallen, sinful power structure of this world in unending struggle," it declared, concluding that "it is evident that the world's system through their agents and institutions for example: government, courts, education, industry, agri-business, finance, real estate, health care, or religion, often foster, perpetuate, and/or facilitate in many ways the dehumanization of individuals, classes, and races of people, especially the poor."[23]

Left evangelicals in the NAE had thus come out strongly in opposition to tendencies within the NAE to sanctify the Cold War order and the American way of life. During an ad hoc meeting at the 1976 NAE convention, they chided the association for promoting "a dangerous degree of civil religion." While maintaining that "we strongly affirm that the Bible teaches respect for government," they warned that "there is a dangerous tendency toward idolatrous patriotism abroad in the land" and expressed hope that future conventions would "avoid mixing patriotism and biblical faith."[24] In the course of the convention, left-leaning groups organized discussion sessions on church-state relations, hunger, the political power of pastors, lifestyle issues, and the relationship between conversion and social attitudes. "How should evangelicals relate to social structures?" they asked, "to capitalism, to democracy?"[25]

Despite the Left's assertiveness, however, ESAC correspondence revealed ongoing tensions over the proper approach to social issues. While commission member H. Wilbert Norton suggested broadening the agenda to include political involvement and structural issues, chairman Theodore Gannon saw social problems as rooted in spiritual deficiencies. He called for "preaching backed by social action" and rejected the notion that people in abject circumstances were the victims of social or economic conditions.[26] Moreover, the liberal rumblings within ESAC, and the Left's attack on what it regarded as mainstream evangelicalism's embrace of civil religion, support for militarism, and indifference to racism, sexism, and economic injustice, caused increasing unease within the NAE establishment, and strengthened the desire on the part of its leadership to rein in ESAC. The NAE began to keep a closer eye on the commission, seeking to control it and replace the transformative social action agenda with a conservative focus on moral issues.

In his report to NAE leaders on the ESAC meeting in May 1976, conservative Gordon Bacon noted both the dangerous influence of the "radical side" and the first successes in containing it. During ESAC discussions on social action, he actively sought to shift the emphasis back to a traditional moralistic agenda. He told the commission in no uncertain terms that evangelical grassroots concerns did not revolve around "world hunger, the arms race, and race issues," but rather: "how do I combat pornography on the local level, how do we combat the breaking up of family life, even in our evangelical churches, what do we do about drugs, alcohol, especially as it relates to our young people, how do we help in the gambling issue." Moreover, he argued that the question "what do we have to say regarding abortion, euthanasia, homosexuality, child abuse and sacredness of life?" increasingly occupied evangelical minds.[27]

Similarly, when the commission decided to rent a booth at the NAE national convention to hand out material "representative of evangelical ministries, such as CHIEF [Christian Hope Indian Eskimo Fellowship] and Voice of Calvary," Bacon warned that "any materials that went out would have to be approved." He also openly opposed efforts to include copies of *Sojourn* in the display. Singling out Rufus Jones, Bacon saw a "radical side present" at the meeting, "where salvation is not by faith alone, but by faith and works." Nonetheless, he expressed relief that the new EASC chairman, John Perkins, "did a very acceptable job" and that "he did not seem to be as far on left field as some others that have had a chair." While many evangelicals "had thought that he had turned liberal," Bacon let the NAE leaders know that "this has now changed and he is accepted more in the evangelical community."[28]

Perkins, an African American minister who had been instrumental in building up Voice of Calvary, was not easily typecast, however. While he recognized the limits of NAE, he urged ESAC to "move heavily to empower the local churches," called for adequate commission staff, and spelled out a vision for ESAC to become an "educational resource" for community church action. He reiterated the need to focus on issues like minority rights, unemployment, and land loss among southern rural blacks. He also embraced closer cooperation with ESA, commending especially Ron Sider for his efforts to generate social awareness in colleges and churches. He even called on ESAC "to help coordinate or to participate in the coordinating of Evangelicals for Social Action's workshops."[29] By 1980 Perkins had hired Rufus Jones as a part-time staff member in the hope of developing seminars and workshops around minority issues. "The liberals had strong programs for minorities. It is time that we evangelicals give biblical leadership to this movement," he declared.[30]

ESAC's attempt to get the NAE to pass a "Right to Food" resolution in 1976 highlights the temporary assertiveness of the evangelical Left, followed by conservative efforts to rein it in and the subsequent turn to the right. The proposed resolution read: "We believe that every person has the basic right to a nutritionally adequate diet." It encouraged churches to increase efforts to feed the hungry, and urged the U.S. government to make this "a cornerstone of national and foreign policy."[31] In February 1976 ESAC scored what seemed to be an important success. The NAE Board of Administration adopted the commission's recommendation to consider "the continuing struggle for racial justice, the issues associated with the problem of poverty and world hunger, the tragedy of violence and oppression as these victimize individuals and threaten free institutions" as "matters of top priority" in the area of social responsibility.[32] At the same time, however, the proposed "Right to Food" resolution was rejected by the NAE Resolutions Committee. Conservative evangelicals, in particular, had expressed serious reservations. David Breese, president of Christian Destiny and member of the NAE Board of Administration, thought this kind of "socialist legislation" simply "absurd" and urged evangelicals not to get involved.[33]

When ESAC decided to bring the resolution to the NAE convention floor, it ran afoul of the NAE establishment's insistence that resolutions had to be reviewed in advance by the proper committee. In turn, George Ford, chairman of the Resolutions Committee, reported back to ESAC a revised resolution on world hunger from which both the right to an adequate diet and the demand for commensurate legislation had been deleted. At the urging of NAE director Billy Melvin, the same meeting asserted that "the family, homosexuality, and pornography" should be the main priorities of ESAC.[34] Although resolutions on hunger continued to feature at NAE conventions, they had effectively been stripped of their radical dimension. By the mid-1980s they typically emphasized that "solutions to hunger and poverty must be grounded in faith in God, commitment to work, personal responsibility and family solidarity," and that "Christians may disagree about appropriate government roles," but "most would agree that government programs alone are no panacea for the problem of poverty."[35]

The growing distrust in the wake of the inerrancy debate widened the developing divide. The repercussions of a letter sent by ESAC member John K. Stoner to Billy Melvin indicate how the allegation of apostasy fed into conservative efforts to purge the commission. Stoner emphasized that he understood infallibility to apply to biblical matters, not to matters of history and science. He rebuked the NAE for accepting people who "support + defend the nation's mad pursuit of nuclear arms supremacy" while excluding "persons who express uncertainty as to whether Cain was a historical Person" and "who are not certain that all human beings except Noah and his family died in a universal flood."[36] In response to subsequent efforts to censor Stoner, ESAC secretary Martin

Schrag reminded Melvin that "I would also make the point that John [Stoner] has signed the NAE statement of faith and raise the question as to whether you can now disbar him from the membership on the Evangelical Social Action Commission."[37]

Throughout the 1970s and 1980s tensions between liberal impulses and conservative control efforts continued to characterize NAE-ESAC relations. In particular, ESAC's efforts to run workshops on inner-city challenges were eyed with suspicion by many conservatives.[38] In 1976 Ron Sider's role as speaker at the urban ministries workshop in Philadelphia caused furrowed eyebrows in the NAE establishment. In a letter to Schrag, Billy Melvin expressed his unease with Sider because of the "impression I got that if one does not agree with his conclusions they are not really Christian." He also noted that ESAC chairman Clarence Hilliard "does seem to struggle with some things that I hope he can overcome."[39] This came in the wake of Melvin's complaints during the previous year about the evangelical credentials of the particular church ESAC had chosen for its urban ministries workshop. He also insisted that Charles Y. Furness of the Department of Social Work at Philadelphia College of Bible be invited as speaker.[40] The angry reaction on the part of Willie Richardson, a "trusted black minister" who was "no radical black," indicated that these interventions continued to touch a raw nerve in the movement. Richardson strongly criticized Philadelphia College of Bible, arguing that it "was paternalistic and was not realistically dealing with the issues of the city."[41]

The NAE files reveal ongoing attempts to monitor and control ESAC, culminating in the appointment of an ESAC liaison officer. The commission, however, continued to infuse liberal voices into the strident conservatism of the NAE, as the correspondence for the 1987 convention indicated: The planned ESAC program listed left evangelicals Jim Wallis and John Howard Yoder as speakers. Nonetheless, conservatives could find comfort in the fact that by the mid-1980s the moral agenda had been satisfactorily asserted over structural issues. If NAE resolutions are an indication of movement dynamics, conservative sentiments were back in the driver's seat, with homosexuality, pornography, obscenity, and gambling dominating the agenda. Likewise, inerrancy had been made the litmus test of evangelical commitment, while lingering doubts about the righteousness of America's global cause and its system of liberal capitalism had been pushed aside.

By the same token, a number of left evangelicals, including those active in Evangelicals for Social Action (ESA), turned conservative in the 1980s. As David R. Swartz has pointed out, former ESA board member Michael Cromartie in the 1980s called many of the organization's positions "bogus," became active in

Charles Colson's Prison Fellowship Ministry, and joined the Ethics and Public Policy Center, a conservative Washington think tank. Clark Pinnock, in the 1970s a liberal evangelical faculty member at Trinity Evangelical Divinity School in Deerfield, Illinois, joined the neo-conservative ranks in the 1980s. He accused Sojourners of subscribing to a "naïve worldview" and of justifying Sandinista violence in the Nicaraguan revolution. And a leader of the Shiloh community in Oregon, who was sent to prison during the Vietnam War for conscientiously objecting, turned "staunchly conservative" in the 1980s.[42]

## Calibrating: The Ideological Foundations of the New Christian Right

The success of the Right cannot be explained solely on the basis of the backlash against perceived moral iniquity, theological apostasy, and political wayward-ness. Instead, like postwar neo-evangelicals and the evangelical Left, the neo-fundamentalists derived ideological and organizational strength from the ability to continue the postwar patterns of transdenominationalism, social action, and cultural accommodation. The neo-evangelical resurgence during and after the Second World War had helped evangelicals regain cultural and political legiti-macy within the political climate of the liberal consensus by softening the hard edges of prewar fundamentalism. The left evangelicals of the 1960s and 1970s had added a public moral and social voice and had helped dissolve counter-cultural impulses into culturally acceptable forms. Despite their denunciations of both the evangelical establishment and leftwing evangelicalism, conservatives benefited from these specific settings and sentiments. They continued postwar evangelicalism's this-worldly turn, in which piety gave way to moralism and theology to religious feeling. Likewise, in insisting on a clear program for social action centered on traditional "social issues," biblical inerrancy, and the sanctification of capitalism, the Right built upon the emphasis on social concern and political involvement that sixties evangelicals had succeeded in placing at the center of the resurgence. In addition, neo-fundamentalism utilized left evangelical linkages with the counterculture. In the process, the Right continued the simultaneous containment and retention of insurgent impulses. It merged traditional moralism with both an embrace of consumer capitalism and the perpetuation of countercultural modes.

Seen from this perspective, the New Christian Right emerges as only one expression of the blend of respectability and rebelliousness, mainstreamization and militancy, ecumenism and orthodoxy, inclusiveness and separation, and traditionalism and modernity that has characterized postwar evangelicalism all along. The key to its success in mobilizing evangelicals for conservative political ends lay once again in combining an insurgent theological, cultural, and political identity with the ability to interact with, adjust to, and appropriate the dynamics of Cold War society and culture. What set the Right apart was that its distinctive merger of insurgent sentiment and cultural affirmation matched post-sixties popular sentiments better than either the domesticated revivalism of postwar establishment evangelicals or the progressive Biblicism of the evangelical Left.

The Right's "morality politics" were indicative of this effort both to reassert traditional pietism and to retain the neo-evangelical and left evangelical impetus for social action. On the one hand, the focus on issues like abortion, homosexuality, and "family values" was designed to head off the broader agenda for social change advocated by leftwing evangelicals. By attributing social wrongs to the sinful nature of man, it shifted the locus of social transformation away from structural evils and back toward individual conversion. On the other hand, the emphasis on moral issues did not simply constitute a return to prewar fundamentalist positions. In fact, prior to the 1970s abortion, homosexuality, and similar issues per se had had remarkably little resonance within the wider evangelical fold. Rather than being dictated by strict religious teachings, these campaigns, therefore, grew out of the conservatives' search for a unifying issue that combined moral orthodoxy with extensive political and social action.[43]

As George Marsden has noted, Jerry Falwell and the Moral Majority "mobilized not so much the political impulse that had been distinctive to fundamentalism, but rather the moral-political impulse that had been part of the revivalist tradition more generally."[44] Denouncing mainstream society on the basis of a millennial and apocalyptic mindset, as Steven Tipton has correctly analyzed and described the process, subsumes a radical political critique.[45] The neo-fundamentalists thus took up Carl Henry's and Francis Schaeffer's critique of the lack of a social program. Similarly, while reducing social problems to sinful individuals and arguing that there was no biblical mandate for state interference with economic activities, *Christianity Today* in the 1970s frequently stressed that God required action in certain areas of the nation's moral life. Single-issue morality politics was thus both pietistic and socially involved.[46]

That social action was a central concern of the neo-fundamentalist resurgence is also borne out by its legacy of community activism. Although many observers considered involvement in social action the clearest difference between theological liberals and conservatives, the numbers do not support this. As James Hunter reminds us, "though liberals emphasize social concern rhetorically, it is the conservatives who are, in actual dollars, far more generous," giving approximately 47 percent more than the liberals.[47] Since frequency of church attendance is the most important indicator of giving, much of the growth of charitable contributions within the Protestant fold can be attributed to fundamentalist Protestants and the organizational prowess of their churches.[48] Similarly, surveys show that faith is an important predictor of voluntary work and that evangelicals are more likely to be involved in charities than non-evangelicals.[49]

What is more, the Right's move toward a broader moral and social agenda owed much to leftwing evangelicalism's engagement with the sixties insurgencies. The anti-abortion campaign, for example, frequently phrased its position in terms of the rights of the unborn child, and lobbying for the Religious Freedom Act employed civil rights rhetoric.[50] Randall Terry of the anti-abortion Operation Rescue wrote "A Letter from Fulton County Jail" and told a reporter that he was at heart a 1960s radical.[51] Meanwhile, the campaigns against abortion and homosexuality retained radical communal and anticorporatist impulses. Christopher Lasch noted that conservative moral indignation at abortion, permissiveness, pornography, welfare dependency, and softness on crime struck a chord with a lower middle class that worried about the ethical bearings of a self-indulgent consumer culture and had experienced socioeconomic decline. Seen from this angle, the anti-abortion campaign reflected a Niebuhrian critique of liberalism as lacking a tragic conception of life and a sense of limits and loss. This was a critique both leftwing and rightwing evangelicals could subscribe to.[52]

Broad-based moralism of this kind also enabled the resurgent Right to downplay its traditional sexism and rabid racism, while simultaneously giving voice to the deep-seated race- and gender-related fears of an embattled lower middle class. Despite its doctrinaire moral absolutism, the New Right had to take into account the fact that social and gender norms both within and outside the evangelical constituency had changed in the wake of the 1960s. As noted in chapter 1, while evangelicals had become more conservative on abortion and pornography, they had also become more liberal on feminism, sex education at school, making birth control available to teens, and gender divisions in the workplace.[53] Similarly, fundamentalist expressions of segregationist sentiments were now frowned upon. In turn, attacks on racism, previously a mainstay of liberal and left evangelicals, had by the 1980s become part of the standard repertoire of the Right, too.[54] A proposed NBEA / NAE Resolution on Racism and Racial Prejudice, for example, which was eventually passed in a significantly altered form in 1991, stated that "society's structures should be designed to provide for those oppressed by racism the opportunities they need to become self-sustaining participants in the benefits and the responsibilities of life in a free society." In a nod to a more individualistic approach, it added that this should be done "with care to affirm the dignity of the oppressed and to foster their advancement in productive citizenship."[55]

At the same time, however, the phasing out of traditional race and gender demarcations came with a conservative moral twist that reintroduced them via the back door. The conservative attack on the welfare state for allegedly generating dependency and encouraging moral iniquity exemplified this strategy. Since the claim that a lack of economic independence translates into the absence of moral self-control had traditionally been used to denigrate blacks and females, conservatives reasserted established race and gender stereotypes via an attack on the beneficiaries of supposedly overgenerous public assistance—namely, African Americans and women. As a result, "racial and social welfare issues quickly became linked in the minds of ordinary citizens."[56] This can be interpreted as a coded reassertion of race and gender divisions. Indeed, it was reminiscent of the way in which the invocation of republican virtues and producer-class ideology in the nineteenth century had legitimized citizenship rights for white males and denied women and minorities the same privileges.[57] This veiled racism and sexism had significant political salience. The raw and divisive battles over busing and affirmative action, for example, which exploded in the 1960s and 1970s, were crucial in the rightwing political mobilization of suburbanites.[58] Likewise, by the 1990s social policy as an effective means of ensuring the loyalty of lower-middle-class southern and western voters to the Democratic party had largely been replaced by welfare reform as an instrument of Republican mobilization of the same voter groups.[59]

Neo-fundamentalism's theology, by merging pietistic orthodoxy with a this-worldly orientation, reveals a similarly ambivalent dynamic. In its insistence on the doctrines of virgin birth, atonement, bodily resurrection, Second Coming, and inerrancy, the New Christian Right is usually associated with asserting a rigid pietism, a narrow-minded moralism, and institutional exclusivism. On the surface, its desire to restore "Christian America" based on a premillennialist eschatology continued to clash with the multicultural realities of American life.[60] Despite these images, however, conservatives continued the postwar trends toward a broad-church Biblicism that sociologists of religion have identified as evangelicalism's accommodation to the cognitive and normative assumptions of modernity, liberal capitalism, and consumer culture. Notwithstanding evangelicalism's insistence on moral transformation through redemptive suffering and holy living, the Christian Right increasingly downplayed theology and promoted lifestyle churches that departed from traditional liturgical evangelicalism. It made the hedonistic celebration of well-being, prosperity, and the personal fulfillment of the converted individual the center of the faith. This subjectivization of the evangelical message, its preoccupation with the self, the good life, and economic success, provided a purely pragmatic inducement to becoming a Christian. It showcased the tendency toward regarding religion as useful for personal and social ends, rather than as an expression of devotion to God. By emphasizing self-help, rather than sin and damnation, faith became a means of social adjustment in this life, rather than a preparation for life after death.[61]

Televangelists Oral Roberts, Jimmy Swaggart, Jim Bakker, and Pat Robertson, for example, illustrated this shift in emphasis toward the experiential and therapeutic aspects of Christianity. While they regarded the Bible as the literal word of God, they located truth in the unmediated experience of the divine and emphasized the direct experience of the spirit to quicken the words of the scripture. Similarly, building edifices for the greater glory of God and admonishing parishioners to reflect upon the cauldrons of hell was a long way from the modern megachurches with their baptized bowling alleys and shopping arcades. "It is probably safe to say that evangelical lifestyle in America today often compromises the biblical doctrine of stewardship," Carl Henry observed in 1980. "Evangelicals too readily forget that many of our economic blessings are a fruit of biblical virtues and, therefore, as the gift of God are at his disposal and not simply something we have achieved by ourselves."[62]

Finally, neo-fundamentalism's economic ideology exemplified successful mediation between potentially exclusive positions. Shedding the last vestiges of traditional uneasiness about unfettered capitalism, the Christian Right was explicit in its embrace of free enterprise, private property, and postwar consumer society. In effect, it sacralized economic growth, spiritualized the American way of life, and sanctioned the socioeconomic status quo. It affirmed materialism and "respectable hedonism" (in James Davison Hunter's phrase) as the normative baseline of postwar society. Conservatives, in effect, replicated in matters of politics and economics liberal Protestantism's accommodation in matters of doctrine and ethics.[63] They legitimated the upwardly mobile lifestyles of people who had benefited from deficit spending, the military buildup, and Cold War social policies. Though avoiding the "New Right" label, the Crystal Cathedral's Robert Schuller, for example, spread a theologically and socially conservative message that sought to "give meaning to lives filled with materialism, while not challenging the grounding of those lives."[64]

At the same time, however, this conservative sanctification of capitalism cannot be separated from the efforts of neo-fundamentalists to position themselves as standard-bearers of the radical promises of nineteenth-century producer-class ideology. Their idolization of the self-made man, disdain for professionals, and admiration for manual workers sought to recapture the emancipatory, egalitarian, and antihierarchical dimensions of traditional republicanism and evangelical social thought. In expressing faith in the moralizing effects of market participation and economic proprietorship, conservatives connected the capitalist ethos with traditional values. They depicted capitalism as a means of nurturing morality and civic virtue through hard work, diligence, thrift, prudence, sobriety, and honesty.[65] As discussed earlier, they sought to employ a nineteenth-century ideology centered on an ethic of self-reliance and self-discipline to provide meaning and justification for a twentieth-century sociocultural reality of consumer culture and the defense-welfare state.

This combination of vindicating consumer capitalism on the one hand, and being dedicated to traditional values on the other, was deeply contradictory. In the nineteenth century, evangelical codes of self-control, personal piety, and stable community and family life had shored up the norms of self-help, independence, and competitive achievement that underlay producer capitalism. They provided the specific meanings and defined the social realities within which "capitalism made sense and became morally binding."[66] The advent of consumer capitalism in the twentieth century changed all this. It resulted in the clash between the evangelical call for moral self-discipline and the hedonistic norms required by a consumer-driven economy. Capitalism was no longer built around self-control and self-reliance, but around immediate gratification and the creation of artificial needs.

Throughout the postwar revival, evangelicals struggled with this tension between a moral code of antimaterialist self-discipline and the sanctification of a booming consumerist setting. As a result, much of evangelical thought was characterized by compartmentalization. While using traditionalist themes in discussing social issues, such as the common good, community ties, and gender roles, conservative Protestants invoked libertarian themes, such as individual opportunity and entrepreneurial self-fulfillment, when discussing economics.[67] The New Christian Right offered a bold new solution to this dilemma of having to navigate between a traditionalist emphasis on moral order and a libertarian emphasis on individual freedom. It did so by merging evangelical and countercultural impulses. In effect, its master stroke was to portray the nineteenth-century moral matrix of the self-controlled market individual in terms derived from sixties themes of personal liberation, authenticity, individual self-actualization, and immediate gratification.[68] Following both religious and secular conservative trailblazers such as Leo Strauss, Eric Voegelin, Robert Nisbet, Russell Kirk, Richard Weaver, and Friedrich von Hayek, the Christian Right located the emergence of the social discipline required for the functioning of society purely in the operations of the free market, rather than in traditional social ties, moral legislation, and regulatory intervention. Together with neo-conservatives like William F. Buckley, Frank Meyer, and M. Stanton Evans, conservative evangelicals depicted neo-liberal policies like supply-side economics and tax cuts simultaneously as morally disciplining instruments and as means of upholding a "countercultural" identity centered on individual self-realization and expressiveness.[69] The rightwing critics of liberalism thus "championed a 'counterculture' of their own, based on biblical injunctions, the patriarchal family, and the economic homilies of nineteenth-century capitalism."[70] In the process, they not only discarded the traditional conservative respect for historically developed norms and practices in favor of a radically foundationalist moral justification for capitalism. They also disregarded the antitraditionalist implications of market commodification.[71]

For all their moral traditionalism, the social and economic theories of the New Christian Right thus shared their adversaries' libertarianism and anti-traditionalist iconoclasm. Its embrace of consumer capitalism, the entrepreneurial individual, and antistatism blended the economic theories adopted from resurgent conservatism with the spirit and methods of the insurgent movements. In short, post-sixties evangelicalism simultaneously restored the notion of the market as a moralizing agency and depicted capitalism as countercultural. This ability to preserve the iconoclasm and anti-establishmentarianism of the 1960s, while at the same time naturalizing the consumerist order, was as important for the cultural resonance of neo-fundamentalism as its unquestioning embrace of liberal capitalism. Radical in upholding a subcultural identity, yet unambiguous in its affirmation of the American social order, rightwing "countercultural capitalism" appealed to both the anti-establishmentarian mood and the desire for moral certainty that characterized the climate of opinion in the aftermath of the 1960s. It depicted the market not only as an instrument of moral resocialization, but also as a means of preserving an anti-establishmentarian identity.

As Jerome Himmelstein has argued, this "paradoxical combination" of respectability and rebelliousness constituted the main strength of resurgent conservatism. It brought together "insider resources—support from business and the upper middle class as well as solid roots within the Republican party— and a capacity to use anti-establishment rhetoric to talk to the growing range of discontents that grew out of the 1960s."[72] Likewise, Lisa McGirr, in describing the appeal of apocalyptic fundamentalism to residents in high-tech Orange County, makes much of the combination of countercultural trappings with a morally and politically conservative message that matched their ambivalence about living in a hypermodern environment.[73] And Phillip Hammond maintains that scholars must look at both the counterculture and the centrist nature of American politics to explain the political turn of an evangelicalism that combines an insurgent "backlash" mobilization with integration into established political structures.[74]

As a result, the subversive potential of evangelical revivalism, which had at times posed a direct challenge to the rise of capitalism, as in the Populist revolt of the late nineteenth century, was channeled into conservative politics that preserved the sense of a spiritual revolution at the core of a countercultural identity, yet sanctified the dominant socioeconomic order. As Marsden has aptly commented, the fundamentalist vindication of free market economics, while attacking the immorality of what this free market produces, reveals how difficult it is to sustain the concept of the evangelical challenge to secular culture. Just as "soft conversionism" sidelined the emphasis on moral earnestness and humility in evangelicalism, the unquestioning neo-fundamentalist embrace of American power and its spiritualization of consumer capitalism pushed aside sociocultural traditionalism.[75] In contrast, many liberal and left-leaning groups within the movement preserved evangelicalism's legacy of socioeconomic criticism. Though they tended to withdraw into a small-groups culture, they continued to attack the military-industrial complex and consumer capitalism from a position of self-imposed communitarian separatism.

Conversely, the counterculture, for all its anti-establishment rhetoric, was thus reintegrated into the dominant socioeconomic order. Although it delegitimated established norms and institutions, the counterculture at the same time affirmed the hedonistic, self-expressive values that are at the core of consumer capitalism.[76] Its insurgent impulses were in many ways more easily reconciled with the normative requirements of consumerism than with the solidaristic impulses of social democracy or the social-relational vision of American progressivism. Contingency, relativism, and situational ethics in themselves did not inherently constitute a radical theory but could be employed to filter into the political process in a way that enabled liberal capitalism to perpetuate itself. As Rebecca Klatch reminds us, even the SDS eventually shifted toward an anti-government and pro-market attitude.[77] Indeed, the political alignments of the 1970s and 1980s "indicated that a defense of values loosely identified with the counterculture was quite compatible with a defense of business and the free market."[78]

This confluence of economic conservatism and countercultural tropes has received only limited scholarly attention. Their complex interaction, however, was a key ingredient in the New Christian Right's popularity and efficacy. By merging biblical values and consumer capitalism, moral self-control and ecstatic emotionalism, countercultural identity and the consecration of dominant economic modes, post-sixties evangelicalism was once again in a position to reconcile the dynamic tension within American society between a broad-based adherence to biblical religion and an equally strong attachment to utilitarian individualism. In essence, the countercultural construction of the converted self matched the normative requirements of consumerist market society in the same way that the moral codes of nineteenth-century evangelicalism had matched the requirements of producer capitalism.

## Networking: The Construction of a Rightwing Movement

What had started as the Right's internal battle against the evangelical Left eventually culminated in a sustained effort to forge a new political movement centered on a campaign against "secular liberalism" that crossed established religious, political, and cultural boundaries.[79] Three main components were crucial in this process: transdenominational coalition-building, new partisan ties, and conservative inroads into the fragmenting counterculture.

Recognizing early on the dangerously disruptive potential of obscure theological debates, Graham, Henry, and other postwar neo-evangelicals had emphasized the need to focus on an inclusive gospel of personal conversion and spiritual regeneration as a way of finding common ground with other faith groups. In marketing a broad-based conversionist theology centered on belief in Christ and the moral essentials of the faith, rather than on liturgical orthodoxy, post-sixties neo-fundamentalists continued this process of reaching out across the denominational divides. In the same vein, the new ecumenical fervor of "open fundamentalism" had by the 1980s toned down the movement's legacy of virulent anti-Catholicism and anti-Semitism.[80]

This new ecumenism allowed the Right to shed its image as a narrowly focused fringe movement and to pitch itself as a standard-bearer of moral propriety in the larger battle against secular humanism. Though causing disquiet among old-style fundamentalists who feared worldly corruption, neo-fundamentalists organized in broad-based groups, such as Christian Voice, Moral Majority, Christian Coalition, and Religious Roundtable, and cooperated with their theological competitors in campaigns against abortion, gay rights, pornography, and other alleged moral ills.[81] Particularly the campaign for religious liberty fostered a new sense of cooperation among conservatives in all three main Judeo-Christian traditions. In 1985, for example, the NAE participated in a conference on religious liberty that was set up in cooperation with the State Department and co-sponsored by the Institute for Religion and Democracy, the American Jewish Committee, the Anti-Defamation League of B'nai B'rith, and the Jacques Maritain Center of Notre Dame University.[82]

Nonetheless, neo-fundamentalists continued to combine moderation with militancy. They adhered to an orthodox stance that rallied believers within a deeply divided and insecure evangelical fold around the comfort of the faith's traditions.[83] In the same vein, ambivalence toward Jews and casting Catholics as the enemy remained powerful mobilizing themes within conservative Protestantism. Despite their unreserved support for Israel and rejection of overt anti-Semitism in response to Nazi atrocities, many neo-fundamentalists remained leery of Judaism. While toning down anti-Semitic rhetoric was a way of adapting to American pluralism, the liberal political attitudes of many Jews continued to clash with evangelical conservatism.[84] Similarly, anti-Catholicism remained virulent. As noted in chapter 2, the NAE's campaign to prevent diplomatic relations with the Holy See continued well into the 1980s. "We have battled this all the way, in keeping with a 1943 NAE resolution, reiterated ten times since," OPA director Robert Dugan reported in 1984 when the Reagan administration appointed an ambassador to the Vatican.[85]

Growing financial and organizational ties between neo-fundamentalism and a newly energized secular conservative movement further aided the right-wing mobilization of evangelicals. These ties built not only on shared backlash sentiments, but also on the links between religious and political conservatives that had developed in the 1950s and 1960s. Leading Republican politicians, such as Senator William Knowland, and conservative organizations, such as the John Birch Society, maintained alliances with a variety of evangelical and fundamentalist groups, including the ACCC, Billy James Hargis's Christian Crusade, and Edgar Bundy's Church League of America. Political crusades like the "Draft Goldwater" movement and Ronald Reagan's 1966 gubernatorial campaign in California appealed to fundamentalists. The struggle to reinstate prayers in public schools, resentment toward the civil rights movement, and support for American involvement in Vietnam meant that many fundamentalists drifted into rightwing politics and blended with northern conservative Republicans or birthright Democrats in the South.[86]

What gave the alliance between religious and political conservatives real punch, however, was business financing. Indeed, the linkage between business funding networks and the electoral power of the New Christian Right was the key to the political effectiveness of the rightwing resurgence.[87] Beginning in the 1970s, big business interests had set up conservative think tanks, such as the

American Enterprise Institute, the Hoover Institution, and the Heritage Foundation. These emerged as clearinghouses for channeling corporate money into conservative projects. Sunbelt corporations, in particular, helped bankroll resurgent conservatism. In addition, local rightwing businessmen began to transfer their resources into conservative nonprofits and into funding single-issue campaigns against obscenity, abortion, or gay rights.[88] By the late 1970s these various rightwing mobilizations came together in the form of a coalition of neoconservative intellectuals, including William F. Buckley, Norman Podhoretz, and Irving Kristol, political conservatives, such as Paul Weyrich, Richard Viguerie, and Howard Phillips, and the New Christian Right, including Jerry Falwell, Pat Robertson, and James Robison.[89]

The mass political mobilization of conservative Protestants for rightwing political goals was essential for the electoral success of resurgent conservatism. On the one hand, social issues allowed the New Right to make headway in conservative religious constituencies, such as southern evangelicals, whose adherents were deeply conservative on moral issues but were traditionally Democratic in their political loyalty.[90] On the other hand, neo-fundamentalism was able to transcend the confines of the religious niche by giving voice to broader lower-middle- and working-class fears that the growth of a "secular humanist" state had relegated traditional religion to the sidelines and that a nihilistic culture of "permissiveness" had undermined family, church, and neighborhood. As noted earlier, particularly in the aftermath of the Supreme Court's 1973 *Roe v. Wade* decision and the struggle for the Equal Rights Amendment in the same decade, the neo-fundamentalist focus on moral issues struck a chord with the lower middle class.[91] The moral values associated with fundamentalism were thus a key factor in drawing together a socioeconomically diverse movement. Indeed, the fundamentalist-evangelical role in the right wing "better accounts both for its ideology . . . and for its relatively diverse base than do alternative explanations."[92] Promising both stability and opportunity, the Christian Right's combination of social conservatism and economic libertarianism formed the ideological core of the populist conservatism that helped politically mobilize groups that would normally support redistributionist and anti-corporatist policies. As the nationalistic and moralistic political climate that characterized southern and western defense-linked affluence increasingly undermined the ties between the New Deal coalition and religious conservatives, the latter succeeded in turning a previously largely Democratic constituency into reliable Republican supporters.[93]

Finally, the New Christian Right thrived organizationally because of its ability to build upon left evangelical inroads into the counterculture. This is one of the least analyzed aspects of rightwing organizing. While scholarship widely acknowledges that conservative Protestantism gained from the backlash against the counterculture, the interaction between the two movements has been largely ignored. Only in the past decade or so has research into the resurgence of evangelicalism created a new awareness of the unexpected ways in which these putatively antagonistic social movements tended to bleed into and shape each other. In her study of Young Americans for Freedom (YAF) and Students for a Democratic Society (SDS), for example, Rebecca Klatch regards the counterculture as the "meeting ground for the varying interests and overlapping impulses of this divided generation" and the place where the antigovernment stance of both organizations formed a common bond. Likewise, Lisa McGirr notes that hippie communities in southern California attracted both counter-cultural teenagers and adult middle-class Orange Countians. And Preston Shires argues that a surprising number of teens and young adults who partici-pated in the 1960s counterculture eventually made their way to the evangelical movement.[94] This rethinking of the relationship between religion and the social movements of the 1960s and 1970s has continued to yield dividends in the form of recent books on Bill Bright and the Campus Crusade for Christ, Billy Graham and the Republican South, and forthcoming work on the Jesus Movement and on religion in the Sunbelt.[95]

Interactions, even borrowings, between sixties movements and the Christian Right were substantial and manifested themselves mainly in two ways. First, conservative evangelicals explicitly appropriated and copied the language, insignia, symbols, and expressive styles, as well as the organizational techniques, of the insurgent movements of the 1960s. The ballooning "counterculture of the Right" bristles with references to "Birkenstocked Burkeans, gun-loving organic gardeners, evangelical free-range farmers, hip homeschooling mamas, right-wing nature lovers" and "Wal-Mart Hippies."[96] This suggests that many of the cultural expressions and energies of the backlash were already present in the antiliberalism of the sixties insurgencies. Indeed, as Todd Gitlin notes, "Today's Christian Coalition deplores the decline of civilization as fervently as the most apocalyptic environmentalist or hippie antimaterialist of the late sixties." In his view, the "style of extremity, millennialism, intolerance of ambiguity is an operating principle" of both the sixties and the backlash.[97]

In the same vein, numerous studies explore the extent to which the inter-action between movement and countermovement produced convergence in movement tactics and even goals. The leftist converts of Jack Sparks's Christian World Liberation Front brought with them guerrilla theater, picketing, leafleting, and direct confrontation.[98] In the iconic Boston school wars, anti-busing activists relied heavily on sixties-style slogans and organizing.[99] The two largest evangeli-cal student organizations, Campus Crusade for Christ and Inter-Varsity Christian Fellowship, sought to appropriate the culture and tactics of leftist student move-ments while still presenting themselves as an antidote to the New Left and the counterculture, and involving evangelicals in conservative political activism.[100] Randall Terry's Operation Rescue used militant tactics borrowed from the civil rights movement.[101] And Phyllis Schlafly opposed the ERA, but spoke out for a range of women's rights.[102] As Richard A. Viguerie, a key architect of the New Right, put it: "Our success is built on four elements—single issue groups, multi-issue conservative groups, coalition politics and direct mail . . . all the New Right has done is copy the success of the old left."[103]

Above and beyond these tactical and linguistic borrowings, the infiltrations and crossovers between the sixties insurgencies and the Christian Right are a prominent feature in the drama of the relationship between movement and countermovement. Studies of the nonprofit sector, for example, have high-lighted the extent to which it allowed for a fairly easy interchange between left-wing and rightwing grassroots organizations.[104] One example was the litigation campaign that led to the court-ordered deinstitutionalization of the mentally disabled and the creation of a vast network of community mental health centers run by nonprofits with public funds in the 1970s and 1980s. Spearheaded by the American Civil Liberties Union (ACLU), the campaign "was based on a loose alliance of right and leftwing critics of the medico-legal establishment, religious conservatives . . . and libertarians of various persuasions."[105] It showed that the formation of a system of nonprofits as a substitute for government-run group homes "was a rallying cry of the Left as well as the Right" that pitted both against unions, social workers, and many old-style liberals.[106] These efforts to create alternative settings for the disabled led to the establishment of a program that steered billions of dollars into acquiring, renovating, and operating facilities and funneled funds into agencies that, in many instances, linked leftwing counter-cultural origins with reliance on rightwing political connections.[107]

Likewise, a number of those who ended up in organizational roles in the religious Right had honed their skills during their participation in sixties-era mobilization and protest. Juli Loesch, for example, was an antiwar activist at Antioch College and a labor activist for Cesar Chavez and the United Farm Workers before becoming a media coordinator for Operation Rescue in the 1980s. Similarly, Catholic civil rights activist, priest, and war protester Daniel Berrigan moved toward protesting abortion in the 1970s.[108] The clearest case of the link between the evangelical Left and the religious Right, however, is Francis Schaeffer, countercultural founder of the L'Abri community in Switzerland.

Schaeffer's critiques of affluence, segregation, the nuclear arms race, and environmental degradation resonated with the left evangelical constituency in the 1960s and 1970s. Yet in the late 1970s Schaeffer took a hard right turn, applying his cultural critiques to abortion, euthanasia, and secular humanism. "By the 1980s he had more clearly aligned himself with Jerry Falwell, Pat Robertson, and the broader religious right, all of whom cited Schaeffer as their inspiration. Many of his surprised disciples . . . followed Schaeffer, who through Jack Kemp helped link evangelical activists to the Republican Party."[109]

Moreover, as indicated in the previous chapter, the links between evangelicalism and the counterculture shed new light on the dynamics of the conservative resurgence. The Jesus Movement in particular marked the beginning of the conservative tendencies of the 1970s. Although it was the evangelical Left that had initially pioneered the conversion of recovering hippies, many countercultural evangelicals were funneled directly into the religious Right as the disenchantment with alternative lifestyles and political radicalism spread.[110] In many instances the transition from hippie to evangelical was characterized less by merging traditional religious precepts with an open, relativistic, live-and-let-live attitude than by the converts' exaggeration of the spiritual misery of their past as a way of establishing their credentials as born-agains. As one convert stated, "If I had never become a hippie, I would never have realized I was a sinner."[111] Similarly, in their own narrative self-definitions many New Christian Rightists exaggerated their history of countercultural depravity.[112] In the end, the neo-fundamentalist spirit of paranoia, moral absolutism, and premillennial expectation offered a more countercultural image to converted hippies than the evangelical Left. Many dropouts and Jesus Freaks shunned the more tolerant approach of progressive groups such as Evangelicals for Social Action, the People's Christian Coalition, and the Christian World Liberation Front.[113]

In turn, the counterculture was partially repoliticized in the framework of the New Christian Right.[114] According to a survey of former Jesus Movement participants, 42 percent defined themselves as politically liberal and only 22 percent as conservative prior to their involvement with the Jesus People. Afterward only 10 percent identified themselves as liberal and 57 percent as conservative.[115] Politicizing this constituency, however, was a gradual process. While converted hippies were frequently more enamored of strict fundamentalism than of mainstream evangelicalism, they were initially not particularly active in conservative political organizations. Indeed, Jesus Movement followers often constituted the less politicized component of the counterculture, with limited commitment to political protest. "I went to marches, but mostly just to hear the bands and get stoned," said one former hippie quoted by Steven Tipton. "My motto was

'Doobies first, then the Revolution.'"[116] The emphasis on seeking spiritual purity through social separation, strict moral teachings, small-group communal practices, and antigovernment ideology resulted in a conservative outlook, but not necessarily an embrace of rightwing politics. Although sectarian, exclusivistic, and authoritarian, many Jesus People groups continued to resent organized, routinized fundamentalism.[117] Nonetheless, the fundamentalist fabric enmeshing converted hippies, ranging from Bible study groups via prayer meetings to self-help groups and therapy sessions, ultimately engaged them not only in middle-class resocialization but also in conservative repoliticization.[118] As Eileen Luhr has shown, the nurturance of a politicized evangelical youth culture from the Jesus Freaks to Christian heavy metal constituted one of the major achievements of late twentieth-century conservatism.[119]

R. Stephen Warner, in his sociological study of a Presbyterian church in California, presents a good illustration of this process. Part of his narrative involves a hippie commune called "the Land," located near Mendocino and led by "hippie queen" Therese and her charismatic lover, Pete. Nudity, sexual freedom, and psychedelic drugs were standard features of life in the commune. The group had adopted a halo of religiosity, which encompassed an eclectic mix of Tibetan Buddhism, Vedic Hinduism, and Native American peyote cult—and "by 1971, some were even experimenting with Christianity."[120] After a series of dramatic events, including the loss of the commune's meeting center, the group came under the purview of a variety of religious newcomers. Filling a void in commune leadership, fundamentalist Marge Schulenberg and her husband in particular provided a new religious focus and effected the first conversions. At the same time, Mark Kimmerly, the pastor of the local Presbyterian church, was also trying to minister to the commune. Christianity emerged as a legitimate religious expression. However, while it was "Kimmerly's intention to promote humane values at the Land," Warner concluded, "most of those who were members later became converts to a fundamentalism far more doctrinally conservative than his own intellectualized faith." Communards began to participate in Antioch Fellowship meetings, and converted members were sent to "religious boot camp" at Beacon House in Eureka. Indeed, a veritable battle ensued when Pete's conversion put pressure on Therese to follow his example, despite her revulsion at what she saw as the Nazi-like fanaticism of the converted.[121]

By the spring of 1972 the Land had a substantial majority of new fundamentalist converts. They demanded behavioral changes among the rest of the members, burned books, and booted off recalcitrants. Work patterns in the commune were regularized and a clear division of sex-roles was imposed, with males acting as decision-makers. Drugs, drinking, smoking, and nudity were no longer allowed, and strict evangelical teachings and observance replaced the earlier spiritual eclecticism. At the same time, the focus on spiritual goals, salvation, and the excitement of the miraculous bridged the old countercultural and new evangelical identities. The Land thus became a resocialization agency that integrated the aging counterculture and revitalized the Mendocino Presbyterian Church. The commune's role in the radical evangelical movement that spread through Mendocino in the early seventies also meant that many former communards retained this combination of a countercultural and an evangelical identity beyond their involvement in the Land.[122]

A plethora of anecdotal evidence corroborates these basic patterns in the transition from being a hippie to being a fundamentalist. The story of Andrea F. is a case in point. The daughter of a refugee from Nazi Germany, Andrea grew up in a leftwing Jewish family in New York. She rebelled against her family, which she described as dysfunctional, by becoming apolitical. Although Andrea briefly became involved in political activism in the 1960s, she soon ended up in a hippie commune in California. Traumatic experiences there led to her disillusionment with hippie life. She witnessed the devastating effects of drugs, the painful breakup of relationships, and the sickness of a close friend who could not be cured by herbal medicines. Andrea then became friends with a Christian couple, who encouraged her to turn to God. They let her find her own way, emphasizing healing and the saving power of God. Later on she became involved with a more rigidly structured fundamentalist church that assigned an elder to guide her. This church demanded complete obedience and prescribed how she should raise her children. It insisted on the need to break their wills and the use of punitive measures. Andrea eventually revolted against the church's hierarchical and authoritarian approach and gradually moved away from it. However, she noted that its appeal had derived from providing clear moral guidance and emphasizing discipline while embracing an anti-establishment message and condoning the expressive styles of hippie culture. Although in her view rightwing politics was an outside intrusion upon the church by those who were looking for a new political constituency, she acknowledged that the anti-abortion campaign in particular was an effective means of politically mobilizing conservative Christians and former hippies.[123]

## Engineering the Right Turn:
## The NAE and Resurgent Conservatism

The previous sections have illustrated how the conservative wing gained dominance within the evangelical movement on the basis of marginalizing intramovement adversaries, mediating between conflicting theo-ideological positions, and networking with outside groups. They suggest that the substance of the New Christian Right was located less in consolidated institutional structures or religious orthodoxy preconditioning evangelicals for rightwing politics than in the political agency of specific groups within a theologically, socioculturally, and politically divided movement. As the main umbrella organization representative of postwar evangelicalism, the NAE exemplified these processes. A look at its inner workings shows that the conservative ascent within the evangelical fold was rooted in the skillful maneuvers of internal actors. The outspoken partisanship of a new generation of NAE leaders in the 1970s and 1980s, such as Robert Dugan and Billy Melvin, asserted a particular conservative vision within a disparate movement. By the 1980s the NAE had effectively become part of the neo-fundamentalist Christian Right and fervently contributed to mobilizing evangelicals for rightwing political causes. Nonetheless, the NAE's move toward the New Right and the Republican party continued to have its critics among rank-and-file evangelicals, many of whom could hardly be accused of harboring leftist sympathies. The NAE's participation in the conservative resurgence, therefore, continued to rely on the ability to walk the line between political neutrality, partisan involvement, and networking with the Christian Right.

In 1978 Robert P. Dugan Jr. took over the NAE's Washington operation as director of the Office of Public Affairs. Dugan was a lifelong Republican from the west-central suburbs of Denver, an ordained Conservative Baptist pastor, and one of Carl Henry's former students. In his new post he embarked on a coordinated campaign to raise the public and political profile of the languishing OPA in particular and the NAE in general. Under his leadership the office expanded and engaged in a range of new activities. He paid particular attention to publicizing the NAE's position by launching *NAE Washington Insight* in 1979 and appearing on Christian radio and television shows.[124] By 1984 Dugan proudly noted the growing media interest in the NAE and the success of the OPA in getting the Equal Access Act passed, hyperbolically calling it the "first victory of the evangelical community on a high profile piece of legislation."[125]

In the same year, Dugan moved the NAE into political broadcasting with *Worldview*, a 30-minute television program on current events with largely conservative political content produced by International Media Service. Dugan hosted and directed the show, and the OPA selected panelists and issues.[126] Although he saw *Worldview* as "maturing nicely," the program eventually ran into trouble, and Dugan announced plans for a new weekly show with "a more high-tech format, perhaps with some of the features of a show like 'Nightline.'" Especially in the aftermath of the 1987 PTL/Jim Bakker debacle, Dugan and other OPA staff were sought-after panelists on both religious and mainstream talk shows, including James Dobson's *Focus on the Family*, *Larry King Live*, and *This Week with David Brinkley*.[127]

Despite these successes, however, Dugan felt handicapped by the lack of funding for the OPA and the subsequent "inability to market our newsletter, which ought to have twenty times the current readership."[128] Calculating that he needed $45,000, he engaged in fundraising for the OPA to increase its political impact, touting the good relationship with the White House and the influence of *NAE Washington Insight* with its 65,000 subscribers.[129] Nonetheless, financial shortfalls continued to stymie his efforts. In most of his reports to the Board of Administration he lamented the lack of funds for what he sought to achieve: to enlarge OPA staff, produce five-minute news broadcasts, send out more copies of *Insight*, produce a film series on political training for evangelicals, and establish a regular polling service.[130] Not until the mid-1980s did his efforts finally appear to have paid off. By hiring an attorney, a public policy analyst, and other staff, he expanded the office to a five-person operation.[131] In 1988 the OPA moved to new premises. Together with EFMA and the Chaplains Commission, it now occupied the entire fifth floor in a building only three blocks from the White House.[132]

In his role as OPA director, Dugan was instrumental in forging new ties with the political Right and in pushing for the Republican mobilization of evangelicals. His inveterate coalition-building efforts, political consciousness raising, and presence in partisan circles made for a busy schedule. He was eager to see evangelicals "become the dominant religious force in reconstructing public policy" and embarked on an "ongoing quest" for the NAE "to be perceived by evangelicals and the media as the consensus authority on certain issues and as the most effective catalyst for influence on public policy."[133] Echoing Richard John Neuhaus, a prominent convert to Catholicism who played a central role in forging an alliance between evangelicals and Catholics and in bringing conservative Christians into the Republican coalition, Dugan saw "the more moderate evangelicals" as destined to assume the major role in "reconstructing the public philosophy of post-secular America" and urged the NAE to be "at the heart of such a nation-shaping role." For this purpose he avidly cultivated ties to the political establishment and government leaders. "We have a fine relationship with the White House and the Reagan Administration, just as we did with the Carter Administration, in its last year," he reported in 1981.[134]

Whether he was recommending appointees to the Reagan administration, supporting anti-abortion legislation, pushing for tuition tax credit bills, or pulling strings to get Reagan to give his famous "evil empire" speech at the 1983 NAE convention in Orlando, Dugan emerged as a ubiquitous Beltway figure who was apparently highly regarded by White House staff members.[135] Despite evangelical misgivings about Reagan's lukewarm approach to social issues, Dugan helped cement a political alliance between conservative Protestants and the Republicans in the 1984 presidential elections. Together with author Tim LaHaye, Christian Voice co-founder Colonel Doner, and NRB executive director Ben Armstrong, he became a member of the Christian Advisory Group of the Reagan-Bush 1984 Campaign Committee, which served as a clearinghouse for pro-Reagan articles in both Christian and secular publications.[136] He also actively used his newsletter to motivate NAE denominations to conduct voter registration drives and put out voter guides.[137] Stewart McLaurin, Christian Voters staff assistant in the Reagan-Bush 1984 campaign committee and former administrative assistant in the Campus Crusade for Christ, wrote in a letter to Dugan, "I personally want to thank you for your guidance and counsel . . . you can be proud of your personal contribution that helped secure the reelection of President Reagan and Vice President Bush."[138]

Dugan also spoke at numerous pastors' meetings in support of conservative congressmen, based on a list sent by Paul Weyrich, who had asked Dugan to "see if there is any way, publicly or privately, you can help some of these candidates."[139] In addition, he supported the campaigns to re-elect Colorado senator William L. Armstrong, a leading figure in nurturing links between the NAE and the Republican party. He also became part of the Conservative Network. These wide-ranging political involvements earned Dugan a measure of influence and respect among conservative activists. In 1987 Doug Wead, George H. W. Bush's campaign liaison, wrote to the rather pleased OPA director that "the Vice President is very well aware of the fact that you are the dean of evangelical lobbyists and power brokers in Washington."[140]

Dugan was particularly intent on using these connections to place evangelicals in high office, and his efforts met with some success. "Through Research Director Robert Cizik, we have succeeded in helping place increasing numbers of evangelicals in government and other Washington offices," he told the NAE Board of Administration in 1983, highlighting the appointment of NAE Executive Committee member John Perkins to the President's Task Force on Food Assistance.[141] On the margins of his March 1989 report to the NAE Board of Administration he counted "Kemp, [Robert] Dole; Wead; Sununu" among evangelicals in the administration.[142] Later in the year he reported on "behind the scenes" maneuvers that had resulted in the appointment of Democrat Ervin S. Duggan as FCC commissioner. Describing Duggan as "a man of evangelical faith," Dugan praised him as a "'family values' Commissioner who wants to rid the airwaves of indecency."[143] Dugan also spearheaded the high-profile involvement of the NAE in the failed effort to appoint Robert Bork to the Supreme Court in 1987.[144]

His Washington Insight Briefings proved to be an especially valuable instrument for forging new ties. They brought evangelical leaders together with politicians, ambassadors, officials, and judges. The meetings included high-profile presenters, such as politicians William L. Armstrong, John McCain, and Charles Stenholm, Deputy National Security Advisor Robert Gates, Ambassador Clyde D. Taylor, accused drug trafficker and Iran-Contra villain Oliver North, National Endowment for the Arts chairman John Frohnmayer, and White House advisor Doug Wead, as well as representatives from the Office of Governmental Affairs of the Lutheran Church–Missouri Synod and the Public Affairs Committee of the Southern Baptist Convention. By 1988 Dugan trumpeted the briefings as a pivotal instrument for building an "informal coalition" between religious and political operators.[145]

Dugan was also in the front line of various efforts to create an organizational center for the New Christian Right. He cooperated with Tim LaHaye and Paul Weyrich in the American Coalition for Traditional Values (ACTV), which sought to give the Christian Right a broader appeal. The organization aimed to develop positions on social policy, engage in voter registration, "build antipathy" to liberalism, forge bipartisan coalitions on specific issues, and court other religious conservatives.[146] By the late 1980s, however, the ACTV was "in apparent hibernation." Other conservative ventures fared little better. The Moral Majority had weakened, and Christian Voice had "merged into the American Freedom Coalition, which will repel evangelicals when they realize that its primary funding source is the Unification Church of Sun Myung Moon." Dugan, however, remained undeterred by this apparent collapse of a number of groups in the Christian Right. He planned to construct a network of evangelical activists across the country who "would be available to trigger grassroots response from their circle of contacts, and would receive more in-depth information about critical issues than our newsletter contains."[147] By 1989 he had gained the Family Research Council (FRC) as a new ally. Led by former Reagan policy advisor Gary Bauer and part of James Dobson's Focus on the Family organization, Dugan viewed FRC as a "co-belligerent" of the NAE.[148] A year later he announced that the "OPA will become the focal point of a newly developing Evangelical Information Exchange, initiated by Dr. Billy Melvin and involving a good number of leading evangelical organizations."[149] By this time he had moved closer to Paul Weyrich and his Free Congress Foundation, sought to strengthen ties with the Heritage Foundation, and participated in "private planning sessions" of the American Congress for

Christian Citizens, organized by Pat Robertson and the Christian Coalition.[150] His intentions were made clear in a letter to Weyrich: "As you know, my book *Winning the New Civil War: Recapturing America's Values* focuses on this conflict. I am strongly committed to calling the evangelical community to a warfare status, with a November to November strategy leading to the 1992 elections."[151]

There was a more controversial side to Dugan's incessant networking, however. Having failed in his 1976 campaign for a congressional seat, his efforts to build coalitions with secular and religious conservatives in the 1980s merged with his personal ambition to obtain a job in the Reagan administration. In a letter to William Armstrong he confessed that, in addition to increasing the presence of evangelicals, "an administration post would give me political experience attainable in no other way" in preparation for another congressional campaign. He suggested that the "office which seems most suited to me . . . is that of an Assistant to the President, with liaison duties to special groups."[152] Armstrong, noting Dugan's "deep involvement in Republican political activities," in turn recommended him to Reagan as someone who "personally served as a 'bridge' between emerging New Right Christians and the mainline denominations."[153]

Although these efforts came to naught, Dugan renewed his attempts to gain political office in the Reagan administration during the 1984 re-election campaign. In January he wrote to Lyn Nofziger and the Reagan-Bush 1984 Committee, proposing himself as a "paid consultant" whose primary task would be "to stimulate voter registration of evangelicals and to secure a large segment of the evangelical vote for Ronald Regan in November." His letter included a detailed campaign plan that urged the development of a "biblical case for registering and voting" through the evangelical media, strengthening evangelical campaign input, and getting evangelical groups involved without jeopardizing their 501(c)(3) tax status. However, he concluded that "no authoritative discussions have yet been held re: remuneration, budget, travel and expenses."[154] By February, a disappointed Dugan acknowledged that his proposal had been put on hold.[155]

None of this dampened Dugan's political enthusiasm. In 1988, despite being urged by old friends to back Pat Robertson's candidacy for the Republican presidential nomination, he came out in support of George H. W. Bush and campaigned for him.[156] In a letter to Doug and Bill Wead, liaison between the Bush campaign and family values groups, Dugan threw his own name into the ring in response to requests for "possible surrogate speakers for the Bush campaign" and invitees for social events with Bush.[157] Wishing for evangelicals to "become footsoldiers" in a way that "reechoed" Falwell, he participated in strategic meetings in the Bush campaign headquarters.[158]

With other like-minded evangelicals, Dugan wrote to Bush with an offer to secure the votes of millions of evangelicals who "lack our understanding of the wide chasm between you and Michael Dukakis, whether in foreign affairs, economic matters, or social values." Emphasizing that the right running mate could "electrify evangelicals," the letter's signatories suggested "Rep. Jack Kemp, Sen. Bill Armstrong, and to a lesser extent, Missouri Gov. John Ashcroft" for the post. At the same time, however, they called for a reciprocal commitment from Bush for an evangelical voice in the campaign and "assurance of access to the White House, a chronic problem during the Reagan Administration." This included demands for evangelical participation in the transition team, key posts in the personnel office, and an evangelical assistant with direct access to the candidate. "Evangelicals may well be the swing vote this November," they reminded Bush, concluding: "Polls show that 43% of us are Democrats and just 38% Republicans, yet 81% of the evangelical vote supported the Reagan-Bush ticket in 1984. We pray that an evangelical block may likewise develop this year."[159]

Bush's reply to "Dear Bob" was noncommittal. "As you know, this isn't the time for me to be making appointments," he wrote, adding that "when this race is over, you can give me some advice on how the evangelicals should best serve."[160] Dugan, however, was unfazed. In response he stressed again that an evangelical should "have a significant position in the White House" in order to "interpret what may be your strongest constituency." He told Bush that it was "critical that your political coalition remain part of your governing coalition, given the opposition that you may face from a Democratic Congress."[161] Following Bush's electoral success, Dugan met with the president-elect to push the case for nurturing the political coalition with evangelicals. Noting that 82 percent of conservative Protestants had voted for Bush, he once again urged the placement of evangelicals in the incoming administration.[162]

As it turned out, the Bush White House failed to satisfy the conservative Protestants. Dugan's reports to the NAE reflected growing dismay about the administration, particularly after Doug Wead, a crucial liaison with the evangelicals, had been fired from his post in the aftermath of the dispute over the "open door policy" toward homosexual activists.[163] Nonetheless, Dugan continued to labor in the vineyard of Republican political mobilization. By 1992 he was gathering names of evangelical leaders and laymen in support of the Bush-Quayle campaign. He was also a prominent member of the campaign's Evangelical Steering Committee, which was chaired by Bill Armstrong and included John Ashcroft, Bill Bright, James Dobson, Jerry Falwell, and Beverly LaHaye.[164]

Throughout his attempts to gain influence and a position for himself within successive Republican administrations, Dugan had to take cognizance of the diversity of the evangelical constituency. He had to strike a fine balance between active partisanship and the NAE's putative political neutrality. Although the NAE files contain a growing body of correspondence from rightwing Christians who, for example, denounced Senator Mark Hatfield as insufficiently pro-family and advocated policies such as AIDS testing at VA hospitals, Dugan was keenly aware of the reluctance of many evangelicals to be identified with the New Christian Right.[165] In turn, he stressed that political efforts were geared toward promoting "individualized political involvement" by Christian citizens who "ran the gamut from liberal to conservative."[166] As late as March 1990, his reports lamented the lack of a coherent evangelical political position and the need for an evangelical consensus on domestic policy issues.[167]

Dugan's precarious position is indicated in a 1979 letter to Eagle Forum founder Phyllis Schlafly. In his missive, he pointed out that the NAE could not share in an *amicus curiae* brief condemning an extension of the approval period for the Equal Rights Amendment, because the 1979 NAE resolution concerning women did not mention the ERA. However, "on the personal level," he added, "let me express gratitude to you for the impact you are making on the nation, particularly pro-family matters."[168] Records of a lunch meeting in 1981 between Dugan and representatives of Prison Fellowship Ministries (PFM), an evangelical agency founded by Charles Colson, reveal a similar level of circumspection. After suggesting that "it may be helpful to have Senator Armstrong author" PFM articles for *Reader's Digest* and *Parade*, Dugan advised the organization "to stay away from Moral Majority and other Christian Right groups for the time being, since those groups will offend many of the moderates whom we will want to involve." At the same time, however, a PFM memo on the meeting recorded that "actually, he was more positive than that. He suggested that we make contact with them a matter of timing, and when we are looking for a few conservative votes, approach them for support."[169]

Similarly, despite his eagerness to engage in partisan politics, Dugan had to take the precarious nonprofit status of the NAE into consideration. He reiterated the mantra that the NAE was nonpartisan and "barred by law from engaging in partisan political activity."[170] At the same time, however, he lobbied for NAE involvement in mobilizing the evangelical electorate and actively linked the NAE to conservative political networks. In his personal résumé, for example, Dugan on the one hand emphasized that the "NAE cannot be involved in elective politics and thus is clearly not part of the so-called New Christian Right." On the other hand, he touted his Republican credentials and involvement in the 1980 Reagan-for-President campaign.[171]

Dugan was occasionally called to task over his political activities. Criticism of his strategy came mainly from political opponents of the Republican administrations and from those who feared that cuddling up to political leaders compromised the religious message of evangelicalism. After reading *NAE Washington Insight*, Barbara Carbone from Connecticut, for example, complained that it "makes me feel I have to be a republican in order to be saved." Indicating the perseverance of left-leaning sentiments on the evangelical grassroots level, she severely chastised Reagan. He "has cut more social programs for the poor and yet this nation has never been so far in debt," she lamented. "He substituted food for bullets. He did away with many restrictions on pollution so that industries and big business could have large profits. He did nothing to clean the environment. . . . His policy on reducing the federal role in social programs only shifts all financial burdens to state and local government." Finally, she called Reagan and Bush to task for seeking to change capital gains taxes "to benefit the rich" and for cutting Medicare.[172]

In an equally articulate follow-up letter, Carbone maintained that the Reagan tax cuts had benefited the rich but penalized the middle classes. "It is like giving you cuff links and taking away your shirt. Many tax breaks that helped middle class + the poor were eliminated." Citing the Iran-Contra scandal and spiraling national debt, she voiced unease about Reagan's religious credentials. "Just because a man *says* he is Born Again, against abortion + for prayer in the school doesn't mean we should promote him from the pulpit. . . . Mr. Reagan didn't go to church, did nothing about the prayer in school, nothing about abortion and most of all he has no compassion for the poor or elderly."[173] In his reply, Dugan weakly defended Reagan's record. He noted that over 80 percent of evangelicals voted for Reagan and Bush, and that it was the Republican party that had adopted an evangelical agenda, rather than vice versa.[174]

In another instance, Paul Doriani, pastor at the Community Congregational Church in Franklin, Indiana, and former member of the state board of the Pennsylvania NAE, wrote in to cancel his subscription to *Insight*. Though acknowledging that the vast majority of his congregation was Republican, he felt that the newsletter was "unfairly partisan." As a result, "we did not distribute the last two months of the *NAE Washington Insight* which we received."[175] In a closely reasoned and detailed reply that betrayed a growing sense of unease about criticism of his partisan stance, Dugan defended his newsletter. He argued that it simply reflected the findings of pollsters that higher levels of religious commitment benefited the Republican party ("in the pews, get the cues"). He also reminded Doriani that the majority of white evangelicals had voted for Bush and that the GOP had cultivated the evangelical vote.[176]

In the early 1990s Dugan's efforts continued to elicit an ambivalent response. David L. Rambo, president of the Christian and Missionary Alliance, a NAE member denomination, declined the invitation to support the Bush-Quayle campaign in 1992. Though personally supportive of Bush, he was sensitive to his denomination's larger constituency, "whose political perspectives often differ greatly from my own."[177] Likewise, Morris H. Chapman, president of the Southern Baptist Convention, and Paul A. Cedar of the Evangelical Free Church of America, turned down the invitation. Despite his personal support for Bush, the latter noted that his position "was prompted by the experience of Billy Graham with Richard Nixon."[178] These ongoing discussions indicate that despite outward appearances, conservative Protestantism was not a monolith in a culture war but a diverse movement whose political allegiances were contingent and contested.

## Conclusion

While the evangelical center was immobilized and the Left was fragmenting in the 1970s, a resurgent Right within conservative Protestantism was overcoming its own internal divisions and experiencing an institutional revival that enabled it to provide a new sense of direction for the movement. In extended battles over issues such as social action, biblical inerrancy, and the virtues of capitalism, conservatives managed to marginalize liberal and leftwing impulses. The structural strains that had beset the NAE since its inception—the combination of drift at the center with remarkable effectiveness on the subagency level—played a key role in this process. By exploiting internecine strife while mobilizing at the fringes, the New Christian Right was able to offer an effective response to intramovement calls for ideological unity and organizational cohesion that had eluded establishment and leftwing evangelicalism.

In this internal contest, the Right proved a seasoned political operator because it provided a particular way of calibrating between the divergent impulses within the evangelical fold. On the surface, the Right asserted a message of religious piety, theological orthodoxy, moral traditionalism, and "redeemer nation" patriotism against the social action impulses, theological softening, and anticapitalist spirit of the evangelical Left. As this chapter shows, however, conservatives in fact moved away from the theological, social, and political margins of the fundamentalist subculture. While the Christian Right's insistence on biblical absolutes reinforced its image as the defender of the true faith, it masked the softening of conversionist theology. Its distinctive amalgamation of the individualistic, experiential, subjectivist trajectories of pentecostal and charismatic Christianity with the authoritarian modes of fundamentalist moral objectivism produced less an assertion of traditional Biblicism than its reduction to generic moral exhortations. Likewise, the Right's emphasis on single-issue moral campaigning can be understood as continuing the social action impulses of left evangelicalism. While dropping the latter's progressive content, conservatives nonetheless borrowed freely from left evangelical modes of organizing and thinking. In the same vein, the Christian Right's return to "traditional values" was in fact indicative of the cultural turn of postwar evangelicalism. While invoking the radical and emancipatory rhetoric of nineteenth-century republican virtues and producer-class ideology, its unabashed pro-capitalist stance amounted to the moralizing of consumer capitalism. In advocating the application of spiritual solutions to social problems without challenging the consumerist order, conservatives defined moral regeneration purely in terms of the economic success of competitive, entrepreneurial individuals. At the same time, however, the traditional values rhetoric projected an image of righteous indignation fighting moral decline in the post-sixties age.

What is more, the hybrid ideology of the neo-fundamentalists owed more to the appropriation of countercultural styles and rhetoric than to outright hostility to hippie iniquities. Many of the cultural expressions and energies of the backlash were generated from within the counterculture. The epistemological subjectivism of conversionist theology shared a deep bond with the anti-establishmentarian impulses of the counterculture; loose church structures were often reminiscent of the formless spontaneity behind sixties happenings; and neo-fundamentalism kept alive the sixties-style rejection of managerial liberalism while reconciling it with the Cold War order. The New Right's "countercultural capitalism" thus preserved insurgent identities while reaffirming the core norms and institutions of American society.

Finally, the resurgent Christian Right thrived because it was able to construct broad-based denominational, political, and cultural networks. Its tremendous organizational efforts and skillful lobbying engineered a transdenominational conservative coalition that extended beyond the postwar religious consensus building of the neo-evangelicals. Evangelicals' willingness to shed their traditional prejudices smoothed these relations. Anti-Semitism, anti-Catholicism, and racism, which had been defining characteristics of fundamentalism, were on the decline. The emphasis on inclusive moral issues at the expense of doctrinal differences put the conservative evangelicals in the vanguard of a post-sixties religious realignment in which the split between theological orthodoxy and theological liberalism partially replaced traditional denominational divides.

Likewise, the postwar construction of lasting coalitions between religious and secular conservatism spurred the political mobilization of evangelicals. Although many partisan ties date back to the 1950s, it was not until the 1980s that leading figures in the NAE, such as Robert Dugan, embarked on a sustained campaign to mobilize conservative Protestants for the Republican party. These efforts proved crucial for the broader resurgence of populist conservatism. On the one hand, evangelicals provided the Republicans with inroads into a lower-middle- and working-class constituency that had previously eluded the party. On the other hand, the Christian Right's distinctive ideology provided the emotional and cultural substructure for the shift away from staid, elitist Republicanism. In combining nineteenth-century producer-class ideology, working-class moral conservatism, and consumer capitalism, it constructed the narrative amalgam of moral propriety, cultural fears, and material aspirations that enabled conservatives to build a broad-based political campaign.

Moreover, the New Christian Right's organizational links with the counterculture contributed to the conservative resurgence by easing the resocialization and normative reintegration of recovering hippies. Indeed, what started out as the success story of the evangelical Left soon revealed itself as the thin end of a conservative wedge. Militant neo-fundamentalism thrived among former hippies, pushing out the left-leaning Jesus Movement leaders who had led the way in the late 1960s and early 1970s in combining the free-flowing expressiveness of hippie culture with the strict moral order of conservative Protestantism.

By the 1970s, a decade of internal division over sociopolitical involvement and scriptural authority had left the movement both divided and adrift. This image of men praying at the 1971 NAE convention in Los Angeles is an evocative illustration of the soul-searching during this period. The simmering tensions erupted into a full-fledged battle for control in the 1970s during which a resurgent Right effectively marginalized liberal and left-leaning groups. (Wheaton College Archives)

At the 1972 NAE convention in St. Louis, president Hudson T. Armerding "passed the gavel" to his successor Myron F. Boyd. The photograph links the generation of neo-evangelicals who pioneered the movement's postwar awakening (Harold J. Ockenga, *sitting*, and Clyde W. Taylor, *second from left*) with a newly assertive generation of conservatives, such as Billy Melvin and Robert Dugan (*third and fourth from left in the background*). In subsequent years the latter helped steer the NAE in the direction of the New Christian Right. (Billy Graham Center Archives, Wheaton College)

Harold Lindsell, pictured here in a photograph from the 1950s, became editor of *Christianity Today* in 1968 and took the magazine in a politically conservative direction. His book *Battle for the Bible*, published in 1976, was a catalyst for the impending showdown between left evangelicals and a resurgent Right. By making inerrancy the benchmark for unadulterated evangelicalism, he and other conservatives crusaded openly against evangelical progressives and effectively split the movement. (Billy Graham Center Archives, Wheaton College)

Francis Schaeffer, evangelical theologian and founder of the L'Abri community in Switzerland, exemplified the transition from progressive to rightwing evangelicalism. Schaeffer's criticism of affluence, segregation, the nuclear arms race, and environmental degradation had resonated with the left evangelical constituency in the 1960s and 1970s. Yet in the late 1970s Schaeffer took a hard right turn, applying his cultural critiques to abortion, euthanasia, and secular humanism. (Billy Graham Center Archives, Wheaton College)

Charles Colson, former Special Counsel to President Nixon convicted on Watergate-related charges, armed himself with the Bible when he visited his former prison, Maxwell Air Force Base Federal Prison Camp in Montgomery, Alabama, in 1981. Five years earlier Colson had founded Prison Fellowship Ministries, which runs biblical immersion courses, lessons in creationism, substance abuse counseling, and vocational training courses. While Colson was a key figure in furthering the conservative turn of the movement, he also cultivated contacts with left evangelical organizations such as ESA, Sojourners, and Voice of Calvary. (Billy Graham Center Archives, Wheaton College)

William L. Armstrong was a leading figure in strengthening the ties between the NAE and the Republican party. The Colorado congressman and senator participated in many political events organized by the NAE's director of public affairs, Robert Dugan, which brought evangelical leaders together with conservative power brokers. The meetings proved to be a valuable means of building an informal coalition between rightwing religious and political operators. (Colorado Christian College, with kind permission of William L. Armstrong)

# Conclusion

## *New Perspectives on American Evangelicalism*

The partisan mobilization of conservative Protestants constitutes one of the most remarkable political developments since World War II and the clearest case of political realignment during the past forty years.[1] In providing a historical perspective on this process, this book suggests some revisions to common assumptions about resurgent neo-fundamentalism. In particular, it questions the notion that the New Christian Right's political ideology and cultural appeal centered mainly on moral traditionalism and theological orthodoxy; that evangelicals would naturally ally themselves with political conservatism; and that the political mobilization of evangelicals was primarily the result of an adversarial backlash against the sociocultural and political turmoil of the 1960s. In contrast, it depicts a diverse movement whose cultural resonance combined anti-establishmentarian impulses with the affirmation of the fundamentals of liberal culture; whose political identities were often rooted in intra-movement realignments and the marginalizing of dissident groups; and whose ideologies and institutions were molded in the process of interacting with and borrowing from the insurgencies of the 1960s.

Drawing upon resource mobilization theory and subcultural identity theory, the findings show, first of all, that the ability to combine an insurgent message with sociocultural integration is a crucial factor in the Christian Right's organizational strength, cultural attractiveness, and political efficacy. Its substance is located less in traditional morality and theological orthodoxy than in the merger of pietism with social activism, subcultural separatism with a new emphasis on ecumenism, rigid Biblicism with therapeutic conversionism, and moral militancy with the active embrace of consumer culture. Hence, the single-issue moralistic

151

politics favored by the New Christian Right were not only indicative of hard-line normative intransigence; they were also part and parcel of the domestication of evangelicalism. Reflecting an ecumenical, postindustrial mindset that re-oriented religious conflict along liberal-orthodox lines, morality politics shifted the emphasis from narrow doctrinalism, racism, and anti-Catholicism toward broad transdenominational moral campaigning. Likewise, the conservatives' religious dogmatism, while suggesting a return to biblical orthodoxy, in effect translated a religious drama based on traditional Protestant concepts of Christo-centrism, salvation through faith, and evangelical mysticism into a quick religious fix that affirmed the dynamic, flexible, entrepreneurial, and self-realizing market subject. With a nod to Max Weber one might argue that this constituted a shift from "inner-worldly asceticism" to "other-worldly hedonism." Moreover, although conservatives continued to preach moral self-discipline, any remaining disquiet about unfettered capitalism gave way to an explicit embrace of the system of free enterprise and the consumerist underpinnings of postwar culture. While the Christian Right's "moralistic materialism" rhetorically recaptured the moral radicalism and emancipatory aspirations of the nineteenth-century producer-class ideology, it helped reconcile them with the libertarian cult of self-indulgence required by consumer capitalism.

Second, this study argues that deducing a pre-existing conservative partisan orientation within evangelicalism from the fact of its later dominance obscures the political diversity within the movement. Such an *a priori* assumption deflects attention from the internal political battles and maneuvers that led to the preponderance of a rightwing political identity, and neglects the potential that existed for different political alignments. In contrast to common perceptions of evangelical Protestantism as a cultural and political monolith, the rightwing political affiliation of evangelicals was contingent upon complex movement dynamics, interactions with social and cultural trends within Cold War society, and external coalition building. Indeed, evangelical political traditions in many ways ran counter to rightwing politics. As indicated above, when the movement entered the political stage with renewed vigor in the 1960s and 1970s, a generation of young, college-trained evangelical leaders called for a new commitment to fighting poverty, oppression, and social injustice. They attacked capitalism, civil religion, militarism, racism, and imperialism. Likewise, the history of the evangelical vote sheds doubt on the notion that social conservatism necessarily translated into support for conservative economic policies. Although by the 1980s evangelicals had become the most reliable constituency for the Republican party, significant parts of the movement remained critical of the iniquities of liberal capitalism, embraced pacifist sentiments, and adhered to strict church-state separationism.

The rise of the New Christian Right thus needs to be understood in the context of an internal backlash. As rightwing evangelicals realized, building an effective evangelical voting bloc within the Republican party required the containment of left and liberal impulses. Indeed, the newly politicized conservatives emerged victorious only after drawn-out struggles within evangelicalism in the late 1960s and 1970s, not just over biblical inerrancy, but also over social action, civil religion, and consumer capitalism. They took advantage of internal rifts within the NAE, pushed aside opponents, and assumed leadership functions via an effective institutional infrastructure and coalitions with other conservatives, both religious and secular.

In so doing, however, the resurgent Right perpetuated the patterns of cultural accommodation and social involvement pioneered by both postwar evangelicalism and the evangelical Left, and built upon their institutional legacy. The postwar neo-evangelicals' desire for social witnessing, cultural resonance, intellectual legitimacy, and political influence had by the 1950s become part and parcel of the movement's larger demarcation as a third force in American Protestantism. Billy Graham, Carl Henry, Harold John Ockenga, and others not only denounced theological liberalism and the social gospel from a position of doctrinal orthodoxy, but also separated themselves from the narrow-minded and isolated prewar fundamentalism. At the same time, the evangelical revival drew strength both from cooperating with conservatives who remained in mainline Protestant denominations and from the subcultural institution building of fundamentalism. Although by the late 1960s the NAE, the paragon of mainstream evangelicalism, was fragmented and weakened in part because it had failed to organize an effective national coordinating body for social action comparable to Catholic Charities USA or the Southern Baptist Convention's Christian Life Commission, the organization had been immensely successful in spawning powerful affiliates and single-issue movements. Many of them, including World Relief and National Religious Broadcasters, eventually formed part of the operating base of resurgent neo-fundamentalism.

Likewise, the left evangelical impulses were picked up by the New Christian Right. The political and cultural upheaval of the 1960s exposed the tensions and contradictions within postwar evangelicalism in new and dramatic ways. As a resurgent evangelical Left mobilized in the context of the civil rights revolution and the anti–Vietnam War protests, it went beyond the individualistic, soul-winning focus of the neo-evangelicals. Left evangelicals rejected Carl F. H. Henry's and Billy Graham's view that cumulative individual spiritual regenerations could solve social problems. Associated with ESA, *The Other Side* magazine, or Wheaton College, they added a structural perspective to the understanding of social problems, and their opposition to the Vietnam War matured into a systematic critique of American society and civil religion.[2] Although the evangelical Left floundered in the aftermath of political disillusionment and internal rifts, its moral fervor, politicization, and renewal of evangelical social action impulses carried over into the resurgent Right. Indeed, "social action" centered on conservative moral issues proved an effective way of rallying evangelicals after a period of painful fragmentation. Moreover, the conservatives continued and amplified the softening of religious dogma, racism, and sexism pioneered by the "worldly evangelicals" of the 1960s.

Finally, the book refutes the notion that resurgent evangelicalism was primarily a reaction against countercultural impulses. In order to understand evangelicalism's political staying power and cultural resonance, we need to move beyond the focus on this alleged antagonism. Analysis of the organizational, personal, and cognitive links between the counterculture and religious conservatism shows that the New Christian Right was forged in the foundry of the sixties insurgencies—less as a reaction to them than as part of their effective co-optation and integration. Seen from this perspective, the conservative political mobilization of evangelicals was predicated less upon the Right's staunch defense of traditional values and resentment against the cultural changes of the 1960s than upon its ability to selectively appropriate, invoke, and identify with the spirit and methods of the insurgent movements. In short, the dynamic interaction and mutual construction of adversarial movements are central to the process of political mobilization.[3]

Ideologically, neo-fundamentalism's concept of moral awakening tapped into sixties spiritualism and rephrased the call for personal liberation in terms of religious conversion. Its gospel of spiritual self-expression and therapeutic conversionism, however, rather than challenging the established order, resocialized individuals as market subjects. It repackaged the sixties agenda of liberation and authenticity in ways that affirmed the entrepreneurial individual. The Right's message of free enterprise picked up on the Left's libertarian and antigovernmental strains and expressed them in the language of "countercultural capitalism." It depicted the entrepreneurial self as inherently moral because of its grounding in an anti-establishmentarian and self-actualizing mindset that shunned the oppressive institutions of the state in favor of the moralizing effects of the market. By integrating the subversive language of cultural transvaluation adopted by the insurgent movements of the 1960s, New Right ideology managed to reinvent capitalism as both a countercultural force and a guardian of moral order.

Institutionally, the merger of evangelical Christianity, countercultural styles, and political organizing allowed for a remarkably smooth interaction between leftwing and rightwing grassroots organizations. As Peter Dobkin Hall has noted, "the so-called 'Conservative Revolution' was only one element of a deep, cross-cutting, and largely apolitical disenchantment with government, established authority, and large organizations."[4] The Jesus Movement, in particular, tapped into the spiritual crisis among hippies in the aftermath of the moral burnout and structural fragility of the counterculture. Strict moral teachings, small-group separatism, antigovernment ideology, and millennial politics sidelined the tolerant, existentialist attitudes of the counterculture. Ranging from Bible study groups and prayer meetings to self-help groups and therapy sessions, the grassroots culture of evangelicalism appealed greatly to former hippies. Crucially, the inroads into the counterculture pioneered by the evangelical Left paved the way for the rise of the New Christian Right. In particular, parachurch organizations that had their origins in the social action resurgence of the 1960s and 1970s, such as Prison Fellowship Ministries, combined an appeal to disillusioned left evangelicals with a drift to the right. Likewise, the anti-abortion campaign replicated the organizational patterns and anticorporatist impulses of the insurgent movements of the 1960s. In other words, the thesis presented in this book, if the reader finds it persuasive, complicates the conventional left-right categorization that underlies many studies of social movements in the United States.

Taken together, these results shed new light on one of the most vexing issues framing discussions about religion in American society—namely, the coexistence of orthodox forms of religion and sociocultural modernity in the United States. The United States is simultaneously the most religious and the most modern country in the Western world. While some of the most orthodox forms of Christianity thrive there, America is also home to the most pronounced manifestations of secular modernity, including libertarian individualism, liberal capitalism, the adulation of science and technology, and the cult of abundance. Similarly, no nation has so trumpeted the cause of individual freedom while simultaneously seeking to control individual moral behavior. Indeed, America has on its statute books tens of thousands of federal, state, and local laws that seek to enforce morality via prohibitions on drinking alcohol, gambling, prostitution, drug taking, and a range of other, more trivial behaviors.[5]

Many observers see the religiously based liberal-orthodox divide that has increasingly characterized American religion and politics since the 1970s as yet another episode in a pervasive normative conflict embedded within the American experience. Scholars, pundits, and religionists alike argue that the country is in the midst of a "culture war" that pits "the repressive, bigoted morality of Christian theocrats" against "the debauched, godless morality of secular humanists."[6] In the same vein, many have warned that the religious realignment underlying the starker normative profile of the feuding political camps threatens to divide American society as the religious divisions that preceded the American Revolution and the Civil War did. Throughout the history of the United States, religious revivals frequently culminated in deep political fissures. Changes in the religious landscape in the aftermath of the First Great Awakening in the eighteenth century, some have argued, shaped the political alignments leading up to the American Revolution. Likewise, the religious divisions generated by the Second Great Awakening fed into the partisan schisms that spawned the Civil War.[7]

In contrast to that alarming scenario, the present study suggests that the Christian Right, rather than being defined by its opposition to the main trends of American society and culture, is in fact the manifestation of another kind of liberalism, or, alternatively, of "reactionary modernism."[8] In secularizing the conversion experience, rationalizing religious divisions, sanctifying consumer capitalism, and reintegrating the counterculture, evangelicals not only happily coexisted with modernity and postmodernity. They also legitimized and shaped its central components, such as free market economics and even the revolution in manners and morals since the 1960s. In combining orthodox faith and the trappings of modern life, evangelicalism continued to clash with the pluralistic reality of American public life, but was nonetheless absorbed into the sociocultural trajectories of modern American society.[9] Postwar evangelicalism is thus part and parcel of the ongoing mutual construction of secular and religious in the United States. Just as American Enlightenment philosophers were rarely deeply anticlerical, and easily reconciled their teleology, rationalism, and utilitarianism with religious thought, so contemporary conservative Protestants have accommodated themselves quite readily to secular liberal society. As George Marsden has noted, while neo-fundamentalism rejected the historicist and culturalist assumptions of modern thought, it embraced both the expressive styles of the counterculture and modern Enlightenment notions of certain and objective knowledge.[10]

Indeed, it was the ability of the Christian Right to combine an antisecularist, militant, and iconoclastic self-image with a basic acceptance and affirmation of the postwar order that undergirded the movement's broader populist appeal. In the polarized and disillusioned atmosphere of the 1970s, evangelicalism's positioning between moralism and consumerism, anti-etatism and statism, radicalism and reaction, became a core component in the ideological amalgam that has sustained the Republican ascendancy since the 1980s. Moral issues mobilized conservative Protestants against a secular trajectory in government that had gradually removed chapel attendance, Bible readings, school prayer, and Christian holiday observances from public institutions in the name of religious neutrality. Evangelicals denounced the liberal state as colluding in moral iniquities, including homosexuality, abortion, and pregnancy out of wedlock. Likewise, by convincingly attributing the social fraying of society to the "moral failures" of the welfare state, the New Christian Right effectively replaced the shared socioeconomic interests that had held together the old Democratic coalition with a set of moral values that allegedly united corporate interests and those of the lower middle class. Using the politics of morality largely as code for voicing the latter's deep-seated racial and gender fears, the New Right was able to deflect traditional lower-middle-class resentment against corporate America and to politically mobilize evangelicals who in the past would have supported redistributionist and anticorporatist policies.

While thriving on an antisecularist and anti-establishmentarian message, however, the New Christian Right simultaneously shored up the normative parameters of the established social order. Neo-fundamentalism's embrace of sociocultural modernity and consumer society, its invocation of traditionalist biblical orthodoxy to provide a spiritual legitimation of liberal capitalism, and its conversion from an ethic of limits to an affirmation of moralistic materialism appealed to those who were among the prime beneficiaries of the dramatic shift in social and economic power since the 1940s from the older commercial centers of the Northeast to the South and the West of the country. Indeed, by merging Puritanism (in the popular understanding of the word) and capitalism, conservatives artfully obscured the inherent contradiction between the traditional values of moral self-discipline and a consumer culture ultimately dependent on hedonism and permissiveness to function at maximum efficiency. This covered up the fact that consumer capitalism itself, in relying upon a libertarian ethic of indulgence, undermined the traditional values cherished by the petty-bourgeois classes.[11]

Likewise, evangelicalism's visceral opposition to big government, managerial liberalism, Washington bureaucrats, and welfare chiselers, in combination with its underlying support for the defense-welfare state, resonated in the evangelical strongholds in the South and West. In the regions' new technocratic suburbs, many people had benefited from, and were largely supportive of, deficit spending, the military buildup, and federal subsidies. At the same time they continued to cultivate antigovernmentalism and a suburban warrior mentality. Combining the sanctification of the Cold War order with an "outsider" message of free enterprise, entrepreneurial individualism, and moral awakening, evangelicals helped mobilize a constituency that was both superpatriotic and antistatist, conservative and anti-establishmentarian, hyperindividualistic and government-subsidized.

Indeed, as I have argued elsewhere, we need to understand the New Christian Right as mediating between postwar conservatives, who had largely accepted the structures of the liberal state, and neo-conservatives, who had a fetishistic conception of the market. Broadly speaking, evangelicalism mirrored the postwar retreat of the political Right from principled antistatism. While anticommunism and large-scale defense spending facilitated the transition of evangelicals from pietistic patriotism to nationalistic statism, public funding policies since the 1940s essentially put the finishing touches on the long-term process by which evangelicals were integrated into the structures of the "subsidiarist" welfare state. These processes transcended the conflict between consensus liberalism and the conservative resurgence. In short, we can talk about two kinds of statism in American society, rather than about liberalism clashing with conservative retrenchment.[12] In fact, religious conservatives in the 1980s and 1990s, such as Richard Viguerie and Paul Weyrich, were significantly less focused on small government than the insurgent conservative "fusionists" of the 1950s and 1960s.[13] These trends continued well into the twenty-first century. The Tea Party movement, for example, whose ranks are swelled by supporters of the Christian Right, showed that this paradoxical attitude has lost none of its vigor. As one Tea Party activist reportedly demanded of South Carolina Republican congressman Robert Inglis: "Keep your government hands off my Medicare."[14]

Finally, the confluence of evangelical Christianity and countercultural ways, rather than their antagonism, turned out to be one of the most enduring legacies of the sixties. The New Christian Right's appropriation of sixties modes undermined leftwing impulses within the evangelical resurgence and reconciled religious revivalism with the liberal socioeconomic order. What is more, it nurtured the conservative components of the counterculture, keeping alive anti-establishmentarian sentiments while at the same time revalidating liberal capitalism. As parts of the counterculture were resocialized and repoliticized within the framework of the New Christian Right, religious commitment once again became primarily an instrument of norm maintenance and social integration, rather than of substantive transformation. Hippie conversions, as Steven Tipton reminds us, adapted and reconciled the postmodern self to the traditional order. They helped realign sixties insurgent sentiments with the core myths of American society, such as the traditional work ethic, entrepreneurial individualism, and free enterprise.[15] In building upon the counterculture's inherent contradiction—delegitimating utilitarian culture and major social institutions while at the same time affirming the hedonistic values that are at the core of consumer capitalism—resurgent evangelicalism became part of the larger story in which capitalism co-opts the cultural transvaluation promoted by the insurgent movements while effectively marginalizing their radical content. In short, the New Christian Right is part and parcel of the socioeconomic rejection, yet sociocultural infusion, of the 1960s that has characterized American politics and society in the past few decades.

As the preceding pages show, the contemporary Christian Right has just enough adversarial content to resonate with the exceptionalist, isolationist, and utopian tropes in American culture—what Abraham Lincoln famously called "the mystic chords of memory" that shape the sense of national identity. At the same time, it has just enough integrationist and accommodationist velocity to fit comfortably within the established norms of a liberal social and economic order. Indeed, one could argue that movements such as the Christian Right constitute no real countermovement to modernity unless they actually start taking their own theological teachings seriously. Instead, their moral revulsion simply generates an attachment to the very system that putatively created the immoral conditions in the first place. As Bethany Moreton has shown, morality politics channels the experience of postindustrial insecurity associated with the decline of unions, corporate takeovers, falling wages, and the growing differential between rich and poor into support for the basic ideology and socioeconomic patterns of liberal capitalism. In post-Vietnam American culture and society, many evangelicals developed a fierce allegiance to laissez-faire economics, eschewed unionization, and accepted low wages out of a deeper faith in the supremacy of family values and the moralizing effects of the market.[16] Likewise, the Christian Right's anti-elitist and anti-establishmentarian rhetoric, though redolent of more radical impulses, has ended up being an instrument of shoring up existing power relations. In effect, it channels post-sixties distrust in government, sense of betrayal, and anti-institutionalist sentiments into the aggrieved individualism of a "libertarian mob" that effectively endorses the corporate consumerist order.[17]

Lest readers despair over this scenario of a social order that perpetuates itself by absorbing its radical critique, this study may as well close with a caveat. Since the eighteenth century, religious revivalism has consistently been one of the most dynamic and volatile forces in American politics and culture. To this day it remains a protean and unpredictable element in the body politic. At any given point in time, the revivalist impulse can therefore inspire social movements with radically different sociocultural and economic agendas.

# *Notes*

## Abbreviations

ESA Records    Evangelicals for Social Action Records, Collection 37, Billy Graham Center Archives, Wheaton, Illinois.

NAE Records    National Association of Evangelicals Records, Collection SC/113, Wheaton College Archives and Special Collections, Buswell Memorial Library, Wheaton College, Illinois.

PFM Records    Prison Fellowship Ministries Records, Collection 274, Billy Graham Center Archives, Wheaton, Illinois.

VoC Records    Records of Voice of Calvary Ministries, Collection 362, Billy Graham Center Archives, Wheaton, Illinois.

## Introduction: Beyond the "Backlash"

1. Lindsell, "An Evangelical Evaluation of the Relationship between Churches and the State in the United States," 11–13 October 1967, NAE Records. On the postwar evangelical debate about capitalism see, for example, Marsden, *Understanding Fundamentalism*, 94–96; Lienesch, *Redeeming America*, 108–10; Ribuffo, *Old Christian Right*, 122–23, 274; Fowler, *New Engagement*, 185.

2. [Henry], "Where Do We Go From Here?" 17.

3. "Resolutions—The Use of Force," 24 February 1977, NAE Records.

4. "Christianity Today Confidential Survey," 29 April 1986, NAE Records.

5. Armstrong, "Christian Responsibility and Government," 18–22 April 1977, NAE Records.

6. Robert P. Dugan Jr. to Michael K. Deaver, 3 December 1982, NAE Records.

7. Gallup and Castelli, *People's Religion*, 217; Davis and Robinson, "War for America's Soul," 42–43; Williams, *Cultural Wars*, 8–10.

8. Butler, "Jack-in-the-Box Faith"; Lasch, *True and Only Heaven*, 505. For good summaries of the backlash thesis see, for example, Liebman and Wuthnow, eds., *New Christian Right*; Wilcox, *Onward Christian Soldiers?*; Bruce, *Conservative Protestant Politics*; Smith, *American Evangelicalism*.

9. See, for example, Miller, *Graham and Republican South*; Dochuk, *From Bible Belt to Sun Belt*; Williams, *God's Own Party*; Turner, *Bill Bright and Campus Crusade*; Hankins, *Uneasy in Babylon*; Layman, *Great Divide*; Kent, *From Slogans to Mantras*; Fogel, *Fourth Great Awakening*; Eskridge and Noll, *More Money, More Ministry*; Emerson and Smith, *Divided by Faith*.

10. Schäfer, "Cold War State and the Resurgence of Evangelicalism"; Schäfer, "Religious Nonprofit Organizations"; and Schäfer, "What Marx, Lenin, and Stalin Needed."

11. Fowler, *New Engagement*, 2.

12. Hunter, *American Evangelicalism*, 47; Carpenter, *Revive Us Again*, 242.

13. Wuthnow, *Consciousness Reformation*, 4–5, 123.

14. Watt, "Private Hopes."

## Chapter 1. The Enigma of Conservative Protestantism

1. Butler, "Jack-in-the-Box Faith." For concise summaries of the Enlightenment paradigm see Bradbury and Gilbert, *Transforming Faith*, ix–x; Gay, *Liberty and Justice*, 173.

2. "Therapy of the Masses," 12.

3. Hixson, *American Right Wing*, xxvi. Social scientists in the 1950s, such as Daniel Bell, Nathan Glazer, and Seymour Martin Lipset, mainly regarded religious orthodoxy as a feature of the paranoid style of the radical Right. They tended to ignore its broader popular base and the "mutually advantageous friendships between Billy Graham and Vice President Richard Nixon." See Ribuffo, "God and Contemporary Politics," 1519. See also Ribuffo, *Old Christian Right*, 261, 270–71.

4. On religion as an important predictor of political attitudes and behavior see Gallup and Castelli, *People's Religion*, 167, 224; Eighmy, *Churches in Cultural Captivity*, 176; Layman, *Great Divide*, 53–60, 243; Kellstedt, "Neglected Variable." On the cultural divide see especially Wuthnow, *Restructuring of Religion*; Hunter, *Culture Wars*.

5. Marsden, *Understanding Fundamentalism*, 63. See also Noll, *Religion and American Politics*; Fogel, *Fourth Great Awakening*.

6. Gallup and Castelli, *People's Religion*, 20. For material on religiousness see ibid., 4, 45, 60–61, 63, 66, 68–69; Oppenheimer, *Knocking on Heaven's Door*, 1–28; "Therapy of the Masses," 13–14; Ostling, "Religious Landscape"; Shorto, "Belief by Numbers"; Warner, *New Wine*, 28.

7. Warner, *New Wine*, 11, 13, 18, 24–25; Noll, *History of Christianity*, 465; Ellwood, *Fifties Spiritual Marketplace*, 5, 9–10, 48–49, 189; Wuthnow, *Restructuring of Religion*, 21, 27–28, 33, 59–60, 144.

8. Gallup and Castelli, *People's Religion*, 4, 218; Noll, *History of Christianity*, 464–65; "Therapy of the Masses," 14.

9. Noll, *History of Christianity*, 465; Gallup and Castelli, *People's Religion*, 93; Ostling, "Religious Landscape," 12; Wacker, "Uneasy in Zion," 378; Wood, "Liberal Protestant Action," 177–79.

10. Gallup and Castelli, *People's Religion*, 208. On the problem of defining evangelicalism see Stone, *Boundaries of Evangelicalism*, 25–38; Kellstedt, "Neglected Variable," 276; Davis and Robinson, "War for America's Soul," 56–57; Dayton and Johnston, *Variety of American Evangelicalism*, 2.

11. Gallup and Castelli, *People's Religion*, xix, 13, 90, 93. See also Hunter, *American Evangelicalism*.

12. Quoted in Johnston, "American Evangelicalism," 261.

13. Quoted in Rothenberg and Newport, *Evangelical Voter*, 25.

14. Bloesch, *Future of Evangelical Christianity*, ix.

15. Rothenberg and Newport, *Evangelical Voter*, 13, 32. Rothenberg has close ties to Paul Weyrich and the Free Congress Foundation.

16. Quoted in Dayton, "Some Doubts," 253. See also Rothenberg and Newport, *Evangelical Voter*, 25, 31–32; Marsden, "Fundamentalism and Evangelicalism," 32–33.

17. Dayton, "Some Doubts," 245; Stone, *Boundaries of Evangelicalism*, 26–31, 35; Williams, *Cultural Wars*, 6; Dayton and Johnston, *Variety of American Evangelicalism*, 1. On defining evangelicalism and fundamentalism see Johnston, "American Evangelicalism," 253–54, 264–68; Marsden, "Fundamentalism and Evangelicalism," 22–27; Marsden, *Understanding Fundamentalism*, 66–68, 100–101; Lienesch, *Redeeming America*, 15; Dayton, "Social and Political Conservatism," 73–74; Gay, *Liberty and Justice*, 4.

18. Noll, *Old Religion*, 155.

19. Quoted in Heclo, *Christianity and American Democracy*, 70. On the historical antecedents see Dayton, "Social and Political Conservatism," 73–74; Johnston, "American Evangelicalism," 254, 262; Marsden, *Understanding Fundamentalism*, 89–91; Hunter, *American Evangelicalism*, 8.

20. Warner, *New Wine*, 33–34, 49–50; Johnston, "American Evangelicalism," 264–68. See also Szasz, *Divided Mind*; Marty, *Fundamentalism and Evangelicalism*; Schmidt, *Souls or the Social Order*; Weber, *Living in the Shadow*; Sandeen, *Roots of Fundamentalism*.

21. Flowers, *Religion in Strange Times*, 44–46; Rothenberg and Newport, *Evangelical Voter*, 16. See also Marsden, "Fundamentalism and Evangelicalism," 29–30. On left evangelicalism in the 1960s and 1970s see, for example, Gay, *Liberty and Justice*. On the development of fundamentalism especially after World War II see also Lienesch, *Redeeming America*, 4–8; Marsden, *Understanding Fundamentalism*, 101.

22. Wuthnow, *Restructuring of Religion*, 133, 157–63; Layman, *Great Divide*, 6, 291.

23. Hunter, *Culture Wars*. See also Williams, *Cultural Wars*, 5–7; Layman, *Great Divide*, 3; Monsma, *Sacred and Secular*, 52–54.

24. Marsden, *Understanding Fundamentalism*, 116–19. See also Wuthnow, *Restructuring of Religion*, 133–72.

25. Lienesch, *Redeeming America*, 50; Thomas Askew quoted in Johnston, "American Evangelicalism," 261.

26. Lienesch, *Redeeming America*, 50.

27. Flowers, *Religion in Strange Times*, 54; Hunter, *American Evangelicalism*, 47; Marsden, *Understanding Fundamentalism*, 1–6; Warner, *New Wine*, 1–30, 59; Rothenberg and Newport,

*Evangelical Voter*, 25; Gallup and Castelli, *People's Religion*, 90; Stone, *Boundaries of Evangelicalism*, 28; McLoughlin, *Revivals, Awakenings*, 213; Schäfer, "Evangelicalism, Social Reform," 251–53.

28. Layman, *Great Divide*, 53–54. See also Guth et al., *Bully Pulpit*, 191–92.

29. Layman, *Great Divide*, 13, 35, 54–57, 64–66, 126–27, 186–93, 199–200, 295. As Gallup and Castelli remind us, religion is a key factor in the way Americans view social and political issues. By the same token, politically active Americans are more likely to be highly religious. See *People's Religion*, 167, 224.

30. Layman, *Great Divide*, 199; Kellstedt and Noll, "Religion, Voting for President," 359–60, 370–76; Smith, *Baptist Republicanism*, 23; Olson and Beck, "Religion and Political Realignment," 207. Olson and Beck maintain that in the 1980s conservative Protestants in the Rocky Mountain states emerged as important independent predictors of Republican performance in all races. Conversely, there was no such link between conservative Protestantism and Republican party preference in the 1950s.

31. Ribuffo, *Old Christian Right*, 260. However, according to a poll in *Christianity Today*, the evangelical clergy was largely Republican. See "Ministers Favor Eisenhower 8 to 1," 28.

32. Layman, *Great Divide*, 175–76, 184, 192, 299. See also Eighmy, *Churches in Cultural Captivity*, 176–77.

33. Kellstedt and Noll, "Religion, Voting for President," 375; Jelen, "Culture Wars and the Party System," 150.

34. In 1988 Bush received the support of 68 percent of white evangelical Protestants, and the 1992 election saw the "largest increase to date in religious polarization of the parties' mass identifiers." Layman, *Great Divide*, 298; see also ibid., 185–86, 189, 243; Himmelstein, *To the Right*, 123; Jelen, "Culture Wars and the Party System," 149. However, John H. Simpson points out that in the 1984 election mainline Protestants voted in higher percentages for Reagan than evangelicals. The main success of the New Christian Right was located less in the mobilization of the born-again vote than in the politicization of moral issues. See Simpson, "Socio-Moral Issues."

35. Layman, *Great Divide*, 199, 171. Evangelicals nowadays make up almost a third of registered voters. However, voting levels remain lower among evangelicals than among white mainline Protestants and Catholics, despite the rise of the Religious Right. In 1990, for example, voter turnout was lower for evangelicals (46 percent) than for mainline Protestants (55 percent). See Kellstedt, "Neglected Variable," 278, 282; Kellstedt and Noll, "Religion, Voting for President," 371. For a detailed study of the Republican mobilization of southern evangelicals see Williams, *God's Own Party*.

36. Manza and Brooks, *Social Cleavages and Political Change*, cited in Butler, "Jack-in-the-Box Faith," 1367; Layman, *Great Divide*, 13.

37. Layman, *Great Divide*, 17, 35, 55–57, 163, 187, 198, 200, 293–95. A key group in this realignment was the evangelical clergy (ibid., 251); Guth et al., *Bully Pulpit*, 191–92. On the link between religious commitment and partisanship see also Kellstedt and Noll, "Religion, Voting for President," 356; Kellstedt, "Neglected Variable," 279–82, 286,

293–95. See also Pew Research Center for the People and the Press, "The 2004 Political Landscape." The Pew surveys suggest that since measurements began in 1987, political identities have become more polarized on a range of issues, including national security, the social safety net, big business, and minority rights. They indicate that the use of government money for either social services or the military is one of the key distinctions between Republicans and Democrats. In particular, the polls suggest that the frequency of church attendance accounts for the sharpest divide in attitudes and that religious practice is an even stronger predictor of partisan behavior than religious belief, which, in itself, is a stronger indicator than income.

38. Layman, *Great Divide*, 27–28, 237, 290–91, 294–97.

39. Kazin, "Grass-Roots Right," 148.

40. Ehrenreich, "New Right Attack," 162; Lasch, *True and Only Heaven*, 477; Himmelstein, *To the Right*, 73, 78–79; Wuthnow, *Restructuring of Religion*, 195; Hamby, *Liberalism and Its Challengers*, 356–57; Hood and Morris, "Boundary Maintenance," 135–36; Layman, *Great Divide*, 7–10, 175–76, 302. On the Christian Right see also Wilcox, *Onward Christian Soldiers?*; Bruce, *Conservative Protestant Politics*; Liebman and Wuthnow, *New Christian Right*.

41. Lienesch, *Redeeming America*, 10–11; Davis and Robinson, "War for America's Soul," 48; Stone, *Boundaries of Evangelicalism*, 41; Hunter, *American Evangelicalism*, 53–56, 117; Smith, *American Evangelicalism*, 75–76; Gallup and Castelli, *People's Religion*, 49, 64, 73–74, 86, 94; Warner, *New Wine*, 59; Marsden, *Understanding Fundamentalism*, 199–201; Dayton, "Social and Political Conservatism," 78; "Therapy of the Masses," 14. For an example of the rural-urban approach see also Hudson, *Religion in America*.

42. McGirr, *Suburban Warriors*, 51–53; Himmelstein, *To the Right*, 75.

43. For good discussions of the status anxiety explanation see Hixson, *American Right Wing*, 9–26; Lasch, *True and Only Heaven*, 476–77. See also Bell, *Radical Right*.

44. Butler, "Jack-in-the-Box Faith."

45. For interpretations linking evangelicalism and modernity see, for example, Berger, *Social Reality of Religion*; Hunter, *Coming Generation*; Shibley, *Resurgent Evangelicalism*, esp. 133–37; Carpenter, *Revive Us Again*; Ellwood, *Fifties Spiritual Marketplace*; Wacker, "Uneasy in Zion"; Carpenter, "Revive Us Again," 105; Stone, *Boundaries of Evangelicalism*, 43–45. See also McBeth, "Baptist Fundamentalism," 210–12; Marsden, *Understanding Fundamentalism*, 108; Dayton, "Some Doubts," 246. For Dayton, the use of "fundamentalist" and "evangelical" as roughly synonymous with "conservative" or "traditional" is purely a legacy of the modernist-fundamentalist debates of the 1920s.

46. Carpenter, "Youth for Christ," 357–58, 363–64; Carpenter, "Revive Us Again," 114.

47. Ellwood, *Fifties Spiritual Marketplace*, 48.

48. Henry, "Dare We Renew the Controversy? The Evangelical Responsibility," 24.

49. Dayton, "Some Doubts," 246–47.

50. Carpenter, "Revive Us Again," 105; Warner, *New Wine*, 72; Hatch and Hamilton, "Taking the Measure," 397–99, 401–2; Marsden, *Understanding Fundamentalism*, 81.

51. Hunter, *Coming Generation*, 47.

52. Ellwood, *Fifties Spiritual Marketplace*, 14–15. On the link between liberalism and the individualism of the evangelical message see also Wuthnow, *Restructuring of Religion*, 55–57.

53. Heclo, *Christianity and American Democracy*, 43, 202; Sweet, "Crisis of Liberal Christianity," 36–37, 39, 43. See also Porterfield, *Transformation of American Religion*. Offering a different reading, Peter Berger links this "back-door secularization" to the rise of left evangelicalism in the 1960s. See Berger, "Introduction," in Gay, *Liberty and Justice*, xi–xii.

54. Carpenter, "Youth for Christ," 372; Carpenter, *Revive Us Again*, 203, 242.

55. Sweet, "Crisis of Liberal Christianity," 35. See also Brereton, *From Sin to Salvation*, 48; Hatch and Hamilton, "Taking the Measure," 402–3.

56. Quoted in Lienesch, *Redeeming America*, 42; see also ibid., 23–51. On the therapeutic impulse and the spiritualization of popular psychology see also Butler, "Jack-in-the-Box Faith," 1374–75; Marsden, *Understanding Fundamentalism*, 78–79; Roof, *Spiritual Marketplace*; Wuthnow, *After Heaven*.

57. [Armerding], Report by Commission for Industrial Chaplaincy, 19–20 September 1945, NAE Records.

58. Armerding, "Chaplain Counselors for Industry," 19–20 September 1945, NAE Records. See also Chase, "The 'Pneuma' Origin of Human Maladjustments," 19–20 September 1945, NAE Records.

59. Hunter, *American Evangelicalism*, 47. On the compatibility of religion and consumer culture see also McDannell, *Material Christianity*.

60. Marsden, *Understanding Fundamentalism*, 80–81. Marsden argues that this process replicated the cognitive adaptation to liberalism that characterized mainline Protestantism in the early part of the century. See also Bell, "Interpretations," 62.

61. Watt, *Transforming Faith*, 24; Wacker, "Uneasy in Zion," 381; Marsden, *Understanding Fundamentalism*, 79. For a good illustration of this transformation see, for example, Trueheart, "Welcome to the Next Church."

62. Hunter, *American Evangelicalism*, 46–47. Hunter cites Martin Marty's conclusion that evangelicals remained a cognitive minority but emerged as a sociocultural majority; Rothenberg and Newport, *Evangelical Voter*, 27, 31–35; Conn, *American City*, 145; Kellstedt and Noll, "Religion, Voting for President," 370–76; Warner, *New Wine*, 61; Wood, "Liberal Protestant Action," 180; Ellwood, *Fifties Spiritual Marketplace*, 9–10; Wuthnow, *Restructuring of Religion*, 36; Lienesch, *Redeeming America*, 10–11. According to Gallup and Castelli, 46 percent of evangelicals live in the South, 25 percent in the Midwest, 15 percent in the West, and 13 percent in the East. See *People's Religion*, 94.

63. Wuthnow, *Restructuring of Religion*, 27–28, 31–33, 35–36; Hall, "Philanthropy," 39; Carpenter, *Revive Us Again*, 240; Gallup, *Unchurched American*, 15; McGirr, *Suburban Warriors*, 8, 48–51, 241–42, 248, 254–56.

64. Butler, "Jack-in-the-Box-Faith," 1375. See also Carlos, "Religious Participation"; Curtis, *Consuming Faith*.

65. Wuthnow, *Restructuring of Religion*, 21; Gallup and Castelli, *People's Religion*, 90; O'Neill, *Third America*, 32–34. See also Diamond, *Souls of the City*; Hudnet-Beumler, *Looking for God*.

66. Moreton, *To Serve God and Wal-Mart*, 100–124.

67. Ellwood, *Fifties Spiritual Marketplace*, 12; see also ibid., 6. On the role of competition and markets in sustaining religiosity see also Finke and Stark, *Churching of America*; Roof, *Spiritual Marketplace*.

68. Fogel, *Fourth Great Awakening*, 179–80, 217. For good discussions of the link between social policy and the New Christian Right see Brown, *Remaking the Welfare State*; Liebman and Wuthnow, *New Christian Right*.

69. Carpenter, "Revive Us Again," 106; Marsden, *Understanding Fundamentalism*, 116–17. See also Lienesch, *Redeeming America*, 20, 47; Wacker, "Uneasy in Zion," 386; Williams, *Cultural Wars*, 6–7; Johnston, "American Evangelicalism," 263; Warner, *New Wine*, 45–46; McLoughlin, *Revivals, Awakenings*, 213–14.

70. Carpenter, "Revive Us Again," 111–12, 116; Carpenter, "Youth for Christ," 359; Carpenter, *Revive Us Again*, 233, 237; Hunter, *American Evangelicalism*, 39, 44; Himmelstein, *To the Right*, 125.

71. Marsden, *Understanding Fundamentalism*, 65–73; Wuthnow, *Restructuring of Religion*, 137–43. See also Hunter, *American Evangelicalism*, 44.

72. Norris and Inglehart, *Sacred and Secular*.

73. Gallup and Castelli, *People's Religion*, 3, 20, quotation on 60. See also Layman, *Great Divide*, 53–60.

74. "Therapy of the Masses," 13–14; Inglehart, "Why Didn't Religion Disappear?"

75. Quoted in Lienesch, *Redeeming America*, 19.

76. Davis and Robinson, "War for America's Soul," 42; Marsden, *Understanding Fundamentalism*, 94–96; Gay, *Liberty and Justice*, 1–2; Lasch, *True and Only Heaven*. For a useful but limited study on the significance of evangelicalism within the Progressive movement see Crunden, *Ministers of Reform*.

77. [Henry], "Where Do We Go from Here?" 18.

78. Wuthnow, "Religious Commitment and Conservatism," 126; see also ibid., 117–32. On the lack of a clear correlation between religious and political conservatism see also Hood and Morris, "Boundary Maintenance," 143; Davis and Robinson, "War for America's Soul," 56–57; Jelen, "Culture Wars and the Party System," 149; Himmelstein, *To the Right*, 121; Williams, "Culture Wars, Social Movements," 285–86.

79. Layman, *Great Divide*, 171–72, 176, 198, 299; Himmelstein, *To the Right*, 78–79, 121–23; Gallup and Castelli, *People's Religion*, 102, 220.

80. Layman, *Great Divide*, 35, 67, 171, 176; Kellstedt and Noll, "Religion, Voting for President," 372–73, 375; Kellstedt, "Neglected Variable," 278, 282; Himmelstein, *To the Right*, 101–3. On limitations on Republican inroads into the evangelical electorate see also Heclo, *Christianity and American Democracy*, 121.

81. Layman, *Great Divide*, 64–70, 193–99; quotation on 301. See also Jelen, "Culture Wars and the Party System," 146, 152–54.

82. Smith, with Emerson, Gallagher et al., "Myth of Culture Wars," 181; see also ibid., 175, 184.

83. Williams, *Cultural Wars*, 10; Williams, "Culture Wars, Social Movements," 286. See also Heclo, *Christianity and American Democracy*, 119–23.

84. Jelen, "Culture Wars and the Party System," 154; Heclo, *Christianity and American Democracy*, 120.

85. "Therapy of the Masses," 14, 16. See also Davis and Robinson, "War for America's Soul," 47–48.

86. Herberg, *Protestant, Catholic, Jew*. On Herberg see Warner, *New Wine*, 12; Wuthnow, *Restructuring of Religion*, 37. On "culture religion" see Ellwood, *Fifties Spiritual Marketplace*, 8, 16.

87. Warner, *New Wine*, 14.

88. Ellwood, *Fifties Spiritual Marketplace*, 5.

89. Hunter, *American Evangelicalism*, 43.

90. Viteritti, *Last Freedom*, 177, 202.

91. Davis and Robinson, "War for America's Soul," 56. See also Williams, "Sex and the Evangelicals."

92. Jelen, "Culture Wars and the Party System," 148–49; Heclo, *Christianity and American Democracy*, 120–21.

93. Gallup and Castelli, *People's Religion*, 217; Davis and Robinson, "War for America's Soul," 42–43; Williams, *Cultural Wars*, 8–10; "Christianity Today Confidential Survey," 29 April 1986, 2–3, NAE Records.

94. Williams, "Culture Wars, Social Movements," 284; Kelley, "Democracy and the New Deal Party System," 185, 191, 194.

95. Layman, *Great Divide*, 249. See also Smith, with Emerson, Gallagher et al., "Myth of Culture Wars," 175; Davis and Robinson, "War for America's Soul," 54, 56–57.

96. Williams, "Culture Wars, Social Movements," 288, 290, 293.

97. Layman, *Great Divide*, 151; see also ibid., 178, 181–83, 299–300.

98. Lasch, *True and Only Heaven*, 506. See also Ehrenreich, "New Right Attack," 174.

99. Kelley, "Democracy and the New Deal Party System," 195–96; Layman, *Great Divide*, 298; Himmelstein, *To the Right*, 104. See also Sundquist, *Dynamics of the Party System*.

100. Kaus, "Revival of Liberalism." See also Brown, "Segmented Welfare System," 198; Kelley, "Democracy and the New Deal Party System," 185, 191, 194–96.

101. Gallup and Castelli, *People's Religion*, 217, 249.

102. Smith, with Emerson, Gallagher et al., "Myth of Culture Wars," 176–77.

103. Lasch, *True and Only Heaven*, 488–89, 491, 506, quotation on 489.

104. Moreton, "Why Is There So Much Sex in Christian Conservatism." See also Moreton, *To Serve God and Wal-Mart*.

105. Hamby, *Liberalism and Its Challengers*, 340, 363–67, 371, 385.

106. Klatch, *Generation Divided*, 146, 148.

107. Carpenter, *Revive Us Again*, 242.

108. Ellwood, *Fifties Spiritual Marketplace*, 48. According to Ellwood, evangelicalism flourished under "medium tension" (ibid., 8).

109. Carpenter, *Revive Us Again*, 243. See also Hammond, "Evangelical Politics," 190. This view can be compared with Himmelstein's interpretation of the success of the New Right in *To the Right*, 78. It also mirrors Mark Noll's argument that Methodism

flourished in the nineteenth century because it combined the democratic style of postrevolutionary America, the emotions and lay involvement of revivalism, and church discipline and uniformity. See Noll, *Old Religion*, 59–60.

110. Smith, *American Evangelicalism*, 153.

111. Stone, *Boundaries of Evangelicalism*, 43–48; see also ibid., 7, 15.

112. Williams, "Culture Wars, Social Movements," 286–87, quotation on 290.

## Chapter 2. The Postwar Neo-Evangelical Awakening

1. Carpenter, *Revive Us Again*, 233; see also ibid., 173–75; Dayton, "Social and Political Conservatism," 74; Hunter, *American Evangelicalism*, 44; Stone, *Boundaries of Evangelicalism*, 113; Wuthnow, *Restructuring of Religion*, 133, 135–37; Taylor, "NAE Celebrates 30 Years." See also Carpenter, "Revive Us Again," 109, 112–16; Carpenter, "Youth for Christ," 368, 374; Hatch and Hamilton, "Taking the Measure"; Warner, *New Wine*, 1–30. "Cooperation without Compromise" was the NAE's motto.

2. Marsden, "Fundamentalism and Evangelicalism," 29–30; Marsden, *Understanding Fundamentalism*, 64–70; Carpenter, "Revive Us Again," 111, 115–16; Carpenter, *Revive Us Again*, 188–89; Hunter, *American Evangelicalism*, 41–45; Stone, *Boundaries of Evangelicalism*, 10; Wuthnow, *Restructuring of Religion*, 137–43; Watt, *Transforming Faith*, 49–71.

3. Nelson, *Making and Unmaking*, 39. The best example of the neo-evangelical critique of the dogmatic separatism and cultural isolationism of prewar fundamentalism is Henry, *Uneasy Conscience*. On postwar neo-evangelicalism see also Carpenter, *Two Reformers*; Marsden, *Reforming Fundamentalism*; Matthews, *Standing Up, Standing Together*.

4. Hunter, *American Evangelicalism*, 45. See also Hunter, *Coming Generation*, 46.

5. Bloesch, *Future of Evangelical Christianity*, vii. See also Marsden, *Understanding Fundamentalism*, 63; Carpenter, *Revive Us Again*, 153.

6. Stone, *Boundaries of Evangelicalism*, 7, 12, 15, 28–29, 83–84, 183. See also Wuthnow, *Restructuring of Religion*, 142–43.

7. "Evangelicals and Fundamentals," 21.

8. Stone, *Boundaries of Evangelicalism*, 76, 102–3.

9. Marsden, *Understanding Fundamentalism*, 67.

10. Dayton, "Social and Political Conservatism," 74; Sandeen quoted in Marsden, "Fundamentalism and Evangelicalism," 25; Marsden, *Understanding Fundamentalism*, 100–101; see also ibid., 72.

11. Quoted in Johnston, "American Evangelicalism," 264–65; see also ibid., 266–68.

12. Quoted in Ford, "Memorandum Containing a Collection of Statements," [1956], 6, NAE Records.

13. Dayton and Johnston, *Variety of American Evangelicalism*, 1. See also Carpenter, *Revive Us Again*, 203, 206–7, 237; Stone, *Boundaries of Evangelicalism*, 37, 102; Marsden, "Fundamentalism and Evangelicalism," 24; Marsden, *Understanding Fundamentalism*, 1, 67; Lienesch, *Redeeming America*, 15.

14. Keillor, *Lake Wobegon Days*, 102.

15. Quoted in Ford, "Memorandum Containing a Collection of Statements," [1956], 3, NAE Records.

16. Marsden, *Understanding Fundamentalism*, 72.

17. Warner, *New Wine*, 33–34, 49–50.

18. Henry, "Dare We Revive the Modernist-Fundamentalist Conflict?," 6. On attempts to demarcate evangelicalism theologically from both fundamentalism and liberalism see also Henry, "Dare We Renew the Controversy? III. The Contemporary Restoration"; Henry, "Dare We Renew the Controversy? The Evangelical Responsibility"; Bromiley, "Fundamentalism—Modernism"; "Resurgent Evangelism."

19. [Henry], "Jonathan Edwards' Still Angry God," 20–21. On Henry see also Weeks, "Henry's Moral Arguments"; Weeks, "Henry on Civic Life." On the intellectual and scholarly aspirations of postwar evangelicals and the formation of the NAE-affiliated Evangelical Theological Society see Hunter, *American Evangelicalism*, 45; Carpenter, *Revive Us Again*, 207–8.

20. Quoted in Ford, "Memorandum Containing a Collection of Statements," [1956], 2, NAE Records. See also Marsden, *Understanding Fundamentalism*, 72.

21. Kamm, "Is America Losing Her Cultural Distinctives?"

22. Henry, *Remaking the Modern Mind*, 22, 265, 267.

23. Henry, "Fragility of Freedom in the West," 8–9; Henry, "Christian-Pagan West," 3–5; Henry, *Remaking the Modern Mind*, 20–21, 25–26, 267. See also Fowler, *New Engagement*, 89.

24. Jellema, "Rise of the Post-Modern Mind." See also Jellema, "Great Silent Shrug"; Jellema, "Strange New Faiths"; De Boer, "John Dewey and the American Spirit."

25. Henry, "Dare We Renew the Controversy? The Evangelical Responsibility," 24.

26. Watson, "God's Program for Governing," 17 April 1944, 4–6, NAE Records.

27. Ibid., 8–9, 11–14.

28. [Henry], "Where Do We Go From Here?" 18.

29. Carpenter, *Revive Us Again*, 183.

30. Henry, *Confessions of a Theologian*, 141. See also Stone, *Boundaries of Evangelicalism*, 29.

31. The NAE and radio-revivalist Charles Fuller are good examples of this. See Marsden, *Understanding Fundamentalism*, 69–70; Hunter, *American Evangelicalism*, 41; Stone, *Boundaries of Evangelicalism*, 33–34, 111–13.

32. Wuthnow, *Restructuring of Religion*, 138–39, 141–42; Carpenter, *Revive Us Again*, 172–73; Carpenter, "Youth for Christ," 367.

33. Wuthnow, *Restructuring of Religion*, 137–38, 140; Marsden, *Understanding Fundamentalism*, 66, 68; Warner, *New Wine*, 56; Stone, *Boundaries of Evangelicalism*, 146–52.

34. Hunter, *American Evangelicalism*, 42.

35. Carpenter, "Revive Us Again," 106–7; Marsden, *Understanding Fundamentalism*, 71; Himmelstein, *To the Right*, 108–10, 113–14.

36. Taylor, "NAE Celebrates 30 Years," 9.

37. "The NAE: Building on Evangelical Consensus," 52. See also Marsden, "Fundamentalism and Evangelicalism," 30; Stone, *Boundaries of Evangelicalism*, 18, 75.

38. Vernon Grounds quoted in Stone, *Boundaries of Evangelicalism*, 100.

39. Taylor, "NAE Celebrates 30 Years," 9. See also Stone, *Boundaries of Evangelicalism*, 76–77, 127, 132; Carpenter, *Revive Us Again*, 153–54, 188–89; Marsden, "Fundamentalism and Evangelicalism," 29–30; Marsden, *Understanding Fundamentalism*, 71–72.

40. "What Protestant Ministers Believe," 30.

41. Minutes of the NAE Staff Retreat in Glen Eyrie, 10–12 January 1961, 6, NAE Records. See also "General Harrison Answers Graham Critics," 28, 33; Stone, *Boundaries of Evangelicalism*, 76, 103, 159; Marsden, *Understanding Fundamentalism*, 73; Marsden, "Fundamentalism and Evangelicalism," 30. See also "The NAE: Building on Evangelical Consensus," 51.

42. Evangelicals, therefore, successfully occupied the middle ground between liberalism and fundamentalism by merging separatism and revivalism, on the one hand, and objectivist theological orthodoxy with an increasingly subjectivistic mindset, on the other. See Smith, *American Evangelicalism*, 11; Marsden, *Understanding Fundamentalism*, 67; Carpenter, "Revive Us Again," 116; Carpenter, "Youth for Christ," 360; Hunter, *American Evangelicalism*, 45, 48.

43. For a good example of the role suburbanization played in mobilizing neo-evangelicals in the postwar period see the records of the NAE Church Extension and Home Mission Commission, especially Ford, "Crisis in Church Extension" [1958], NAE Records.

44. Carpenter, *Revive Us Again*, 161–65; Marsden, *Understanding Fundamentalism*, 119–21; see also ibid., 82.

45. Henry, *Uneasy Conscience*, 22; Henry, *Remaking the Modern Mind*, 266. See also Marsden, *Understanding Fundamentalism*, 119; Ellwood, *Fifties Spiritual Marketplace*, 12; Carpenter, *Revive Us Again*, 180.

46. Ellwood, *Fifties Spiritual Marketplace*, 13, 48; see also ibid., 49, 189; Hunter, *American Evangelicalism*, 44; Marsden, *Understanding Fundamentalism*, 73. A good discussion of Graham can be found in Lippy, *Twentieth-Century Shapers*, 179–86.

47. Martin, *With God on Our Side*, 29–30.

48. Taylor, "Citizens of Heaven and Earth," 8 August 1954, 7, NAE Records.

49. Smith, *American Evangelicalism*, 11.

50. Henry, *Confessions of a Theologian*, 119, 181. See also Marsden, *Understanding Fundamentalism*, 62, 72.

51. Carpenter, *Revive Us Again*, 191–204; Ellwood, *Fifties Spiritual Marketplace*, 10–11, 14; Henry, *Confessions of a Theologian*, 114–43.

52. Henry, *Confessions of a Theologian*, 144; see also ibid., 141–43, 145–74; Marsden, *Understanding Fundamentalism*, 73; Martin, *With God on Our Side*, 42.

53. Henry, "Why 'Christianity Today,'" 20–21. See also "Declaration of Principles," 20; Ellwood, *Fifties Spiritual Marketplace*, 134.

54. Quoted in Henry, *Confessions of a Theologian*, 141. On *Christianity Today* as part of the drive for ecumenism see also Stone, *Boundaries of Evangelicalism*, 105.

55. Henry, "Why 'Christianity Today,'" 22–23.

56. Henry, *Confessions of a Theologian*, 176. See also "Christian Responsibility," 24.

57. On evangelical prophetic belief and Israel see, for example, Harrison, "Reminiscences and a Prophecy," 14. On evangelical attitudes toward Jews and Israel see Lienesch, *Redeeming America*, 228–33; Boyer, *When Time Shall Be No More*, 185–87, 208–24; Bailey, *Southern White Protestantism*, 136; Mearsheimer and Walt, *The Israel Lobby*; Marsden, "US–Israel Relations."

58. Miller, *Graham and Republican South*. Miller sees Graham as representative of the peculiarly evangelical nature of the South's rapprochement with modernity. While embracing traditional forms of belief, he supplied an acceptable path upon which white Southern moderates could back away from Jim Crow in ways that portended the rise of "color blindness" within popular conservatism. See also Fowler, *New Engagement*, 65–66, 171–73. Fowler maintains that the stance on race separated mainstream evangelicals from fundamentalists, who, as in the case of Bob Jones University, frequently retained segregationist policies. On evangelicals and race see also Bailey, *Southern White Protestantism*, 136; Noll, *Race, Religion, and Reform*; Newman, *Getting Right with God*; Chappell, *Stone of Hope*; Emerson and Smith, *Divided by Faith*.

59. Hunter, *American Evangelicalism*, 43–45. See also "What Is the Target?"; Martin, *With God on Our Side*, 35–39; Ribuffo, *Old Christian Right*.

60. Arnold, "Communism Report," 10–12 January 1961, NAE Records.

61. Bailey, *Southern White Protestantism*, 145.

62. Discussion of Rutherford L. Decker's message "How Others Look at Us," 6–7 February 1961, NAE Records.

63. Lienesch, *Redeeming America*, 231–32; Boyer, *When Time Shall Be No More*, 208–24; Watt, *Transforming Faith*, 58. Conversion also remained the goal as far as Catholics were concerned. In outlining the evangelical strategy "for the Roman Catholic problem," Clyde Taylor suggested at a staff retreat "to evangelize the Catholics as an answer to the problem." See Minutes of the NAE Staff Retreat in Glen Eyrie, 10–12 January 1961, 8, NAE Records.

64. Ockenga, "Communist Issue Today," 12. See also Lienesch, *Redeeming America*, 213.

65. See, for example, "Billy Graham and the Pope's Legions"; "Bigotry or Smear?"

66. Henry, "Christian-Pagan West," 4, 5. On Catholicism being perceived as a perverted form of Christianity see Watt, *Transforming Faith*, 57.

67. Taylor, Mid-Year Report, Secretary of Affairs, 1 October 1952, NAE Records.

68. Taylor, Report of the Office of Public Affairs to the NAE Board of Administration, 7 October 1963, 2, NAE Records. See also Wuthnow, *Restructuring of Religion*, 143.

69. See, for example, Taylor, Report of the Evangelical Action Commission and the NAE Office of Public Affairs, 14 April 1969, NAE Records. See also Dugan, NAE Office of Public Affairs Annual Report, 5 March 1984, NAE Records.

70. Carpenter, *Revive Us Again*, 188; Stone, *Boundaries of Evangelicalism*, 28–29; Wuthnow, *Restructuring of Religion*, 142–43. See also Young, "We Gather Together?"

71. "Temporary Committee for United Action," [1941], NAE Records; Stone, *Boundaries of Evangelicalism*, 122, 132; Carpenter, *Revive Us Again*, 144, 153–54; Taylor, "NAE Celebrates 30 Years."

72. Ostling, "Religious Landscape," 12; Carpenter, *Revive Us Again*, 150. See also National Association of Evangelicals, "History of the NAE."

73. "NAE's Role in the Future," 40; Carpenter, *Revive Us Again*, 158–59.

74. Marsden, "Fundamentalism and Evangelicalism," 29.

75. Carpenter, *Revive Us Again*, 150, 154.

76. Ford, "Memorandum Containing a Collection of Statements," [1956], 1, NAE Records.

77. Hankins, *Uneasy in Babylon*, 40.

78. Taylor, "NAE Celebrates 30 Years," 10; see also ibid., 8–12, 14, 40–41. On the NRB see "NAE's Role in the Future"; "Thirty Short Months," 19–20 September 1945, 14b–14c, NAE Records.

79. Section II, Sectional Reports, 7 October 1980, NAE Records. Opposed to the increasing dialogue between the NAE and the mainline NCCC, NRB decided to formally end its relationship with the NAE on 9 February 2001.

80. Taylor, "NAE Celebrates 30 Years," 10.

81. "Thirty Short Months," 19–20 September 1945, 14b, NAE Records.

82. Taylor, "NAE Celebrates 30 Years," 10–11.

83. Minutes of the NAE Staff Retreat in Glen Eyrie, 10–12 January 1961, 4, NAE Records. See also Taylor, "Dynamic Performance," 4 April 1957, 5, NAE Records.

84. Taylor, "NAE Celebrates 30 Years," 11; "The NAE: Building on Evangelical Consensus," 51.

85. Carpenter, *Revive Us Again*, 183–86. See also Carpenter, "Revive Us Again," 115–16; Carpenter, "Youth for Christ," 368.

86. Taylor, "NAE Celebrates 30 Years," 9; "The Washington Office," 53. On problems with the FCC regarding the renewal of licenses for religious broadcasters see also Taylor, Supplementary Report on Legislation, 9 October 1961, 2, NAE Records.

87. Taylor, "NAE Celebrates 30 Years," 12.

88. "The Washington Office," 53.

89. "Thirty Short Months," 19–20 September 1945, 14b–14c, NAE Records; Taylor, "NAE Celebrates 30 Years," 12.

90. Minutes of the Evangelical Action Committee, 5 June 1957, 1, NAE Records.

91. Taylor, "NAE Celebrates 30 Years," 11–12. See also "Thirty Short Months," 19–20 September 1945, 14b–14c, NAE Records. I discuss World Relief and its participation in government foreign aid programs in detail in Schäfer, "What Marx, Lenin, and Stalin Needed."

92. "The NAE: Building on Evangelical Consensus," 51; Clyde W. Taylor to Billy Graham, 6 December 1968, NAE Records.

93. Report of the Executive President, 28 April 1948, NAE Records. In 1979 Executive Director Billy Melvin attributed the increase in the NAE deficit to the "expanded ministry of the Office of Public Affairs." See Minutes of the Board of Administration, 7–8 October 1980, 3, NAE Records.

94. Photocopy of unsigned letter to the NAE Board of Administration, 21 January 1954, NAE Records.

95. See, for example, the report on the crisis in operational costs in [Ford], "Urgent," 9 June 1958, NAE Records.

96. Minutes of Special Board of Administration, 20 January 1964, NAE Records. By the 1960s the NAE budget had reached the six-figure region—it stood close to $150,000 by 1960 and over $300,000 by 1968.

97. J. Howard Pew to Clyde W. Taylor, 30 January 1968, NAE Records.

98. [Dugan], "Sample to individuals," 18 November 1981, NAE Records.

99. Robert P. Dugan Jr. to Arthur E. Gay, 2 November 1982, NAE Records.

100. "The NAE: Building on Evangelical Consensus," 52–53.

101. Minutes of the NAE Staff Retreat in Glen Eyrie, 10–12 January 1961, 7, NAE Records. On occasional contacts with the NCC see also "NAE's Role in the Future."

102. Rees, "Address of Paul S. Rees," 20–21 January 1954, 2, NAE Records.

103. A good example of this is Paul P. Petticord's memorandum to Herbert Mekeel in the run-up to the NAE's church-state conference in 1961. See Petticord, "Observations-Objectives," 6–7 February 1961, NAE Records.

104. [Ford], Report of the Executive Director to the Board of Administration, 8–9 October 1962, NAE Records.

105. "NAE's Role in the Future."

## Chapter 3. The Evangelical Left and the 1960s

1. Moberg, *Great Reversal*; Marsden, *Fundamentalism and American Culture*, 85–93; Dayton, "Social and Political Conservatism," 72. See also Eighmy, *Churches in Cultural Captivity*, xix; Flowers, *Religion in Strange Times*, 54. As Ronald White has aptly pointed out, however, "to define the Social Gospel as liberal is to miss the diversity of the movement." Indeed, Progressive-era activism was characterized by a simultaneous interest in Bible study and social reform. See White, *Liberty and Justice for All*, xx, xxiii.

2. Watt, *Transforming Faith*, 53; Fowler, *New Engagement*, 89.

3. Gay, *Liberty and Justice*, 1–2. On anticapitalist sentiments in postwar evangelicalism see Lienesch, *Redeeming America*, 108–10; Ribuffo, *Old Christian Right*, 122–23, 274; Fowler, *New Engagement*, 185. See also Cerillo, "Survey of Recent Evangelical Social Thought," 273. On postwar evangelical political orientations see Marsden, *Understanding Fundamentalism*, 94–96.

4. Fowler, *New Engagement*, 189; Marsden, *Understanding Fundamentalism*, 105; Wuthnow, *Restructuring of Religion*, 144, 159–60; Hunter, *American Evangelicalism*, 45–46.

5. Marsden, *Understanding Fundamentalism*, 75, 95. On evangelical divisions see also Stone, *Boundaries of Evangelicalism*, 159, 171–72, 175–76; Wuthnow, *Restructuring of Religion*, 145–48; Wuthnow, *Struggle for America's Soul*, 35.

6. Stone, *Boundaries of Evangelicalism*, 160; Marsden, *Understanding Fundamentalism*, 63, 74.

7. For an insightful analysis that traces the rightwing political mobilization of evangelicals to developments in the 1940s and 1950s while acknowledging the significance of an indigenous evangelical Left see Watt, *Transforming Faith*, 49–71.

8. Quoted in Stone, *Boundaries of Evangelicalism*, 97. See also Carpenter, *Revive Us Again*, 202.

9. Gallup and Castelli, *People's Religion*, 20, 60; Carpenter, *Revive Us Again*, 242; McGirr, *Suburban Warriors*, 248.

10. Schaeffer, "The Modern Drift," 6. On Schaeffer as an inspiration for younger evangelical intellectuals see Fowler, *New Engagement*, 61–62.

11. Gaebelein quoted in [Henry], "Low Tide in the West," 22.

12. Fowler, *New Engagement*, 78; Stone, *Boundaries of Evangelicalism*, 18, 80–81; Hunter, *Coming Generation*, 41. See also Lindner, "Resurgence of Evangelical Social Concern."

13. Henry, *Uneasy Conscience*, 16, 20, 30, 32; Reid, "Age of Anxiety"; Stone, *Boundaries of Evangelicalism*, 88–93, 138; Marsden, *Understanding Fundamentalism*, 64.

14. Henry, "Evangelicals in the Social Struggle," 5. See also "Evangelism: By Isolation or by Participation."

15. Henry, *Uneasy Conscience*, 68; see also ibid., 76, 80.

16. Ibid., 17.

17. [Henry], "Future of the American Worker."

18. Fowler, *New Engagement*, 66–68, 70–71.

19. Stone, *Boundaries of Evangelicalism*, 105; Fowler, *New Engagement*, 47, 49, 54; Hatch and Hamilton, "Taking the Measure," 400–401.

20. Henry, "Evangelicals in the Social Struggle," 10. See also Henry, *Confessions of a Theologian*, 158.

21. Henry, "Evangelicals in the Social Struggle," 10–11; Hatch and Hamilton, "Taking the Measure," 400–401; Fowler, *New Engagement*, 46. See also Miller, *Graham and Republican South*.

22. Henry, "Evangelicals in the Social Struggle," 5–6. See also Henry, *Uneasy Conscience*, 23, 69; Van Riessen, "The Church and Social Problem"; [Henry], "Will the 'Y' Recover Its Gospel."

23. Henry, "Evangelicals in the Social Struggle," 5. See also Stone, *Boundaries of Evangelicalism*, 119, 141; Cerillo, "Survey of Recent Evangelical Social Thought," 273–74; Fowler, *New Engagement*, 80.

24. Lienesch, *Redeeming America*, 50; Fowler, *New Engagement*, 48.

25. Henry, "Evangelicals in the Social Struggle," 6, 11.

26. The four agencies are the NAE's World Relief Commission, World Vision, Medical Assistance Program, and Compassion. See also Hunter, *Coming Generation*, 256, n. 28.

27. "The NAE: Building on Evangelical Consensus," 50.

28. Minutes of the Executive Committee Meeting, 6 March 1956, NAE Records. The reference to social consciousness as a "new concept" is found in Minutes of the NAE Staff Retreat in Glen Eyrie, 10–12 January 1961, 3, NAE Records.

29. Zahniser, Report of the Commission on Social Action, 6–10 April 1959, NAE Records.

30. [Smith], Report of the Social Action Commission, 8–9 October 1962, NAE Records.

31. Eighmy, *Churches in Cultural Captivity*, xix; Henderson, "Social Action in a Conservative Environment," 247.

32. Stone, *Boundaries of Evangelicalism*, 197, n. 12. See also Carpenter, *Revive Us Again*, 159–60; Fowler, *New Engagement*, 77–78, 81, 85.

33. Minutes of the NAE Staff Retreat in Glen Eyrie, 10–12 January 1961, 3, 5, NAE Records. Gill ran the OPA's Community Relations program. The idea was to create a regular department of the NAE where regional directors could receive help for local and regional work. The program, however, was largely confined to studying a typical American community (Portland, Maine), since the OPA found it "impossible to proceed very much further without working through the regional offices." See Taylor, Report of the Office of Public Affairs to NAE Executive Committee, 14 September 1961, 6, NAE Records.

34. Stone, *Boundaries of Evangelicalism*, 145.

35. [Henry], "Where Do We Go From Here?" 18; Stone, *Boundaries of Evangelicalism*, 142; Fowler, *New Engagement*, 81, 85, 88.

36. Henry, "Evangelicals in the Social Struggle," 5; Cerillo, "Survey of Recent Evangelical Social Thought," 273–74; Fowler, *New Engagement*, 26–27.

37. See, for example, Stob, "Labor Needs a Conscience."

38. Hunt, "Christians and the Economic Order."

39. Howard, "Christian Approach to Economics." See also Howard, *Christian Alternative to Socialism*. On constructing a biblical sanctioning of capitalism and free enterprise see also Watt, *Transforming Faith*, 65–67.

40. Dayton, "Social and Political Conservatism," 71; Stone, *Boundaries of Evangelicalism*, 173; Fowler, *New Engagement*, 44–47.

41. Richard Pierard to W. T. Miller, 15 November 1972, ESA Records. On evangelicals in the sixties see Quebedeaux, *Young Evangelicals*, 38; Quebedeaux, *Worldly Evangelicals*, xi, 147–62. In a conversation with the author, Pierard argued that Quebedeaux's focus on the "young evangelicals" underestimated the role older evangelicals played in the emergence of the evangelical Left in the 1970s. See also Flowers, *Religion in Strange Times*, 55–56; Cerillo, "Survey of Recent Evangelical Social Thought," 276–80; Marsden, *Understanding Fundamentalism*, 74–76; Erickson, *Evangelical Left*. For a detailed analysis of leftwing evangelicalism see Swartz, "Left Behind"; Swartz, "Identity Politics."

42. Gay, *Liberty and Justice*, 22–30, 34–40.

43. Ibid., 42, 45–51, 59–60. The Left's view of poverty also indicates that evangelicalism not only contains individualistic moralistic dimensions and serves as a normative

legitimation for liberal capitalism, but also includes solidaristic, even collectivist impulses. Timothy Clydesdale, for example, has identified three main historical strands of evangelical thought. In his view, "indifferent evangelicals," including George Whitefield and Dwight Moody, saw poverty as an individual problem to be addressed via evangelism and spiritual regeneration. "Dutiful stewards," including Jonathan Edwards, understood poverty in terms of spiritual and economic causes, but warned against giving to the "lazy." And "Prophets of Justice," such as Jonathan Blanchard and Jim Wallis, located poverty in structural evil, requiring societal protection for the oppressed. See Clydesdale, "Soul-Winning and Social Work," 188–92, 197.

44. Wuthnow, *Restructuring of Religion*, 153–54, 156–57, 162–63; Quebedeaux, *Worldly Evangelicals*, 86, 152, 164; Gay, *Liberty and Justice*, 14; Hunter, *Coming Generation*, 43; Flowers, *Religion in Strange Times*, 42–43; Marsden, *Understanding Fundamentalism*, 74.

45. Gallup and Castelli, *People's Religion*, 4, 13.

46. Gay, *Liberty and Justice*, 14. See also Hunter, *Coming Generation*, 43.

47. Evangelicals for McGovern, Circular, [1972], ESA Records.

48. Marsden, *Understanding Fundamentalism*, 74; Sweet, "Crisis of Liberal Christianity," 44. See also Tseng and Furness, "Reawakening of Social Consciousness."

49. Carroll, "New Populists," 528, 539; Clydesdale, "Soul-Winning and Social Work," 196; Warner, *New Wine*, 15–17, 45; Hunter, *Coming Generation*, 42.

50. Garr, *Reinvesting in America*, xii, 32, 43–45, 77, 89–90, 169–70, 196. See also Miles, *Evangelism and Social Involvement*, 102–22.

51. Conn, *American City*, 153, 159.

52. Hunter, *Coming Generation*, 257, n. 35.

53. For an insightful discussion of the role of philanthropy in the black community see Carson, "Patterns of Giving."

54. Marsden, *Understanding Fundamentalism*, 103–5; Flowers, *Religion in Strange Times*, 52; Hunter, *American Evangelicalism*, 46.

55. Dayton, "Social and Political Conservatism," 79; Quebedeaux, *Worldly Evangelicals*, 84–85, 88–89, 98–100; Hunter, *Coming Generation*, 43–44; Flowers, *Religion in Strange Times*, 42–43; Wuthnow, *Restructuring of Religion*, 194; Berger, "Introduction," xi–xii.

56. Quebedeaux, *Worldly Evangelicals*, 90–97; Stone, *Boundaries of Evangelicalism*, 164–66; Wuthnow, *Struggle for America's Soul*, 35; Fowler, *New Engagement*, 56–58; Pierard, *Unequal Yoke*, 185–86.

57. [Henry], "Where Do We Go from Here?" 18.

58. Henry, "Evangelicals: Out of the Closet but Going Nowhere?"

59. Cerillo and Dempster, *Salt and Light*, 18.

60. Minutes of the Executive Committee Meeting, 22 June 1956, NAE Records.

61. Minutes of the Social Action Commission, 6 October 1956, NAE Records.

62. [Ford], Executive Director's Report to the Board of Administration, 2–4 April 1957, 4, 6, NAE Records.

63. Taylor, Report of the Secretary of Public Affairs, 1 April 1957, 1, NAE Records. See also "Seminar on Federal Service," 4, NAE Records.

64. Cairns, "Church-State Relations in the United States," 6–7 February 1961, 10, NAE Records.

65. Zahniser, Report of the Commission on Social Action, 6–10 April 1959, 1, NAE Records; [Smith], Report of the Social Action Commission, 8–9 October 1962, 1–2, NAE Records.

66. Minutes of the Social Action Commission, 7 October 1963, 3, NAE Records.

67. "Social Action Committee Meeting," 8 September 1965, NAE Records.

68. Ibid.; Commission on Social Concern, Social Concern Breakfast Meeting, 19 April 1966, NAE Records.

69. Thursday Morning Breakfast Meeting of Social Concern Commission, 21 April 1966, NAE Records.

70. Annual Report of the Commission on Social Concern, April 1966, 1–2, NAE Records.

71. Report of the Social Concern Commission, 13 April 1967, NAE Records.

72. Report of the Social Concern Commission, 5–6 October 1970, NAE Records.

73. Report of the Social Concern Commission, 6 April 1970, NAE Records.

74. Report of the Commission on Social Concern, 4–5 October 1971, NAE Records.

75. T. E. Gannon to Executive Committee, Commission on Social Concern, 27 October 1972, NAE Records. Gambling in particular was a powerful mobilizing issue on the grassroots level. As a conservative pastor in a liberal denomination in California wrote, the daily routine of his antigambling campaign included testifying before committees, appearing on radio and television, organizing telephone and personal contacts, and helping politicians answer letters from their constituents. "My modus operandi is to work with individual Assemblymen and Senators on an eyeball-to-eyeball basis," he proudly reported. "This year's reapportionment has created many new legislative districts with no incumbents, and we are trying to get new Christian men elected to the California legislature." See Harvey Chinn to Edward J. Hales, 15 May 1974, NAE Records.

76. Evangelical Social Action Commission, Report to the Board of Administration, 8–9 October 1973, NAE Records.

77. [Van Elderen], "Calvin Theol. Sem., 12/5/74," ESA Records.

78. Ron Sider to David O. Moberg, 19 May 1973, ESA Records. See also Minutes of the Social Concerns Commission, 1–3 May 1973, 5, NAE Records.

79. Sider, "News Release," 27 November 1973, 1–2, NAE Records. On ESA see also Flowers, *Religion in Strange Times*, 55–57.

80. "A Declaration of Evangelical Social Concern," 27 November 1973, 1–2, NAE Records.

81. [Van Elderen], "Calvin Theol. Sem., 12/5/74," 1, ESA Records.

82. Sweet, "Crisis of Liberal Christianity," 44.

83. [Van Elderen], "Calvin Theol. Sem., 12/5/74," 4–5, ESA Records.

84. "A Declaration of Evangelical Social Concern," 27 November 1973, 2, NAE Records. See also Quebedeaux, *Worldly Evangelicals*, 84; Flowers, *Religion in Strange Times*, 56.

85. "Questionnaire for Original Signatories of the Chicago Declaration," [1975], ESA Records. The planning committee established for the 1974 workshop included Michaelson, Gaebelein, Paul Henry, Rufus Jones, Pierard, Wallis, Sider, and Nancy Hardesty. See Minutes, Planning Committee, 20 April 1974, ESA Records.

86. Henry, "Evangelical Social Concern," 99–100.

87. [Van Elderen], "Calvin Theol. Sem., 12/5/74," 3–4, 7, ESA Records.

88. "Suggested Concrete Proposals for Action," 23–25 November 1973, 1, ESA Records.

89. Ibid., 1–4.

90. Rufus Jones to Ron Sider, 15 May 1973, ESA Records.

91. "Suggestions for Specific Action," [1970s], ESA Records.

92. John Alexander to Rufus Jones, [November 1973], ESA Records.

93. [Alexander], "Action Proposal," [1973], ESA Records.

94. [Van Elderen], "Calvin Theol. Sem., 12/5/74," 11, ESA Records.

95. Mott and Roberts, A Report on the Second Thanksgiving Workshop, 29 November–1 December 1974, ESA Records. The meeting was dominated by "continued debate" among the 117 participants "between those who favor a counter-culture model for social change and those who prefer changing social structures from within." See "News Release 'Evangelicals for Social Action,'" 3 December 1974, ESA Records.

96. "Action Proposals Accepted at the Second Thanksgiving Workshop," 1974, ESA Records.

97. Sider, "A Personal Reflection," 16 December 1974, ESA Records.

98. Rufus Jones to Rev. Pamela J. Cole, 11 December 1974, ESA Records.

99. Quebedeaux, *Worldly Evangelicals*, 146–48; Cerillo, "Survey of Recent Evangelical Social Thought," 278–79.

100. Brown, "Christian Social Responsibility," [1975], ESA Records.

101. Quebedeaux, *Worldly Evangelicals*, 149; Cerillo, "Survey of Recent Evangelical Social Thought," 272.

102. [Van Elderen], "Calvin Theol. Sem., 12/5/74," 5, ESA Records.

103. Quebedeaux, *Worldly Evangelicals*, 152–53. See also Pierard, *Unequal Yoke*, 177–85.

104. David O. Moberg to Ronald J. Sider, 27 February 1973, ESA Records.

105. [Van Elderen], "Calvin Theol. Sem., 12/5/74," 8, ESA Records. On evangelicals, race, and the civil rights movement in general see Wuthnow, *Restructuring of Religion*, 145–48.

106. Greene, "Confrontation in Black and White," 25, ESA Records.

107. "Chicago Crisis," 57.

108. Greene, "Confrontation in Black and White," 26, ESA Records. At the 1974 ESA workshop Perkins had suggested a project on "Community Development through the Training of Black Christian Leaders." See "Action Proposals Accepted at the Second Thanksgiving Workshop," 1974, ESA Records.

109. Judy Brown Hull to "Whoever is interested" on "The Past, Present, and Future of E.S.A.," 1975, ESA Records.

110. "Chicago Crisis," 57.

111. Minutes of the Evangelical Social Action Commission Executive Committee, 10 April 1975, NAE Records.

112. Minutes of the Business Meeting of ESAC, 8–10 April 1975, NAE Records.

113. Martin H. Schrag to ESAC Executive Committee, 20 August 1975; [Schrag], "The Biblical Basis for Social Action," [1975], NAE Records.

114. Rufus Jones to Hugh J. Lind, 17 March 1976. See also Hugh J. Lind to Rufus Jones, 2 March 1976; Betty L. Philpott to Rufus Jones, 18 February 1976; Rufus Jones to Betty L. Philpott, 26 February 1976; all in ESA Records.

115. Rufus Jones to Judy Hull, 21 May 1976, ESA Records.

116. Lucille Sider Dayton to Martin H. Schrag, 6 April 1975, NAE Records.

117. Hilliard, "2. A Dissent," 15–16, NAE Records.

118. "Planning for Action."

119. Fowler, *New Engagement*, 34, 84.

120. Paul B. Henry to Ronald J. Sider, 23 August 1973, ESA Records.

121. Ira Gallaway to Robert Pierard, 17 December 1976, ESA Records.

122. "Planning for Action."

123. Memorandum from Mike [Cromartie] to Gordon [Loux?], 17 January 1978, PFM Records.

124. Quebedeaux, *Worldly Evangelicals*, 146.

125. Robert P. Dugan Jr. to David McKenna, 23 March 1972, NAE Records.

126. David McKenna to Robert P. Dugan Jr., 27 March 1972, NAE Records. See also Hudson T. Armerding to Robert P. Dugan Jr., 28 March 1972, NAE Records.

127. Donald B. Patterson to NAE leaders, 8 May 1973, NAE Records; Robert P. Dugan to Myron F. Boyd, 23 October 1973, NAE Records.

128. Henry, "Evangelicals: Out of the Closet but Going Nowhere?" 16–17.

129. Ibid., 17–20.

130. Ibid., 18–20.

131. Taylor, Report of the General Director, 7 October 1974, NAE Records.

132. "NAE Task Force on Long-Range Planning," 8 October 1980, 1, NAE Records.

133. Ibid., 2–3, 5–6.

134. Henry, "Evangelicals: Out of the Closet but Going Nowhere?," 20–22.

135. Wacker, "Uneasy in Zion," 379, 380–81; Streiker, *Jesus Trip*, 62.

136. On the link between evangelicalism and the insurgent movements of the 1960s see Isserman and Kazin, *America Divided*, 241–59; Ribuffo, "God and Contemporary Politics," 1526; Balmer, *Mine Eyes Have Seen the Glory*, 19–25; Carpenter, "Revive Us Again," 105; Warner, *New Wine*, 72, 141–53. See also Oppenheimer, *Knocking on Heaven's Door*; Kent, *From Slogans to Mantras*; Rossinow, *Politics of Authenticity*; Tipton, *Saved from the Sixties*.

137. Swartz, "Left Behind," 69; Leland, "Rebels with a Cross."

138. Wuthnow, *Consciousness Reformation*, 4–5, 123; Sweet, "Crisis of Liberal Christianity," 37. Gallup and Castelli offer a good indication of the countercultural

nature of the post-sixties religious revival. Their findings indicate that in 1990, 33 percent of Americans claimed to have had a "religious experience, a particularly powerful religious insight or awakening" that falls into the categories of an "'otherworldly' feeling of union with a divine being, forgiveness of sin and promise of salvation, a spiritual awakening related to nature, experiences related to healing, experiences involving visions, voices, and dreams, sudden insight and turning to God in moments of crisis." This was the same percentage as in 1976, but had increased from 20 percent in 1962. See *People's Religion*, 68–69.

139. Tipton, *Saved from the Sixties*, 17; see also ibid., 15–16, 24.

140. Enroth, Ericson, and Peter, *Jesus People*, 231.

141. Wuthnow, *Consciousness Reformation*, 123.

142. Sweet, "Crisis of Liberal Christianity," 37. See also Warner, *New Wine*, 39–41.

143. Swartz, "Left Behind," 277–78; Marsh, "Confession: Among the Jesus Freaks."

144. Balmer, *Mine Eyes Have Seen the Glory*, 19–20.

145. Enroth, Ericson, and Peter, *Jesus People*.

146. McGirr, *Suburban Warriors*, 242–43; Tipton, *Saved from the Sixties*, 18, 23; Marsden, *Understanding Fundamentalism*, 104. See also Gallup and Castelli, *People's Religion*, 70.

147. McLoughlin, *Revivals, Awakenings*, 213. McLoughlin sees the consciousness of the 1960s as the basis for a new value system springing from renewed respect for life and its mysterious source (ibid., 216). Though he may have had Charles Reich in mind, this statement might be equally applicable to anti-abortion campaigners. See also Warner, *New Wine*, 44–45; James, *Varieties of Religious Experience*, esp. Lecture III.

148. [Van Elderen], "Calvin Theol. Sem., 12/5/74," 6–7, ESA Records.

149. Gish quoted in Gay, *Liberty and Justice*, 55–56.

150. Hunter, *American Evangelicalism*, 46; Fowler, *New Engagement*, 143. See also Rossinow, *Politics of Authenticity*; Isserman and Kazin, *America Divided*; Shires, *Hippies of the Religious Right*.

151. Rev. Robert Spike quoted in Jellema, "Strange New Faiths," 16.

152. Wuthnow, *Consciousness Reformation*, 30, 37–39, 41. The five groups Wuthnow studied were the pentecostals, the Christian World Liberation Front, the Children of God, Jews for Jesus, and the Campus Crusade for Christ.

153. Shires, *Hippies of the Religious Right*; Eynon, "Cast upon the Shore," 560–61.

154. Gallup and Castelli, *People's Religion*, 13.

155. Flowers, *Religion in Strange Times*, 50–51. See also Turner, *Bill Bright and Campus Crusade*; Swartz, "Left Behind"; Young, "Hippies to Jesus Freaks."

156. Eskridge and DiSabatino, *Remembering the Jesus Movement*, 3.

157. Marsden, *Understanding Fundamentalism*, 104; Gallup and Castelli, *People's Religion*, 4, 11.

158. Tipton, *Saved from the Sixties*, 29, 41, 53; Enroth, Ericson, and Peter, *Jesus People*, 228, 236.

159. See also interview with Andrea F. in chapter 4.

160. Tipton, *Saved from the Sixties*, 30; see also ibid., 58.

161. Quoted in Lyra, "Rise of the Jesus Movement," 57.

162. Streiker, *Jesus Trip*, 9, 62, 65. See also Balmer, *Mine Eyes Have Seen the Glory*, 21. See also Lyra, "Rise of the Jesus Movement"; Fowler, *New Engagement*, 148–50.

163. Quebedeaux, *Worldly Evangelicals*, 146, 149; Lyra, "Rise of the Jesus Movement," 53–54.

164. Balmer, *Mine Eyes Have Seen the Glory*, 22–23; McGirr, *Suburban Warriors*, 243.

165. Tipton, *Saved from the Sixties*, 36.

166. Streiker, *Jesus Trip*, 16; Lyra, "Rise of the Jesus Movement," 52, 54–56; Enroth, Ericson, and Peter, *Jesus People*, 237, 241–46. On the decline and continuity of the Jesus Movement see Flowers, *Religion in Strange Times*, 52–53.

167. Quoted in Lindsey, "Aquarians and Evangelicals."

168. Quotations from Tipton, *Saved from the Sixties*, 55, 58, 61. See also Flowers, *Religion in Strange Times*, 48.

169. Quotations from Tipton, *Saved from the Sixties*, 49, 58–60.

170. Lyra, "Rise of the Jesus Movement," 51.

171. Balmer, *Mine Eyes Have Seen the Glory*, 21, 24–25; Enroth, Ericson, and Peter, *Jesus People*, 223, 227; Marsden, *Understanding Fundamentalism*, 78; Stone, *Boundaries of Evangelicalism*, 27, 33–34; Lienesch, *Redeeming America*, 15–16.

172. Quoted in Tipton, *Saved from the Sixties*, 57; see also ibid., 61.

173. Quoted in Enroth, Ericson, and Peter, *Jesus People*, 243. See also Sweet, "Crisis of Liberal Christianity," 34–35.

174. Eskridge and DiSabatino, *Remembering the Jesus Movement*, 6. The figures on speaking in tongues can be found in an earlier version of the survey. See Eskridge and DiSabatino, "Jesus People Survey Tabulations & Comments: First 400," 13–14.

175. Quoted in Tipton, *Saved from the Sixties*, 64; see also ibid., 65–68, 74–75, 77; Enroth, Ericson, and Peter, *Jesus People*, 228, 236; Warner, *New Wine*, 72.

176. Streiker, *Jesus Trip*, 64–65.

177. Tipton, *Saved from the Sixties*, 29, 72–73, 78–80, 85.

178. Warner, *New Wine*, 85. The author cites Italian sociologist Francesco Alberoni's distinction between nascent and institutional religion, which extends into social and political life as an alteration between states of emotional exhilaration and states of bureaucratic routine. See ibid., 45–46.

179. Tipton, *Saved from the Sixties*, 64; see also ibid., 43, 52.

180. Hatch and Hamilton, "Taking the Measure," 402–3; Sweet, "Crisis of Liberal Christianity," 34–35, 37–39, 43; Marsden, *Understanding Fundamentalism*, 78.

181. McLoughlin, *Revivals, Awakenings*, 213–14; Lienesch, *Redeeming America*, 47.

182. Tipton, *Saved from the Sixties*, 93; see also ibid., 72.

183. Sweet, "Crisis of Liberal Christianity," 30.

184. Henry, "Evangelicals: Out of the Closet but Going Nowhere?," 17.

185. Ibid.

186. Hunter, *American Evangelicalism*, 46.

187. Quebedeaux, *Worldly Evangelicals*, 164.

## Chapter 4. The Rise
## of the Christian Right

1. Marsden, *Understanding Fundamentalism*, 76–77, 105; Ribuffo, "God and Jimmy Carter," 141, 146, 149–50, 152, 155–56; Lienesch, *Redeeming America*, 2, 7–8; Quebedeaux, *Worldly Evangelicals*, 145; McLoughlin, *Revivals, Awakenings*, 212.

2. Carroll, "New Populists," 539–40.

3. Wuthnow, *Struggle for America's Soul*, 35.

4. Henry, "Evangelical Social Concern," 99–100.

5. Marsden, *Understanding Fundamentalism*, 95–96.

6. Quoted in [Dugan], "Dr Martin Marty," 5–6 October 1982, NAE Records.

7. Himmelstein, *To the Right*, 5.

8. See also Stone, *Boundaries of Evangelicalism*, 12, 183.

9. Marsden, *Understanding Fundamentalism*, 77.

10. Wuthnow, *Struggle for America's Soul*, 35. See also Davis and Robinson, "War for America's Soul," 56–57; Ribuffo, "God and Jimmy Carter," 155.

11. Lindsey, "Aquarians and Evangelicals."

12. [Dugan], "Dr Martin Marty," 5–6 October 1982, NAE Records.

13. On the funding of postwar evangelicalism see Eskridge and Noll, *More Money, More Ministry*.

14. Gay, *Liberty and Justice*, 14, 17–18; Lienesch, *Redeeming America*, 118; Fowler, *New Engagement*, 47.

15. Stone, *Boundaries of Evangelicalism*, 163–64, 166, 171; Carpenter, *Revive Us Again*, 206; Quebedeaux, *Worldly Evangelicals*, 87; Gay, *Liberty and Justice*, 17.

16. Marsden, *Understanding Fundamentalism*, 76; Stone, *Boundaries of Evangelicalism*, 166, 168; Fowler, *New Engagement*, 23.

17. Dugan, Semi-Annual Report to the Board of Administration, 6–7 October 1987, NAE Records.

18. Fowler, *New Engagement*, 24; Marsden, "Fundamentalism and Evangelicalism," 31–32; Himmelstein, *To the Right*, 123. See also Morgan, *The New Crusades*; Ammermann, *Baptist Battles*.

19. Robert P. Dugan Jr. to John Sununu, 2 August 1989, NAE Records.

20. Gay, *Liberty and Justice*, 3, 12, 67, 73–79, 84–100; Fowler, *New Engagement*, 23, 26–27, 154, 185–87; Stone, *Boundaries of Evangelicalism*, 166; Cerillo, "Survey of Recent Evangelical Social Thought," 273–74; Dayton, "Social and Political Conservatism"; McGirr, *Suburban Warriors*, 163–64, 169; Himmelstein, *To the Right*, 59; Lienesch, *Redeeming America*, 108, 110–14, 119; Hamby, *Liberalism and Its Challengers*, 356–57. See also "Inflation and the Breakdown of Trust"; Howard, "Christian Approach to Economics"; Elzinga, "Demise of Capitalism."

21. [Schrag], "Tentative Report," [1976], NAE Records.

22. Minutes—Business Meeting of ESAC at NAE Convention, 23 February 1976, NAE Records; H. Wilbert Norton to Martin H. Schrag, 11 June 1976, NAE Records.

23. "Evangelical Social Action Commission Statement: Biblical-Theological Basis for Social Action," in Schrag, Report of the Evangelical Social Action Commission, 28 December 1977, NAE Records.

24. "Ad-Hoc Meeting Regarding Civil Religion," 25 February 1976, NAE Records.

25. Schrag, "Summarization of Issues," 25 February 1976, NAE Records.

26. H. Wilbert Norton to Martin H. Schrag, 11 June 1976, NAE Records; T. E. Gannon to Martin H. Schrag, 14 June 1976, NAE Records.

27. Bacon, Report—Evangelical Social Action Commission, 2–3 May 1978, NAE Records.

28. Ibid.

29. Perkins, Report to the Social Action Committee, 18 September 1978, VoC Records.

30. Section II, Sectional Reports, 7 October 1980, NAE Records.

31. Minutes of Second Business Meeting of the 1976 NAE Convention of the ESAC, 25 February 1976, NAE Records.

32. Minutes of the Board of Administration, 22–25 February 1976, NAE Records; see also Minutes—Business Meeting of ESAC at NAE Convention, 23 February 1976, NAE Records.

33. David Breese to Billy Melvin, 16 April 1976, NAE Records.

34. Minutes of the ESAC Executive Committee Meeting, 17 June 1976, NAE Records.

35. "Resolution on Hunger and Poverty," in General Session Minutes, 5 March 1986, NAE Records.

36. John K. Stoner to Billy Melvin, 26 April 1976, NAE Records.

37. Martin H. Schrag to Billy Melvin, 30 April 1976, NAE Records.

38. Evangelical Social Action Commission, Report to the General Board, 6 October 1975, NAE Records.

39. Billy Melvin to Martin H. Schrag, 20 April 1976, NAE Records.

40. Billy Melvin to Martin H. Schrag, 6 November 1975, NAE Records.

41. Recounted in Martin H. Schrag to Billy Melvin, 21 November 1975, NAE Records.

42. Swartz, "Left Behind," 580. See also Swartz, "Identity Politics."

43. Fowler, *New Engagement*, 24, 155, 194–98.

44. Marsden, *Understanding Fundamentalism*, 107.

45. Tipton, *Saved from the Sixties*, 85–92.

46. Marsden, "Fundamentalism and Evangelicalism," 32; Fowler, *New Engagement*, 35–39; Bloesch, *Future of Evangelical Christianity*, 135.

47. Hunter, *Coming Generation*, 256, n. 30. Charitable giving and belief in charity are also important differences between religious and secular conservatives. See Lienesch, *Redeeming America*, 124–25.

48. White, "Philanthropic Giving," 69.

49. Clydesdale, "Soul-Winning and Social Work," 200–202; Conn, *American City*, 193.

50. Ribuffo, "God and Contemporary Politics," 1527.

51. Swartz, "Left Behind," 542.

52. Lasch, *True and Only Heaven*, 486–89, 491, 495. See also Himmelstein, *To the Right*, 52; Ehrenreich, "New Right Attack," 174, 190.

53. Jelen, "Culture Wars and the Party System," 148–49; Davis and Robinson, "War for America's Soul," 56; Dayton, "Some Doubts," 246–47; Fowler, *New Engagement*, 193.

54. McGirr, *Suburban Warriors*, 183; Marsden, *Understanding Fundamentalism*, 95–96.

55. Dick Blackbourn to Social Action Commission members, 15 November 1989, NAE Records.

56. Layman, *Great Divide*, 254–55. See also Carroll, "New Populists," 534; Ehrenreich, "New Right Attack," 189.

57. Handler and Hasenfeld, *Moral Construction*, 207. See also Brown, "Segmented Welfare System," 196; Lienesch, *Redeeming America*, 131; Jacobson, *Whiteness of a Different Color*.

58. Lasch, *True and Only Heaven*, 497, 504; McGirr, *Suburban Warriors*, 239.

59. Hixson, *American Right Wing*, xxv; Layman, *Great Divide*, 302.

60. Carpenter, "Youth for Christ," 370; Wacker, "Uneasy in Zion," 384–86.

61. Marsden, *Understanding Fundamentalism*, 78–79, 116–19; Sweet, "Crisis of Liberal Christianity," 45; Hatch and Hamilton, "Taking the Measure," 402–3; Gallup and Castelli, *People's Religion*, 5; McGirr, *Suburban Warriors*, 251.

62. Henry, "Evangelicals: Out of the Closet but Going Nowhere?," 21.

63. Sweet, "Crisis of Liberal Christianity," 45; Watt, *Transforming Faith*, 53, 65–67; Hunter, *American Evangelicalism*, 42.

64. McGirr, *Suburban Warriors*, 253.

65. Lienesch, *Redeeming America*, 107–9, 121; Ehrenreich, "New Right Attack," 163–64; Gay, *Liberty and Justice*, 84, 92; Carroll, "New Populists," 534; Ribuffo, "God and Contemporary Politics," 1524; Lasch, *True and Only Heaven*, 531. See also Carwardine, *Evangelicals and Politics*; Wilentz, *Chants Democratic*.

66. Thomas, *Revivalism and Cultural Change*, 22. See also Hixson, *American Right Wing*, xxvi–xxvii.

67. Himmelstein, *To the Right*, 89.

68. Tipton, *Saved from the Sixties*, 72–73, 79–80, 85; Thomas, *Revivalism and Cultural Change*, 3; McGirr, *Suburban Warriors*, 163–64. See also Kintz, *Between Jesus and the Market*.

69. Himmelstein, *To the Right*, 56, 59–60, 92; Ehrenreich, "New Right Attack," 163–64.

70. Isserman and Kazin, "Failure and Success," 237. Research into the evangelical resurgence has spawned a new awareness that evangelical religion traditionally conceived of itself as countercultural. In the mid-eighteenth-century South, John Boles reminds us, Baptists and Methodists "represented an intentionally oppositional culture" with a strong sense of separate identity. Likewise, historians of the more recent religious resurgence, such as Joel Carpenter, argue that evangelicals built up an entire parallel subcultural infrastructure that provided the institutional backdrop for the postwar

resurgence. More recently, the rise of this Christian counterculture could be seen most dramatically in the separatist Christian homeschooling movement. See Boles, "The Southern Way of Religion"; Carpenter, "Revive Us Again," 109, 111–14, 116; Clarkson, "The Institutionalization of the Christian Right."

71. Himmelstein, *To the Right*, 13, 31, 45; Hixson, *American Right Wing*, xxvi–xxvii. See also Lasch, *True and Only Heaven*, 528.

72. Himmelstein, *To the Right*, 78.

73. McGirr, *Suburban Warriors*, 245–46, 247–48.

74. Hammond, "Evangelical Politics," 190.

75. Marsden, *Understanding Fundamentalism*, 82.

76. Tipton, *Saved from the Sixties*, 18, 23. Francis Schaeffer argues that because they lacked absolute morals, hippies were trapped by the culture they rejected. See Fowler, *New Engagement*, 70.

77. Klatch, *Generation Divided*, 148–49, 215.

78. Lasch, *True and Only Heaven*, 515.

79. Stone, *Boundaries of Evangelicalism*, 82; Marsden, *Understanding Fundamentalism*, 76, 95–96; Himmelstein, *To the Right*, 118; Lienesch, *Redeeming America*, 3, 12–14.

80. Wuthnow, *Restructuring of Religion*, 156; Hatch and Hamilton, "Taking the Measure," 402–3; Ribuffo, "God and Contemporary Politics," 1531; McGirr, *Suburban Warriors*, 183.

81. Marsden, "Fundamentalism and Evangelicalism," 32; McGirr, *Suburban Warriors*, 230.

82. Dugan, NAE Office of Public Affairs Annual Report, 4 March 1985, NAE Records.

83. Stone, *Boundaries of Evangelicalism*, 29; Marsden, *Understanding Fundamentalism*, 101.

84. Marsden, *Understanding Fundamentalism*, 77; Ribuffo, *Old Christian Right*, 266.

85. Dugan, NAE Office of Public Affairs Annual Report, 5 March 1984, NAE Records. On the perseverance of anti-Catholic sentiments in evangelicalism see Wuthnow, *Restructuring of Religion*, 142–43; Young, "We Gather Together?"

86. Rothenberg and Newport, *Evangelical Voter*, 4; Hixson, *American Right Wing*, xxv; Himmelstein, *To the Right*, 66–68; McGirr, *Suburban Warriors*, 113–15; Hunter, *American Evangelicalism*, 45; Marsden, *Understanding Fundamentalism*, 94.

87. Himmelstein, *To the Right*, 8, 97, 164. On the funding of postwar evangelicalism see Eskridge and Noll, *More Money, More Ministry*. On postwar networks that united Sunbelt entrepreneurs, evangelicals, and free-market activists see also Moreton, *To Serve God and Wal-Mart*; Dochuk, "Prairie Fire."

88. McGirr, *Suburban Warriors*, 224, 226–28.

89. Lienesch, *Redeeming America*, 8; Ribuffo, *Old Christian Right*, 263.

90. Ehrenreich, "New Right Attack," 162. According to a 1986 poll conducted by *Christianity Today*, 31 percent of evangelicals picked "passing a constitutional amendment prohibiting abortion except to save the life of the mother" as the most important "social issue," with 76 percent supporting it. This was followed by 20 percent viewing "electing

a president who will appoint conservative judges who favor judicial restraint" as the most important issue, receiving the support of 79 percent. "Seeing the welfare system reformed" came third, garnering the support of 94 percent. When asked whether there was one single issue on which they would base their vote for a presidential candidate, 10 percent of those polled listed opposition to abortion. See "Christianity Today Confidential Survey," 29 April 1986, NAE Records.

91. Bloesch, *Future of Evangelical Christianity*, 140; Lasch, *True and Only Heaven*, 486–88.

92. Hixson, *American Right Wing*, xxvi. See also McGirr, *Suburban Warriors*, 186; Himmelstein, *To the Right*, 104.

93. Smith, with Emerson, Gallagher et al., "Myth of Culture Wars," 176–77; Rothenberg and Newport, *Evangelical Voter*, 10. According to an NAE straw poll among 110 evangelical leaders, pastors, and laypersons gathered at the biennial Washington Insight Briefing in 1986, 88 percent would have voted for a Republican and 12 percent for a Democrat if the presidential election had been held then. However, Vice President Bush, the Republican front-runner, ran well behind other Republicans as the preferred choice for presidential candidate. See "Evangelical Voters Divided According to Presidential Straw Poll," 29 April 1986, NAE Records.

94. Klatch, *Generation Divided*, 134; see also ibid., 148–49, 155–56; McGirr, *Suburban Warriors*, 244; Shires, *Hippies of the Religious Right*.

95. Turner, *Bill Bright and Campus Crusade*; Miller, *Graham and Republican South*. See also Harvey, "John Wilson, American Religious Historians, and the 1960s."

96. Quoted from original subtitle of Dreher, *Crunchy Cons*; Brooks, "The Wal-Mart Hippies." See also Walker, "The Traditionalist Counterculture"; Moreton, "Why Is There So Much Sex in Christian Conservatism."

97. Gitlin, "Straight from the Sixties," 56.

98. Swartz, "Left Behind," 277–78.

99. Kazin, "Grass-Roots Right," 150.

100. Turner, *Bill Bright and Campus Crusade*.

101. Ribuffo, "God and Contemporary Politics," 1527.

102. Lo, "Countermovements and Conservative Movements," 119.

103. Viguerie, "New Right Activist," 647–48.

104. Hall, "Welfare State and Careers," 381; Ehrenreich, "New Right Attack," 168.

105. Hall, "Philanthropy," 31.

106. Smith and Stone, "Unexpected Consequences," 236.

107. Hall, "Welfare State and Careers," 380–81.

108. Swartz, "Left Behind," 541–42, 544. See also Cromartie, "Fixing the World," 25.

109. Swartz, "Left Behind," 533–34.

110. Eynon, "Cast upon the Shore"; Flowers, *Religion in Strange Times*, 42–43, 48, 50. See also Warner, *New Wine*, 29–30; Quebedeaux, *Worldly Evangelicals*, 146; Heclo, *Christianity and American Democracy*, 107; Swartz, "Left Behind," 541–42; Shires, *Hippies of the Religious Right*; DiSabatino, "History of the Jesus Movement"; Lindsey, "Aquarians and Evangelicals."

111. Quoted in Tipton, *Saved from the Sixties*, 58.

112. Warner, *New Wine*, 83. Other examples include Lon Mabon, founder of the Oregon Citizens Alliance, and Randall A. Terry, founder of the anti-abortion group Operation Rescue.

113. Warner, *New Wine*, 68, 82; Quebedeaux, *Worldly Evangelicals*, xi; Flowers, *Religion in Strange Times*, 55–56.

114. Marsden, *Understanding Fundamentalism*, 95–96.

115. Eskridge and DiSabatino, *Remembering the Jesus Movement*, 3. The number of those who saw themselves as "moderate" remained roughly the same, dropping only slightly from 27 to 25 percent.

116. Tipton, *Saved from the Sixties*, 36.

117. Ibid., 93; Streiker, *Jesus Trip*, 10–12, 59, 65; Balmer, *Mine Eyes Have Seen the Glory*, 21.

118. Tipton, *Saved from the Sixties*, 94.

119. Luhr, *Witnessing Suburbia*.

120. Warner, *New Wine*, 141.

121. Ibid., 145–48. Warner notes that Therese had been a member of the Hitler youth movement in the 1930s, most likely the Bund Deutscher Mädel (BDM).

122. Ibid., 148–54.

123. Interview conducted in Eugene, Oregon, 20 October 2003. The name has been changed.

124. Robert P. Dugan Jr. to the Editor of *Christianity Today*, 27 October 1986, NAE Records; Dugan, NAE Office of Public Affairs Semi-Annual Report, 4–5 October 1983, NAE Records; Dugan, NAE Office of Public Affairs Semi-Annual Report, 6–7 October 1981, NAE Records.

125. Dugan, NAE Office of Public Affairs Semi-Annual Report, 2–3 October 1984, NAE Records. The Equal Access Act requires federally funded secondary schools to provide equal access to meeting spaces and school publications to most extracurricular clubs. These include programs organized for religious purposes, such as prayer and Bible study sessions, unless a school "opts out" of the act by prohibiting all non-curriculum clubs.

126. Ibid.; Dugan, NAE Office of Public Affairs Report, 8–9 October 1985, NAE Records; Dugan, NAE Office of Public Affairs Semi-Annual Report, 2–3 October 1990, NAE Records; Dugan, NAE Office of Public Affairs Semi-Annual Report, 9 October 1991, NAE Records.

127. Dugan, NAE Office of Public Affairs Report, 8–9 October 1985, NAE Records; Dugan, Semi-Annual Report to the Board of Administration, 6–7 October 1987, NAE Records.

128. Dugan, NAE Office of Public Affairs Semi-Annual Report, 6–7 October 1981, NAE Records.

129. [Dugan], "Sample to individuals," 18 November 1981, NAE Records.

130. Dugan, NAE Office of Public Affairs Semi-Annual Report, 4–5 October 1983, NAE Records; Dugan, NAE Office of Public Affairs Annual Report, 5 March 1984, NAE Records.

131. Dugan, NAE Office of Public Affairs Semi-Annual Report, 3–4 October 1989, NAE Records; Dugan, NAE Office of Public Affairs Annual Report, 4 March 1985, NAE Records.

132. Dugan, NAE Office of Public Affairs Annual Report, 6 March 1989, NAE Records.

133. [Dugan], "Sample to individuals," 18 November 1981, NAE Records; Dugan, NAE Office of Public Affairs Semi-Annual Report, 4–5 October 1983, NAE Records.

134. Dugan, NAE Office of Public Affairs Semi-Annual Report, 6–7 October 1981, NAE Records.

135. Robert P. Dugan Jr. to The President, 13 October 1983, NAE Records; Spring, "Bob Dugan: Representing Evangelicals in Washington," April 1984, 6–7, NAE Records.

136. Stewart McLaurin to Christian Advisory Group, 4 May 1984, NAE Records; Stewart McLaurin to Christian Advisory Group, 31 May 1984, NAE Records. The folder also contains Dugan's handwritten minutes of the group's meetings.

137. Dugan, NAE Office of Public Affairs Annual Report, 5 March 1984, NAE Records; Dugan, NAE Office of Public Affairs Semi-Annual Report, 2–3 October 1984, NAE Records. See also Marsden, *Understanding Fundamentalism*, 77.

138. Stewart McLaurin to Robert P. Dugan, 8 November 1984, NAE Records.

139. Paul Weyrich to Robert P. Dugan, 18 June 1984, NAE Records. See also John Paul Stark to Robert P. Dugan, 23 July 1984, NAE Records; JoAnne Jankowski to Robert P. Dugan, 24 May 1984, NAE Records.

140. Doug Wead to Robert P. Dugan, 11 March 1987, NAE Records.

141. Dugan, NAE Office of Public Affairs Semi-Annual Report, 4–5 October 1983, NAE Records.

142. Dugan, NAE Office of Public Affairs Annual Report, 6 March 1989, NAE Records.

143. Dugan, NAE Office of Public Affairs Semi-Annual Report, 3–4 October 1989, NAE Records.

144. Dugan, Semi-Annual Report to the Board of Administration, 6–7 October 1987, NAE Records.

145. Dugan, NAE Office of Public Affairs Semi-Annual Report, 4–5 October 1988, NAE Records; Dugan, NAE Office of Public Affairs Semi-Annual Report, 2–3 October 1990, NAE Records.

146. [Dugan], "Tim La Haye, Phone discussion, 11/16/83," NAE Records; [Dugan], handwritten notes on ACTV meeting with Paul Weyrich, 15 November 1984, NAE Records.

147. Dugan, NAE Office of Public Affairs Annual Report, 6 March 1989, NAE Records.

148. Robert P. Dugan Jr. to Gary Bauer, 22 March 1990, NAE Records.

149. Dugan, NAE Office of Public Affairs Annual Report, 5 March 1990, NAE Records.

150. Robert P. Dugan to Paul Weyrich, 12 August 1991, NAE Records; Pat Robertson to Robert P. Dugan, 10 January 1990, NAE Records; Pat Robertson to Robert P. Dugan,

9 February 1990, NAE Records; Pat Robertson to Robert P. Dugan, 29 March 1990, NAE Records.

151. Robert P. Dugan to Paul Weyrich, 12 August 1991, NAE Records.

152. Robert P. Dugan Jr. to William L. Armstrong, 17 November 1980, NAE Records. The NAE files contain numerous letters from Dugan to members of Reagan's transition team.

153. William L. Armstrong to Ronald Reagan, 2 December 1980, NAE Records.

154. Robert P. Dugan Jr. to Lyn Nofziger, 26 January 1984; Robert P. Dugan to Reagan-Bush 1984 Committee, 26 January 1984, NAE Records.

155. Robert P. Dugan Jr. to Herbert Ellingwood, 21 February 1984, NAE Records.

156. Herbert Ellingwood to Robert P. Dugan, [Spring 1988], NAE Records.

157. Robert P. Dugan Jr. to Doug and Bill Wead, 29 July 1988, NAE Records.

158. [Dugan], "Bush Hdqter, 3:00," [Fall 1988], NAE Records.

159. Tim LaHaye, Robert P. Dugan Jr., William R. Bright, D. James Kennedy, Paul Pressler, Jerry Rose to George Bush, "Ad Hoc Coalition of Evangelical Leaders," 8 August 1988, NAE Records.

160. George Bush to Robert P. Dugan Jr., 1 October 1988, NAE Records.

161. Robert P. Dugan Jr. to George Bush, 17 November 1988, NAE Records.

162. Dugan, NAE Office of Public Affairs Annual Report, 6 March 1989, NAE Records.

163. Dugan, NAE Office of Public Affairs Semi-Annual Report, 2–3 October 1990, NAE Records.

164. "Memorandum to Members of Evangelical Steering Committee, Bush/Quayle," 22 June 1992, NAE Records.

165. Suzanne Robbins and Barbara Monteith to Robert P. Dugan Jr., 25 January 1988, NAE Records; [Dugan], "Dr Martin Marty," 5–6 October 1982, NAE Records.

166. Spring, "Bob Dugan: Representing Evangelicals in Washington," April 1984, NAE Records.

167. Dugan, NAE Office of Public Affairs Annual Report, 5 March 1990, NAE Records.

168. Robert P. Dugan Jr. to Phyllis Schlafly, 23 August 1979, NAE Records.

169. DvN [Daniel van Ness] to RDV [Ralph D. Veerman] and GDL [Gordon Loux], 24 September 1981, PFM Records.

170. Robert P. Dugan Jr., Memo to Colonel Doner, 15 November 1984, NAE Records.

171. Dugan, resume, 1980, NAE Records.

172. Barbara Carbone to Robert P. Dugan Jr., 9 March 1989, NAE Records.

173. Barbara Carbone to Robert P. Dugan Jr., 30 March 1989, NAE Records.

174. Robert P. Dugan to Barbara Carbone, 23 March 1989, NAE Records.

175. Paul M. Doriani to Robert P. Dugan Jr., 18 December 1992, NAE Records.

176. Robert P. Dugan Jr. to Paul M. Doriani, 23 December 1992, NAE Records.

177. David L. Rambo to Robert P. Dugan Jr., 30 June 1992, NAE Records.

178. Paul A. Cedar to Robert P. Dugan Jr., 1 July 1992, NAE Records; Morris H. Chapman to Robert P. Dugan Jr., 14 July 1992, NAE Records.

## Conclusion: New Perspectives on American Evangelicalism

1. Layman, *Great Divide*, 199. See also Green, Guth, and Hill, "Faith and Election."
2. Swartz, "Left Behind."
3. Lo, "Countermovements and Conservative Movements."
4. Hall, "Philanthropy," 25.
5. Woodiwiss, *Crime, Crusades, and Corruption*.
6. Heclo, *Christianity and American Democracy*, 205.
7. Marsden, *Understanding Fundamentalism*, 63; Noll, *Religion and American Politics*; Fogel, *Fourth Great Awakening*. See also Heimert, *Religion and the American Mind*.
8. In Jeffrey Herf's apt phrase. See Herf, *Reactionary Modernism*.
9. Carpenter, "Youth for Christ," 373–74. The tension between individualistic, even libertarian, impulses and a strong public moralistic dimension has a long history in conservative Protestantism, particularly in the conflicts between Lutheran and Calvinist traditions. See Noll, *Old Religion*.
10. Marsden, *Understanding Fundamentalism*, 116–19.
11. According to Christopher Lasch, this was the most important contribution of neoconservative intellectuals to the rise of the New Right. Lasch, *True and Only Heaven*, 509, 512, 516, 518; Ehrenreich, "New Right Attack," 175.
12. I have explored this in more detail in Schäfer, "Cold War State and the Resurgence of Evangelicalism"; Schäfer, "Religious Nonprofit Organizations"; and Schäfer, "What Marx, Lenin, and Stalin Needed."
13. See also Offenbach, "Re-examining the Birth of the New Right."
14. Rucker, "S.C. Senator Is a Voice of Reform Opposition." See also Benen, "Political Animal."
15. Tipton, *Saved from the Sixties*, 72–73, 79–80, 85.
16. Moreton, *To Serve God and Wal-Mart*.
17. Lilla, "Tea Party Jacobins."

# Bibliography

### Archival Materials

#### Minutes

Board of Administration. National Association of Evangelicals. Minutes of the Meeting of the NAE Board of Administration, 19–20 September 1945. NAE Records.

———. Minutes of Special Board of Administration, 20 January 1964. NAE Records.

———. Minutes of the Board of Administration, Second Session, 22–25 February 1976. NAE Records.

———. Minutes of the Board of Administration, NAE, 7–8 October 1980. NAE Records.

Commission on Social Action. National Association of Evangelicals. Minutes of the Social Action Commission, 6 October 1956. NAE Records.

———. Minutes of the Social Action Commission, 7 October 1963. NAE Records.

———. Social Action Committee Meeting, 8 September 1965. NAE Records.

Commission on Social Concern. National Association of Evangelicals. Social Concern Breakfast Meeting, 19 April 1966. NAE Records.

———. Thursday Morning Breakfast Meeting of Social Concern Commission, 21 April 1966. NAE Records.

———. Minutes of the Social Concerns Commission, 1–3 May 1973. NAE Records.

Evangelical Action Committee. National Association of Evangelicals. Minutes of the Evangelical Action Committee [Clyde W. Taylor], 5 June 1957. NAE Records.

Evangelicals for Social Action. Planning Committee. Minutes, Thanksgiving Workshop, 20 April 1974. ESA Records.

Evangelical Social Action Commission. National Association of Evangelicals. Minutes of the Business Meeting of ESAC at NAE Convention, 8–10 April 1975. NAE Records.

———. Minutes of the Evangelical Social Action Commission Executive Committee, 10 April 1975. NAE Records.

———. Minutes—Business Meeting of ESAC at NAE Convention, 23 February 1976. NAE Records.

————. Minutes of Second Business Meeting of the 1976 NAE Convention of the ESAC of the NAE, 25 February 1976. NAE Records.

————. Minutes of the ESAC Executive Committee Meeting, 17 June 1976. NAE Records.

Executive Committee. National Association of Evangelicals. Minutes of the Executive Committee Meeting, 6 March 1956. NAE Records.

————. Minutes of the Executive Committee Meeting, 22 June 1956. NAE Records.

National Association of Evangelicals. Minutes of the NAE Staff Retreat in Glen Eyrie, 10–12 January 1961. NAE Records.

### Reports, News Releases, Statements, Memoranda, Circulars, etc., without Named Authors

"Action Proposals Accepted at the Second Thanksgiving Workshop, ESA, 1974." Evangelicals for Social Action, 1974. ESA Records.

"Ad-Hoc Meeting Regarding Civil Religion." Annual Convention. National Association of Evangelicals, 25 February 1976. NAE Records.

"Christianity Today Confidential Survey of Subscribers: A Political Opinion Poll." 29 April 1986. NAE Records.

Commission on Social Concern. National Association of Evangelicals. Annual Report of the Commission on Social Concern. National Association of Evangelicals, April 1966. NAE Records.

————. Report of the Social Concern Commission to the Board of Administration, 13 April 1967. NAE Records.

————. Report of the Social Concern Commission, 6 April 1970. NAE Records.

————. Report of the Social Concern Commission, 5–6 October 1970. NAE Records.

————. Report of the Commission on Social Concern, 4–5 October 1971. NAE Records.

"A Declaration of Evangelical Social Concern." Circular. National Association of Evangelicals, 27 November 1973. NAE Records.

"Evangelicals for McGovern." Circular, [1972]. ESA Records.

Evangelical Social Action Commission. National Association of Evangelicals. Report to the Board of Administration, 8–9 October 1973. NAE Records.

————. Report to the General Board, 6 October 1975. NAE Records.

————. "Evangelical Social Action Commission Statement: Biblical-Theological Basis for Social Action." In Report of the Evangelical Social Action Commission to the NAE Board of Administration, by Martin H. Schrag. National Association of Evangelicals, 28 December 1977. NAE Records.

"Evangelical Voters Divided According to Presidential Straw Poll." NAE News Release. National Association of Evangelicals, 29 April 1986. NAE Records.

Executive President. National Association of Evangelicals. Report of the Executive President to the Board of Administration of the NAE, 28 April 1948. NAE Records.

"Memorandum to Members of Evangelical Steering Committee, Bush/Quayle." National Association of Evangelicals, 22 June 1992. NAE Records.

"NAE Task Force on Long-Range Planning." Survey (labeled "McKenna Report"). National Association of Evangelicals, 8 October 1980. NAE Records.

"News Release 'Evangelicals for Social Action.'" Evangelicals for Social Action, 3 December 1974. ESA Records.

Photocopy of unsigned letter to the Board of Administration, National Association of Evangelicals, 21 January 1954. NAE Records.

"Questionnaire for Original Signatories of the Chicago Declaration on Evangelical Social Concern." Submitted by J. Robert Ross (marked "Tally revised as of July 29, 1975"). Evangelicals for Social Action, 1975. ESA Records.

"Resolution on Hunger and Poverty." In General Session Minutes, NAE Convention. National Association of Evangelicals, 5 March 1986. NAE Records.

"Resolutions—The Use of Force." In General Session Minutes. Second Session. National Association of Evangelicals, 24 February 1977. NAE Records.

Section II, Sectional Reports. NAE Board of Administration. National Association of Evangelicals, 7 October 1980. NAE Records.

"Seminar on Federal Service." In "Spiritual Unity in Action: The Program of the N.A.E. for 1963." National Association of Evangelicals, 1963. NAE Records.

"Suggested Concrete Proposals for Action." Thanksgiving Workshop on Evangelicals and Social Concern. Evangelicals for Social Action, 23–25 November 1973. ESA Records.

"Suggestions for Specific Action." Handwritten note, [1970s]. ESA Records.

"Temporary Committee for United Action among Evangelicals." Circular. National Association of Evangelicals, [1941]. NAE Records.

"Thirty Short Months: A Partial Record of the Achievements of the National Association of Evangelicals since Its Organization Was Completed in May 1943." In Minutes of the Meeting of the Board of Administration. National Association of Evangelicals, 19–20 September 1945. NAE Records.

*Reports, News Releases, Memoranda, Notes, etc., with Named Authors*

[Alexander, John]. "Action Proposal." Evangelicals for Social Action, [1973]. ESA Records.

Armerding, A. Herman. "Chaplain Counselors for Industry—A New Development in Human Relations Announced by the Industrial Chaplaincy Commission." In Minutes of the Meeting of the NAE Board of Administration. National Association of Evangelicals, 19–20 September 1945. NAE Records.

[———]. Report by Commission for Industrial Chaplaincy. In Minutes of the Meeting of the NAE Board of Administration. National Association of Evangelicals, 19–20 September 1945. NAE Records.

Armstrong, William L. "Christian Responsibility and Government." Address given at the Washington Leadership Briefing sponsored by the NAE. National Association of Evangelicals, 18–22 April 1977. NAE Records.

Arnold, Ron. "Communism Report." In Minutes of the NAE Staff Retreat in Glen Eyrie. National Association of Evangelicals, 10–12 January 1961. NAE Records.

Bacon, Gordon. Report—Evangelical Social Action Commission. National Association of Evangelicals, 2–3 May 1978 (dated "May 4th"). NAE Records.

Brown, Dale W. "Christian Social Responsibility—An Anabaptist Model," [1975]. ESA Records.

Cairns, Earle. "Church-State Relations in the United States." Conference on Church-State Relations. Appendix B. National Association of Evangelicals, 6–7 February 1961. NAE Records.

Chase, Ernest L. "The 'Pneuma' Origin of Human Maladjustments." In Minutes of the Meeting of the NAE Board of Administration. National Association of Evangelicals, 19–20 September 1945. NAE Records.

[Cromartie], Mike, to Gordon [Loux?]. Memorandum, 17 January 1978. PFM Records.

Dugan, Robert P., Jr. Resume, 1980. NAE Records.

———. NAE Office of Public Affairs, Semi-Annual Report to the Board of Administration. National Association of Evangelicals, 6–7 October 1981. NAE Records.

[———]. "Sample to individuals." Letter. National Association of Evangelicals, 18 November 1981. NAE Records.

[———]. "Dr Martin Marty, 'Evangelicalism Today'—Response Dr. Kenneth Kantzer and David Breese." Handwritten notes. In "Agenda, Board of Administration NAE." National Association of Evangelicals, 5–6 October 1982. NAE Records.

———. NAE Office of Public Affairs Semi-Annual Report to the Board of Administration. National Association of Evangelicals, 4–5 October 1983. NAE Records.

[———]. "Tim La Haye, Phone discussion, 11/16/83." Handwritten notes. National Association of Evangelicals, 16 November 1983. NAE Records.

———. NAE Office of Public Affairs Annual Report to the Board of Administration. National Association of Evangelicals, 5 March 1984. NAE Records.

———. NAE Office of Public Affairs Semi-Annual Report to the Board of Administration. National Association of Evangelicals, 2–3 October 1984. NAE Records.

———. Memorandum to Colonel Doner. 15 November 1984. NAE Records.

[———]. Handwritten notes on ACTV meeting with Paul Weyrich, 15 November 1984. NAE Records.

———. NAE Office of Public Affairs Annual Report to the Board of Administration. National Association of Evangelicals, 4 March 1985. NAE Records.

———. NAE Office of Public Affairs Report to the Board of Administration. National Association of Evangelicals, 8–9 October 1985. NAE Records.

———. Semi-Annual Report to the Board of Administration. [With marginalia.] National Association of Evangelicals, 6–7 October 1987. NAE Records.

[———]. "Bush Hdqter, 3:00." Handwritten notes. National Association of Evangelicals, [Fall 1988]. NAE Records.

———. NAE Office of Public Affairs Semi-Annual Report to the Board of Administration. [With marginalia.] National Association of Evangelicals, 4–5 October 1988. NAE Records.

———. NAE Office of Public Affairs Annual Report to the Board of Administration. [With marginalia.] National Association of Evangelicals, 6 March 1989. NAE Records.

———. NAE Office of Public Affairs Semi-Annual Report to the Board of Administration. [With marginalia.] National Association of Evangelicals, 3–4 October 1989. NAE Records.

———. NAE Office of Public Affairs Annual Report to the Board of Administration. [With marginalia.] National Association of Evangelicals, 5 March 1990. NAE Records.

———. NAE Office of Public Affairs Semi-Annual Report to the Board of Administration. [With marginalia.] National Association of Evangelicals, 2–3 October 1990. NAE Records.

———. NAE Office of Public Affairs Semi-Annual Report to the Board of Administration. National Association of Evangelicals, 9 October 1991. NAE Records.

Ford, George L. "Memorandum Containing a Collection of Statements from Individual NAE Leaders in Answer to Questions by Mr. George Cornell of Associated Press." National Association of Evangelicals, [1956]. NAE Records.

[———]. Executive Director's Report to the Board of Administration. National Association of Evangelicals, 2–4 April 1957. NAE Records.

———. "The Crisis in Church Extension for Evangelicals." National Association of Evangelicals, [1958]. NAE Records.

[———]. "Urgent." National Association of Evangelicals, 9 June 1958. NAE Records.

[———]. Report of the Executive Director to the Board of Administration. National Association of Evangelicals, 8–9 October 1962. NAE Records.

Greene, Bonnie M. "Confrontation in Black and White: Evangelicals for Social Action, Third Annual Workshop." *Vanguard*, September–October 1975, 25–26. ESA Records.

Hilliard, Clarence. "2. A Dissent." Photocopy of unidentified magazine article, [c. 1975]. NAE Records.

Hull, Judy Brown, to "Whoever is interested" on "The Past, Present, and Future of E.S.A." Thanksgiving Week 1975. ESA Records.

LaHaye, Tim, Robert P. Dugan Jr., William R. Bright, D. James Kennedy, Paul Pressler, Jerry Rose to George Bush. "Ad Hoc Coalition of Evangelical Leaders." 8 August 1988. NAE Records.

Lindsell, Harold. "An Evangelical Evaluation of the Relationship between Churches and the State in the United States." Consultation on the Church in a Secular World. National Association of Evangelicals, 11–13 October 1967. NAE Records.

Mott, Stephen, and Wesley Roberts. A Report on the Second Thanksgiving Workshop. Evangelicals for Social Action, 29 November–1 December 1974. ESA Records.

Perkins, John M. Report to the Social Action Committee of the National Association of Evangelicals, 18 September 1978. VoC Records.

Petticord, Paul P. "Observations-Objectives." Conference on Church-State Relations. Appendix C. National Association of Evangelicals, 6–7 February 1961. NAE Records.

Rees, Paul S. "Address of Paul S. Rees, President, National Association of Evangelicals to the Board of Administration in Session at Lorimer Baptist Church [Chicago]." National Association of Evangelicals, 20–21 January 1954. NAE Records.

[Schrag, Martin H.]. "The Biblical Basis for Social Action." [1975]. NAE Records.

[———]. "Tentative Report on Securing Information and Counsel from NAE-related Denominations and from ESAC Members-at-large." National Association of Evangelicals, [1976]. NAE Records.

———. "Summarization of Issues Discussed by Several Small Groups at NAE Convention." National Association of Evangelicals, 25 February 1976. NAE Records.

———. Report of the Evangelical Social Action Commission to the NAE Board of Administration. National Association of Evangelicals, 28 December 1977. NAE Records.

Sider, Ronald J. "News Release." 27 November 1973. NAE Records.

———. "A Personal Reflection on the 1974 Thanksgiving Workshop." Evangelicals for Social Action, 16 December 1974. ESA Records.

[Smith, Frank]. Report of the Social Action Commission to the Board of Administration. National Association of Evangelicals, 8–9 October 1962. NAE Records.

Spring, Beth. "Bob Dugan: Representing Evangelicals in Washington." *Focus on the Family*, April 1984, 6–7. NAE Records.

Taylor, Clyde W. Mid-Year Report, Secretary of Affairs, Washington, DC, Office to NAE Board of Administration. National Association of Evangelicals, 1 October 1952. NAE Records.

———. "Citizens of Heaven and Earth." Typescript "condensed from address given at Winona Lake, Indiana." "Broadcast over WBMI-Chicago." National Association of Evangelicals, 8 August 1954. NAE Records.

———. Report of the Secretary of Public Affairs to the NAE Board of Administration. National Association of Evangelicals, 1 April 1957. NAE Records.

———. "The Dynamic Performance of an Alert Minority." Address given at the fifteenth Annual Convention of the National Association of Evangelicals, Buffalo, NY, 4 April 1957. NAE Records.

———. Report of the Office of Public Affairs to the NAE Executive Committee. National Association of Evangelicals, 14 September 1961. NAE Records.

———. Supplementary Report on Legislation. In Report to the Mid-Year Meeting, NAE Board of Administration. National Association of Evangelicals, 9 October 1961. NAE Records.

———. Report of the Office of Public Affairs to the NAE Board of Administration. National Association of Evangelicals, 7 October 1963. NAE Records.

———. Report of the Evangelical Action Commission and the NAE Office of Public Affairs to the Board of Administration. National Association of Evangelicals, 14 April 1969. NAE Records.

———. Report of the General Director, Board of Administration. National Association of Evangelicals, 7 October 1974. NAE Records.

[Van Elderen, Marlin]. "Calvin Theol. Sem., 12/5/74." Typescript with revisions. ESA Records.

[Van Ness, Daniel], to RDV [Ralph D. Veerman] and GDL [Gordon Loux]. Memorandum "Re: Meeting with Bob Dugan." 24 September 1981. PFM Records.

Watson, Claude A. "God's Program for Governing." Second Annual Conference. National Association of Evangelicals, 17 April 1944. NAE Records.

Zahniser, Arthur. Report of the Commission on Social Action to the Board of Administration. National Association of Evangelicals, 6–10 April 1959. NAE Records.


## Secondary Sources

Ammermann, Nancy. *Baptist Battles: Social Change and Religious Conflict in the Southern Baptist Convention.* New Brunswick, NJ: Rutgers University Press, 1990.

Bailey, Kenneth K. *Southern White Protestantism in the Twentieth Century.* New York: Harper and Row, 1964.

Balmer, Randall. *Mine Eyes Have Seen the Glory: A Journey into the Evangelical Subculture in America.* New York: Oxford University Press, 1989.

Bell, Daniel. "Interpretations of American Politics." In *The Radical Right: The New American Right,* ed. Daniel Bell, 39–61. Rev. ed. Garden City, NY: Doubleday, 1963.

———, ed. *The Radical Right: The New American Right.* Rev. ed. Garden City, NY: Doubleday, 1963.

Benen, Stephen. "Political Animal." *Washington Monthly,* 29 July 2009, http://www.washingtonmonthly.com/archives/individual/2009_07/019271.php. 1 September 2010.

Berger, Peter L. "Introduction." In *With Liberty and Justice for Whom? The Recent Evangelical Debate over Capitalism,* by Craig Gay, xi–xii. Grand Rapids, MI: Eerdmans, 1991.

———. *The Social Reality of Religion.* Harmondsworth: Penguin Books, 1973.

"Bigotry or Smear?" *Christianity Today,* 1 February 1960, 20–21.

"Billy Graham and the Pope's Legions." *Christianity Today,* 22 July 1957, 20–21.

Bloesch, Donald G. *The Future of Evangelical Christianity: A Call for Unity amid Diversity.* Garden City, NY: Doubleday, 1983.

Boles, John B. "The Southern Way of Religion." http://www.vqronline.org/articles/1999/spring/boles-southern-way-religion/. 27 March 2009.

Boyer, Paul S. *When Time Shall Be No More: Prophecy Belief in Modern American Culture.* Cambridge, MA: Belknap Press of Harvard University Press, 1992.

Bradbury, Malcolm L., and James B. Gilbert, eds. *Transforming Faith: The Sacred and Secular in Modern American History.* New York: Greenwood Press, 1989.

Brereton, Virginia Lieson. *From Sin to Salvation: Stories of Women's Conversions, 1800 to the Present.* Bloomington: Indiana University Press, 1991.

Bromiley, Geoffrey W. "Fundamentalism—Modernism: A First Step in the Controversy." *Christianity Today,* 11 November 1957, 3–5.

Brooks, David. "The Wal-Mart Hippies." *New York Times*, 4 March 2010, http://www
.nytimes.com/2010/03/05/opinion/05brooks.html. 30 April 2011.

Brown, Michael K., ed. *Remaking the Welfare State: Retrenchment and Social Policy in America and Europe*. Philadelphia: Temple University Press, 1988.

———. "The Segmented Welfare System: Distributive Conflict and Retrenchment in the United States, 1968–1984." In *Remaking the Welfare State: Retrenchment and Social Policy in America and Europe*, ed. Michael K. Brown, 182–210. Philadelphia: Temple University Press, 1988.

Bruce, Steve. *Conservative Protestant Politics*. Oxford: Oxford University Press, 1999.

Butler, Jon. "Jack-in-the-Box Faith: The Religion Problem in Modern American History." *Journal of American History* 90 (2004): 1357–78.

Carlos, Serge. "Religious Participation and the Urban-Suburban Continuum." *American Journal of Sociology* 75 (1970): 742–59.

Carpenter, Joel A. "Revive Us Again: Alienation, Hope, and the Resurgence of Fundamentalism, 1930–1950." In *Transforming Faith: The Sacred and Secular in Modern American History*, ed. Malcolm L. Bradbury and James B. Gilbert, 105–25. New York: Greenwood Press, 1989.

———. *Revive Us Again: The Reawakening of American Fundamentalism*. New York: Oxford University Press, 1997.

———. *Two Reformers of Fundamentalism: Harold John Ockenga and Carl F. H. Henry*. New York: Garland, 1988.

———. "Youth for Christ and the New Evangelicals." In *Reckoning with the Past: Historical Essays on American Evangelicalism from the Institute for the Study of American Evangelicals*, ed. D. G. Hart, 354–75. Grand Rapids, MI: Baker Books, 1995.

Carroll, Peter N. "The New Populists, the New Right, and the Search for the Lost America." In *Conflict and Consensus in Modern American History*, ed. Allen F. Davis and Harold D. Woodman, 527–40. 7th ed. Lexington, MA: D. C. Heath, 1988.

Carson, Emmett D. "Patterns of Giving in Black Churches." In *Faith and Philanthropy in America: Exploring the Role of Religion in America's Voluntary Sector*, ed. Robert A. Wuthnow, Virginia Hodgkinson, and Associates, 232–52. San Francisco: Jossey-Bass, 1990.

Carwardine, Richard. *Evangelicals and Politics in Antebellum America*. New Haven: Yale University Press, 1993.

Cerillo, Augustus, Jr. "A Survey of Recent Evangelical Social Thought." *Christian Scholar's Review* 5 (March 1976): 272–80.

Cerillo, Augustus, Jr., and Murray W. Dempster. *Salt and Light: Evangelical Political Thought in Modern America*. Grand Rapids, MI: Baker Book House, 1989.

Chappell, David L. *A Stone of Hope: Prophetic Religion, Liberalism, and the Death of Jim Crow*. Chapel Hill: University of North Carolina Press, 2003.

"Chicago Crisis." *Christianity Today*, 10 October 1975, 57.

"Christian Responsibility in Political Affairs." *Christianity Today*, 1 August 1960, 24.

Clarkson, Frederick. "The Institutionalization of the Christian Right." http://www
.publiceye.org/magazine/v15n1/State_of_Christian_Rt-10.html. 29 March 2009.

Clydesdale, Timothy T. "Soul-Winning and Social Work: Giving and Caring in the Evangelical Tradition." In *Faith and Philanthropy in America: Exploring the Role of Religion in America's Voluntary Sector*, ed. Robert A. Wuthnow, Virginia Hodgkinson, and Associates, 187–210. San Francisco: Jossey-Bass, 1990.

Conn, Harvie M. *The American City and the Evangelical Church: A Historical Overview.* Grand Rapids, MI: Baker Books, 1994.

Cromartie, Michael. "Fixing the World: From Nonplayers to Radicals to New Right Conservatives: The Saga of Evangelicals and Social Action." *Christianity Today*, 27 April 1992, 25.

Crunden, Robert M. *Ministers of Reform: The Progressives' Achievement in American Civilization, 1889–1920.* New York: Basic Books, 1982.

Curtis, Susan. *A Consuming Faith: The Social Gospel and Modern American Culture.* Baltimore: Johns Hopkins University Press, 1991.

Davis, Nancy J., and Robert V. Robinson. "A War for America's Soul? The American Religious Landscape." In *Cultural Wars in American Politics: Critical Reviews of a Popular Myth*, ed. Rhys H. Williams, 39–61. New York: de Gruyter, 1997.

Dayton, Donald W. "The Social and Political Conservatism of Modern American Evangelicalism: A Preliminary Search for the Reasons." *Union Seminary Quarterly Review* 22 (Winter 1977): 71–80.

———. "Some Doubts about the Usefulness of the Category 'Evangelical.'" In *The Variety of American Evangelicalism*, ed. Donald W. Dayton and Robert K. Johnston, 245–51. Knoxville: University of Tennessee Press, 1991.

Dayton, Donald W., and Robert K. Johnston, eds. *The Variety of American Evangelicalism.* Knoxville: University of Tennessee Press, 1991.

De Boer, Cecil. "John Dewey and the American Spirit." *Christianity Today*, 27 May 1957, 8–10.

"Declaration of Principles." *Christianity Today*, 14 October 1957, 20–21.

Diamond, Etan. *Souls of the City: Religion and the Search for Community in Postwar America.* Bloomington: University of Indiana Press, 2003.

DiSabatino, David. "History of the Jesus Movement." http://www.ottawainnercity ministries.ca/newsArticlesStats/Jesus_Movement.htm. 27 March 2009.

Dochuk, Darren T. *From Bible Belt to Sun Belt: Plain Folk Religion, Grassroots Politics, and the Rise of Evangelical Conservatism.* New York: W.W. Norton & Company, 2011.

———. "Prairie Fire: The New Evangelical Right and the Politics of Oil, Money, and Moral Geography." Paper presented at the David Bruce Centre for American Studies Colloquium "New Perspectives on American Evangelicalism and the 1960s." Keele University, UK, 16–19 April 2011.

Dreher, Rod. *Crunchy Cons: The New Conservative Counterculture and Its Return to Roots.* New York: Three Rivers Press, 2006.

Ehrenreich, Barbara. "The New Right Attack on Social Welfare." In *The Mean Season: The Attack on the Welfare State*, ed. Fred Block et al., 161–95. New York: Pantheon Books, 1987.

Eighmy, John Lee. *Churches in Cultural Captivity: A History of the Social Attitudes of Southern Baptists.* Knoxville: University of Tennessee Press, 1972.

Ellwood, Robert S. *The Fifties Spiritual Marketplace: American Religion in a Decade of Conflict.* New Brunswick, NJ: Rutgers University Press, 1997.

Elzinga, Kenneth G. "The Demise of Capitalism and the Christian's Response." *Christianity Today,* 7 July 1972, 12–16.

Emerson, Michael O., and Christian Smith. *Divided by Faith: Evangelical Religion and the Problem of Race in America.* New York: Oxford University Press, 2000.

Enroth, Ronald M., Edward E. Ericson Jr., and C. Breckinridge Peter. *The Jesus People: Old-Time Religion in the Age of Aquarius.* Grand Rapids, MI: Eerdmans, 1972.

Erickson, Millard J. *The Evangelical Left: Encountering Postconservative Evangelical Theology.* Grand Rapids, MI: Baker Books, 1997.

Eskridge, Larry, and David DiSabatino. "Jesus People Survey Tabulations & Comments: First 400." http://one-way.org/jesusmovement/. 9 January 2008.

———. "Remembering the Jesus Movement" Survey Highlights, http://one-way.org/jesusmovement/. 29 July 2008.

Eskridge, Larry, and Mark A. Noll, eds. *More Money, More Ministry: Money and Evangelicals in Recent North American History.* Grand Rapids, MI: Eerdmans, 2000.

"Evangelicals and Fundamentals." *Christianity Today,* 16 September 1957, 20–21.

"Evangelism: By Isolation or by Participation." *Christianity Today,* 29 April 1957, 23.

Eynon, Bret. "Cast upon the Shore: Oral History and New Scholarship on the Movements of the 1960s." *Journal of American History* 83 (1996): 560–70.

Finke, Roger, and Rodney Stark. *The Churching of America, 1776–1990: Winners and Losers in Our Religious Economy.* New Brunswick, NJ: Rutgers University Press, 1992.

Flowers, Ronald B. *Religion in Strange Times: The 1960s and 1970s.* Macon, GA: Mercer University Press, 1984.

Fogel, Robert William. *The Fourth Great Awakening and the Future of Egalitarianism.* Chicago: University of Chicago Press, 2000.

Fowler, Robert Booth. *A New Engagement: Evangelical Political Thought, 1966–1976.* Grand Rapids, MI: Eerdmans, 1987.

Gallup, George, Jr. *The Unchurched American.* Princeton: Princeton Religious Research Center, 1978.

Gallup, George, Jr., and Jim Castelli. *The People's Religion: American Faith in the 90s.* New York: Macmillan, 1989.

Garr, Robin. *Reinvesting in America: The Grassroots Movements That Are Feeding the Hungry, Housing the Homeless, and Putting Americans Back to Work.* Reading, MA: Addison-Wesley, 1995.

Gay, Craig. *With Liberty and Justice for Whom? The Recent Evangelical Debate over Capitalism.* Grand Rapids, MI: Eerdmans, 1991.

"General Harrison Answers Graham Critics." *Christianity Today,* 21 January 1957, 28, 33.

Gitlin, Todd. "Straight from the Sixties: What Conservatives Owe to the Decade They Hate." *American Prospect* 26 (May–June 1996): 54–59.

Green, John C., James L. Guth, and Kevin Hill. "Faith and Election: The Christian Right in Congressional Campaigns 1978–1988." *Journal of Politics* 55 (1993): 80–91.

Guth, James L., John C. Green, Corwin E. Smidt, Lyman A. Kellstedt, and Margaret M. Poloma. *The Bully Pulpit: The Politics of Protestant Clergy.* Lawrence: University Press of Kansas, 1997.

Hall, Peter Dobkin. "Philanthropy, the Welfare State, and the Transformation of American Public and Private Institutions, 1945–2000." *Working Paper* no. 5. Cambridge, MA: Hauser Center for Nonprofit Organizations, Harvard University, 2000, http://www.hks.harvard.edu/hauser/PDF_XLS/workingpapers/working paper_5.pdf. 7 December 2008.

———. "The Welfare State and the Careers of Public and Private Institutions Since 1945." In *Charity, Philanthropy and Civility in American History*, ed. Lawrence J. Friedman and Mark D. McGarvie, 363–83. Cambridge: Cambridge University Press, 2003.

Hamby, Alonzo. *Liberalism and Its Challengers: From F.D.R. to Bush.* New York: Oxford University Press, 1992.

Hammond, Phillip E. "Evangelical Politics: Generalizations and Implications." *Review of Religious Research* 27 (1985): 189–92.

Handler, Joel, and Yeheskel Hasenfeld. *The Moral Construction of Poverty: Welfare Reform in America.* Newbury Park: Sage Publications, 1991.

Hankins, Barry. *Uneasy in Babylon: Southern Baptist Conservatives and American Culture.* Tuscaloosa: University of Alabama Press, 2002.

Harrison, William K. "Reminiscences and a Prophecy." *Christianity Today*, 4 March 1957, 14.

Harvey, Paul. "John Wilson, American Religious Historians, and the 1960s." *Religion in American History* [group blog], 30 September 2007, http://usreligion.blogspot.com/2007/09/john-wilson-american-religious.html. 27 March 2009.

Hatch, Nathan O., and Michael S. Hamilton. "Taking the Measure of the Evangelical Resurgence, 1942–1992." In *Reckoning with the Past: Historical Essays on American Evangelicalism from the Institute for the Study of American Evangelicals*, ed. D. G. Hart, 395–412. Grand Rapids, MI: Baker Books, 1995.

Heclo, Hugh. *Christianity and American Democracy.* Cambridge, MA: Harvard University Press, 2007.

Heimert, Alan. *Religion and the American Mind from the Great Awakening to the Revolution.* Cambridge, MA: Harvard University Press, 1966.

Henderson, Stephen T. "Social Action in a Conservative Environment." *Foundations* 23 (1980): 245–51.

Henry, Carl F. H. "The Christian-Pagan West." *Christianity Today*, 24 December 1956, 3–5, 34.

———. *Confessions of a Theologian: An Autobiography.* Waco, TX: Word Books, 1986.

———. "Dare We Renew the Controversy? III. The Contemporary Restoration." *Christianity Today*, 8 July 1957, 15–18.

———. "Dare We Renew the Controversy? The Evangelical Responsibility." *Christianity Today*, 22 July 1957, 23–26, 38.

———. "Dare We Revive the Modernist-Fundamentalist Conflict?" *Christianity Today*, 10 June 1957, 3–6.

———. "Evangelical Social Concern." *Christianity Today*, 1 March 1974, 99–100.

———. "Evangelicals in the Social Struggle." *Christianity Today*, 8 October 1965, 3–11.

———. "Evangelicals: Out of the Closet but Going Nowhere?" *Christianity Today*, 4 January 1980, 16–22.

———. "The Fragility of Freedom in the West." *Christianity Today*, 15 October 1956, 8–11, 17.

[———]. "Future of the American Worker." *Christianity Today*, 13 May 1957, 20–22.

[———]. "Jonathan Edwards' Still Angry God." *Christianity Today*, 6 January 1958, 20–21.

[———]. "Low Tide in the West." *Christianity Today*, 24 December 1956, 20–24.

———. *Remaking the Modern Mind*. Grand Rapids, MI: Eerdmans, 1946.

———. *The Uneasy Conscience of Modern Fundamentalism*. Grand Rapids, MI: Eerdmans, 1947.

[———]. "Where Do We Go from Here?" *Christianity Today*, 12 November 1956, 16–18.

———. "Why 'Christianity Today.'" *Christianity Today*, 15 October 1956, 20–23.

[———]. "Will the 'Y' Recover Its Gospel." *Christianity Today*, 11 November 1957, 20–21.

Herberg, Will. *Protestant, Catholic, Jew: An Essay in American Religious Sociology*. Garden City, NY: Doubleday, 1955.

Herf, Jeffrey. *Reactionary Modernism: Technology, Culture, and Politics in Weimar and the Third Reich*. New York: Cambridge University Press, 1984.

Himmelstein, Jerome L. *To the Right: The Transformation of American Conservatism*. Berkeley: University of California Press, 1990.

Hixson, William B., Jr. *Search for the American Right Wing: An Analysis of the Social Science Record, 1955–1987*. Princeton: Princeton University Press, 1992.

Hood, Ralph W., and Ronald J. Morris. "Boundary Maintenance, Social-Political Views, and the Presidential Preference among High and Low Fundamentalists." *Review of Religious Research* 27 (1985): 134–45.

Howard, Irving E. *The Christian Alternative to Socialism*. Arlington, VA: Better Books, 1966.

———. "Christian Approach to Economics." *Christianity Today*, 18 August 1958, 7–9.

Hudnet-Beumler, James. *Looking for God in the Suburbs: The Religion of the American Dream and Its Critics*. New Brunswick, NJ: Rutgers University Press, 1994.

Hudson, Winthrop S. *Religion in America*. New York: Scribner's Sons, 1965.

Hunt, Norman C. "Christians and the Economic Order." *Christianity Today*, 2 September 1957, 5–8.

Hunter, James Davison. *American Evangelicalism: Conservative Religion and the Quandary of Modernity*. New Brunswick, NJ: Rutgers University Press, 1983.

———. *Culture Wars: The Struggle to Define America*. New York: Basic Books, 1992.

———. *Evangelicalism: The Coming Generation*. Chicago: University of Chicago Press, 1987.

"Inflation and the Breakdown of Trust." *Christianity Today*, 6 January 1958, 21–23.

Inglehart, Ronald. "Why Didn't Religion Disappear? The Sacred and the Secular." *WZB Mitteilungen* 105 (September 2004): 7–10.

Isserman, Maurice, and Michael Kazin. *America Divided: The Civil War of the 1960s*. New York: Oxford University Press, 2000.

———. "The Failure and Success of the New Radicalism." In *The Rise and Fall of the New Deal Order, 1930–1980*, ed. Steve Fraser and Gary Gerstle, 212–42. Princeton: Princeton University Press, 1989.

Jacobson, Matthew Frye. *Whiteness of a Different Color: European Immigrants and the Alchemy of Race*. Cambridge, MA: Harvard University Press, 1998.

James, William. *The Varieties of Religious Experience: A Study in Human Nature*. New York: Longmans, Green, 1917.

Jelen, Ted. "Culture Wars and the Party System: Religion and Realignment, 1972–1993." In *Cultural Wars in American Politics: Critical Reviews of a Popular Myth*, ed. Rhys H. Williams, 145–57. New York: de Gruyter, 1997.

Jellema, Dirk. "The Great Silent Shrug." *Christianity Today*, 23 May 1960, 9–11.

———. "The Rise of the Post-Modern Mind." *Christianity Today*, 9 May 1960, 12–13, 27–28.

———. "Strange New Faiths." *Christianity Today*, 6 June 1960, 14–16.

Johnston, Robert K. "American Evangelicalism: An Extended Family." In *The Variety of American Evangelicalism*, ed. Donald W. Dayton and Robert K. Johnston, 252–72. Knoxville: University of Tennessee Press, 1991.

Kamm, S. Richey. "Is America Losing Her Cultural Distinctives?" *Christianity Today*, 8 July 1957, 3–5.

Kaus, Mickey. "The Revival of Liberalism." *New York Times*, 9 August 1996.

Kazin, Michael. "The Grass-Roots Right: New Histories of U.S. Conservatism in the Twentieth Century." *American Historical Review* 97 (1992): 136–55.

Keillor, Garrison. *Lake Wobegon Days*. New York: Viking, 1985.

Kelley, Stanley. "Democracy and the New Deal Party System." In *Democracy and the Welfare State*, ed. Amy Gutman, 185–206. Princeton: Princeton University Press, 1988.

Kellstedt, Lyman A. "Religion, the Neglected Variable: An Agenda for Future Research on Religion and Political Behavior." In *Rediscovering the Religious Factor in American Politics*, ed. David C. Leege and Lyman A. Kellstedt, 273–303. Armonk, NY: M. E. Sharpe, 1993.

Kellstedt, Lyman A., and Mark A. Noll. "Religion, Voting for President, and Party Identification, 1948–1984." In *Religion and American Politics*, ed. Mark A. Noll, 355–79. New York: Oxford University Press, 1990.

Kent, Stephen A. *From Slogans to Mantras: Social Protest and Religious Conversion in the Late Vietnam War Era*. Syracuse, NY: Syracuse University Press, 2001.

Kintz, Linda. *Between Jesus and the Market: The Emotions That Matter in Right-Wing America*. Durham, NC: Duke University Press, 1997.

Klatch, Rebecca E. *A Generation Divided: The New Left, the New Right, and the 1960s*. Berkeley: University of California Press, 1999.

Lasch, Christopher. *The True and Only Heaven: Progress and Its Critics*. New York: W. W. Norton, 1991.

Layman, Geoffrey. *The Great Divide: Religious and Cultural Conflict in American Party Politics*. New York: Columbia University Press, 2001.

Leland, John. "Rebels With a Cross." *New York Times*, 2 March 2006, http://www.ny times.com/2006/03/02/fashion/thursdaystyles/02rebels.html?page wanted=print. 27 March 2009.

Liebman, Robert, and Robert Wuthnow, eds. *The New Christian Right: Mobilization and Legitimation.* New York: Aldine, 1983.

Lienesch, Michael. *Redeeming America: Piety and Politics in the New Christian Right.* Chapel Hill: University of North Carolina Press, 1993.

Lilla, Mark, "The Tea Party Jacobins." *New York Review of Books*, 27 May 2010, http://www.nybooks.com/articles/archives/2010/may/27/tea-party-jacobins. 13 May 2011.

Lindner, Robert D. "The Resurgence of Evangelical Social Concern (1925–75)." In *Evangelicals: What They Believe, Who They Are, Where They Are Changing*, ed. David F. Wells and John D. Woodbridge, 189–210. Grand Rapids, MI: Baker Book House, 1977.

Lindsey, Brink. "The Aquarians and the Evangelicals: How Left-wing Hippies and Right-wing Fundamentalists Created a Libertarian America." *Reason Magazine*, July 2007, http://www.reason.com/news/show/120265.html. 27 March 2009.

Lippy, Charles H., ed. *Twentieth-Century Shapers of American Popular Religion.* New York: Greenwood Press, 1989.

Lo, Clarence Y. H. "Countermovements and Conservative Movements in the Contemporary U.S." *Annual Review of Sociology* 8 (1982): 107–34.

Luhr, Eileen. *Witnessing Suburbia: Conservatives and Christian Youth Culture.* Berkeley: University of California Press, 2009.

Lyra, Synesio, Jr. "The Rise and Development of the Jesus Movement." *Calvin Theological Journal* 8 (April 1973): 40–61.

Manza, Jeff, and Clem Brooks. *Social Cleavages and Political Change: Voter Alignments and U.S. Party Coalitions.* New York: Oxford University Press, 1999.

Marsden, George M. *Fundamentalism and American Culture: The Shaping of Twentieth-Century Evangelicalism, 1870–1925.* New York: Oxford University Press, 1980.

———. "Fundamentalism and American Evangelicalism." In *The Variety of American Evangelicalism*, ed. Donald W. Dayton and Robert K. Johnston, 22–35. Knoxville: University of Tennessee Press, 1991.

———. *Reforming Fundamentalism: Fuller Seminary and the New Evangelicalism.* Grand Rapids, MI: Eerdmans, 1987.

———. *Understanding Fundamentalism and Evangelicalism.* Grand Rapids, MI: Eerdmans, 1991.

Marsden, Lee. "US-Israel Relations: A Special Friendship." In *America's 'Special Relationships': Foreign and Domestic Aspects of the Politics of Alliance*, ed. John Dumbrell and Axel R. Schäfer, 191–207. London: Routledge, 2009.

Marsh, Charles. "Confession: Among the Jesus Freaks." 6 July 2001, http://killingthe buddha.com/mag/confession/among-the-jesus-freaks/. 27 March 2009.

Martin, William. *With God on Our Side: The Rise of the Religious Right in America.* New York: Broadway Books, 1996.

Marty, Martin E., ed. *Modern American Protestantism and Its World: Historical Articles on Protestantism in American Religious Life.* Vol. 10: *Fundamentalism and Evangelicalism.* Munich: K. G. Saur, 1993.

Matthews, Arthur H. *Standing Up, Standing Together: The Emergence of the National Association of Evangelicals.* Carol Stream, IL: National Association of Evangelicals, 1992.

McBeth, Leon. "Baptist Fundamentalism: A Cultural Interpretation." In *Fundamentalism and Evangelicalism*, ed. Martin Marty, 205–13. Munich: K. G. Saur, 1993.

McDannell, Colleen. *Material Christianity: Religion and Popular Culture in America.* New Haven: Yale University Press, 1996.

McGirr, Lisa. *Suburban Warriors: The Origins of the New American Right.* Princeton: Princeton University Press, 2001.

McLoughlin, William. *Revivals, Awakenings, and Reform: An Essay on Religion and Social Change in America, 1607–1977.* Chicago: University of Chicago Press, 1978.

Mearsheimer, John J., and Stephen M. Walt. *The Israel Lobby and U.S. Foreign Policy.* New York: Farrar, Straus and Giroux, 2007.

Miles, Delos. *Evangelism and Social Involvement.* Nashville: Broadman Press, 1986.

Miller, Steven P. *Billy Graham and the Rise of the Republican South.* Philadelphia: University of Pennsylvania Press, 2009.

"Ministers Favor Eisenhower 8 to 1." *Christianity Today*, 29 October 1956, 28.

Moberg, David O. *The Great Reversal: Evangelism and Social Concern.* Rev. ed. Philadelphia: Lippincott, 1977.

Monsma, Stephen V. *When Sacred and Secular Mix: Religious Nonprofit Organizations and Public Money.* Lanham, MD: Rowman and Littlefield, 1996.

Moreton, Bethany. *To Serve God and Wal-Mart: The Making of Christian Free Enterprise.* Cambridge, MA: Harvard University Press, 2009.

———. "Why Is There So Much Sex in Christian Conservatism and Why Do So Few Historians Care Anything about It?" *Journal of Southern History* 75 (2009): 717–38.

Morgan, David T. *The New Crusades, the New Holy Land: Conflict in the Southern Baptist Convention, 1969–1991.* Tuscaloosa: University of Alabama Press, 1996.

"The NAE: Building on Evangelical Consensus: An Interview with Billy Melvin." *Christianity Today*, 8 October 1982, 50–53.

"NAE's Role in the Future: Some Distinguished Evangelicals Offer Criticism and Hope about the Future of NAE." *Action*, Spring 1972, 14, 40–41.

National Association of Evangelicals. "History of the NAE." http://www.nae.net/index.cfm?FUSEACTION=nae.history. 24 July 2008.

Nelson, Rudolph. *The Making and Unmaking of an Evangelical Mind: The Case of Edward Carnell.* Cambridge: Cambridge University Press, 1987.

Newman, Mark. *Getting Right with God: Southern Baptists and Desegregation, 1945–1995.* Tuscaloosa: University of Alabama Press, 2001.

Noll, Mark A. *A History of Christianity in the United States and Canada.* Grand Rapids, MI: Eerdmans, 1992.

———. *The Old Religion in a New World: The History of North American Christianity.* Grand Rapids, MI: Eerdmans, 2002.

———. *Race, Religion, and Reform: Political Upheaval from Nat Turner to George W. Bush.* Princeton: Princeton University Press, 2008.

———, ed. *Religion and American Politics: From the Colonial Period to the 1980s.* New York: Oxford University Press, 1989.

Norris, Pippa, and Ronald Inglehart. *Sacred and Secular: Religion and Politics Worldwide.* Cambridge: Cambridge University Press, 2004.

Ockenga, Harold John. "The Communist Issue Today." *Christianity Today,* 22 May 1961, 9–12.

Offenbach, Seth. "Heed the Grassroots: Re-examining the Birth of the New Right." Paper presented at the Policy History Conference, Columbus, Ohio, 3–6 June 2010.

Olson, John Kevin, and Ann C. Beck. "Religion and Political Realignment in the Rocky Mountain States." *Journal of the Scientific Study of Religion* 29 (1990): 198–209.

O'Neill, Michael. *The Third America: The Emergence of the Nonprofit Sector in the United States.* San Francisco: Jossey-Bass, 1989.

Oppenheimer, Mark. *Knocking on Heaven's Door: American Religion in the Age of Counterculture.* New Haven: Yale University Press, 2003.

Ostling, Richard N. "America's Ever-Changing Religious Landscape." *Brookings Review* 17 (Spring 1999): 10–13.

Pew Research Center for the People and the Press. "The 2004 Political Landscape; Evenly Divided and Increasingly Polarized, 1987–2003 Values Surveys." Combined dataset, data archive, 5 November 2003, http://people-press.org/dataarchive/. 20 July 2008.

Pierard, Richard V. *The Unequal Yoke: Evangelical Christianity and Political Conservatism.* Philadelphia: Lippincott, 1970.

"Planning for Action." *Christianity Today,* 19 November 1976, 52.

Porterfield, Amanda. *The Transformation of American Religion: The Story of a Late Twentieth-Century Awakening.* Oxford: Oxford University Press, 2001.

Quebedeaux, Richard. *The Worldly Evangelicals.* San Francisco: Harper and Row, 1978.

———. *The Young Evangelicals: Revolution in Orthodoxy.* New York: Harper and Row, 1974.

Reid, W. Stanford. "The Age of Anxiety: A Call to Christian Action." *Christianity Today,* 18 August 1958, 3–4.

"Resurgent Evangelism." *Christianity Today,* 9 June 1958, 20–22.

Ribuffo, Leo. "God and Contemporary Politics." *Journal of American History* 79 (1993): 1515–33.

———. "God and Jimmy Carter." In *Transforming Faith: The Sacred and Secular in Modern American History,* ed. Malcolm L. Bradbury and James B. Gilbert, 141–59. New York: Greenwood Press, 1989.

———. *The Old Christian Right: The Protestant Far Right from the Great Depression to the Cold War.* Philadelphia: Temple University Press, 1983.

Roof, Wade Clark. *Spiritual Marketplace: Baby Boomers and the Remaking of American Religion.* Princeton: Princeton University Press, 1999.

Rossinow, Doug. *The Politics of Authenticity: Liberalism, Christianity and the New Left in America.* New York: Columbia University Press, 1998.

Rothenberg, Stuart, and Frank Newport. *The Evangelical Voter: Religion and Politics in America.* Washington, DC: Institute for Government and Politics, 1984.

Roundtable on Religion and Social Welfare Policy. Americans United for Separation of Church and State et al. v. Warden Terry Mapes, Prison Fellowship Ministries, InnerChange Freedom Initiative et al. (United States District Court, Southern District of Iowa, suit filed 2/12/03), http://www.religionandsocialpolicy.org/legal/legal_update_display.cfm?id=13. 19 August 2008.

Rucker, Philip. "S.C. Senator Is a Voice of Reform Opposition: DeMint a Champion of Conservatives." *Washington Post,* 28 July 2009, http://www.washingtonpost.com/wp-dyn/content/article/2009/07/27/AR2009072703066.html. 1 September 2010.

Sandeen, Ernest R. *The Roots of Fundamentalism and American Millenarianism, 1800–1930.* Chicago: University of Chicago Press, 1970.

Schaeffer, Francis A. "The Modern Drift: Is Nobody Home in This World?" *Christianity Today,* 20 June 1960, 3–6.

Schäfer, Axel R. "The Cold War State and the Resurgence of Evangelicalism: A Study of the Public Funding of Religion since 1945." *Radical History Review* 99 (Fall 2007): 19–50.

———. "Evangelicalism, Social Reform and the U.S. Welfare State, 1970–1996." In *Religious and Secular Reform in America: Ideas, Beliefs and Social Change,* ed. David K. Adams and Cornelius A. van Minnen, 249–73. New York: New York University Press, 1999.

———. "Religion, the Cold War State, and the Resurgence of Evangelicalism in the U.S., 1942–1990." *ZENAF Arbeits- und Forschungsbericht (ZAF),* 1/2006, Center for North American Studies, Johann Wolfgang Goethe-Universität Frankfurt, http://web.uni-frankfurt.de/zenaf/zenaf/schaefer_zaf.pdf. 6 December 2008.

———. "Religious Nonprofit Organizations, the Cold War, the State and Resurgent Evangelicalism, 1945–1990." In *The US Government, Citizen Groups and the Cold War: The State-Private Network,* ed. Helen Laville and Hugh Wilford, 175–93. London: Routledge, 2006.

———. "What Marx, Lenin, and Stalin Needed Was . . . to Be 'Born Again': U.S. Foreign Policy, Church-State Relations and Evangelicals during the Cold War." In *America's 'Special Relationships': Foreign and Domestic Aspects of the Politics of Alliance,* ed. John Dumbrell and Axel R. Schäfer, 223–41. London: Routledge, 2009.

Schmidt, Jean Miller. *Souls or the Social Order: The Two-Party System in American Protestantism.* Brooklyn: Carlson Publishing, 1991.

Shibley, Mark A. *Resurgent Evangelicalism in the United States.* Columbia: University of South Carolina Press, 1996.

Shires, Preston. *Hippies of the Religious Right.* Waco, TX: Baylor University Press, 2007.

Shorto, Russell. "Belief by the Numbers." *New York Times Magazine,* 7 December 1997, 60–61.

Simpson, John H. "Socio-Moral Issues and Recent Presidential Elections." *Review of Religious Research* 27 (1985): 115–23.

Smith, Christian. *American Evangelicalism: Embattled and Thriving.* Chicago: Chicago University Press, 1998.

Smith, Christian, with Michael Emerson, Sally Gallagher et al. "The Myth of Culture Wars: The Case of American Protestantism." In *Cultural Wars in American Politics: Critical Reviews of a Popular Myth,* ed. Rhys H. Williams, 175–95. New York: de Gruyter, 1997.

Smith, Oran P. *The Rise of Baptist Republicanism.* New York: New York University Press, 1995.

Smith, Stephen Rathgeb, and Deborah A. Stone. "The Unexpected Consequences of Privatization." In *Remaking the Welfare State: Retrenchment and Social Policy in America and Europe,* ed. Michael K. Brown, 232–52. Philadelphia: Temple University Press, 1988.

Stob, George. "Labor Needs a Conscience." *Christianity Today,* 2 September 1957, 17–18, 23–24.

Stone, Jon R. *On the Boundaries of American Evangelicalism: The Postwar Evangelical Coalition.* New York: St. Martin's Press, 1997.

Streiker, Lowell D. *The Jesus Trip: Advent of the Jesus Freaks.* Nashville: Abingdon Press, 1971.

Sundquist, James L. *Dynamics of the Party System.* Washington, DC: Brookings Institution, 1983.

Swartz, David R. "Identity Politics and the Fragmenting of the 1970s Evangelical Left." *Religion and American Culture* 21 (Winter 2011): 81–120.

———. "Left Behind: The Evangelical Left and the Limits of Evangelical Politics, 1965–1988." PhD diss., University of Notre Dame, 2008.

Sweet, Leonard. "The 1960s: The Crisis of Liberal Christianity and the Public Emergence of Evangelicalism." In *Evangelicalism and Modern America,* ed. George M. Marsden, 29–45. Grand Rapids, MI: Eerdmans, 1984.

Szasz, Ferenc Morton. *The Divided Mind of Protestant America, 1880–1930.* Tuscaloosa: University of Alabama Press, 1982.

Taylor, Clyde W. "NAE Celebrates 30 Years of Service." *Action,* Spring 1972, 8–12.

"Therapy of the Masses: Americans Are Becoming More Religious, but Not Necessarily More Censorious." In "A Nation Apart: A Survey of America." *The Economist,* 8 November 2003, 12–16.

Thomas, George M. *Revivalism and Cultural Change: Christianity, Nation Building, and the Market in the Nineteenth-Century United States.* Chicago: University of Chicago Press, 1989.

Tipton, Steven M. *Getting Saved from the Sixties: Moral Meaning in Conversion and Cultural Change.* Berkeley: University of California Press, 1982.

Trueheart, Charles. "Welcome to the Next Church." *Atlantic Monthly*, August 1996, 37–58.

Tseng, Timothy, and Janet Furness. "The Reawakening of the Evangelical Social Consciousness." In *The Social Gospel Today*, ed. Christopher Evans, 114–25. Louisville, KY: Westminster/John Knox, 2001.

Turner, John G. *Bill Bright and the Campus Crusade for Christ: The Renewal of Evangelicalism in Postwar America.* Chapel Hill: University of North Carolina Press, 2008.

Van Riessen, H. "The Church and Social Problem." *Christianity Today*, 22 July 1957, 3–5.

Viguerie, Richard A. "A New Right Activist Explains Conservative Successes, 1980." In *Major Problems in American History since 1945*, ed. Robert Griffith, 647–48. Lexington, MA: D.C. Heath, 1992.

Viteritti, Joseph P. *The Last Freedom: Religion from the Public School to the Public Square.* Princeton: Princeton University Press, 2007.

Wacker, Grant. "Uneasy in Zion: Evangelicals in Postmodern Society." In *Reckoning with the Past: Historical Essays on American Evangelicalism from the Institute for the Study of American Evangelicals*, ed. D. G. Hart, 376–93. Grand Rapids, MI: Baker Books, 1995.

Walker, Jesse. "The Traditionalist Counterculture." Review of Rod Dreher, *Crunchy Cons: The New Conservative Counterculture and Its Return to Roots. First Principles*, 4 February 2008, http://www.firstprinciplesjournal.com/print.aspx?article=31&loc=b&type=cbbp. 27 March 2009.

Warner, R. Stephen. *New Wine in Old Wineskins: Evangelicals and Liberals in a Small-Town Church.* Berkeley: University of California Press, 1988.

"The Washington Office: A Voice above the Clamor." *Christianity Today*, 8 October 1982, 53.

Watt, David Harrington. "The Private Hopes of American Fundamentalists and Evangelicals, 1925–1975." *Religion and American Culture* 1 (Summer 1991): 155–75.

———. *A Transforming Faith: Explorations of Twentieth-Century American Evangelicalism.* New Brunswick, NJ: Rutgers University Press, 1991.

Weber, Timothy. *Living in the Shadow of the Second Coming: American Premillennialism, 1875–1982.* Chicago: University of Chicago Press, 1987.

Weeks, David L. "Carl F. H. Henry's Moral Arguments for Evangelical Political Activism." *Journal of Church and State* 40 (Winter 1998): 83–106.

———. "Carl F. H. Henry on Civic Life." In *Evangelicals in the Public Square: Four Formative Voices on Political Thought and Action*, ed. J. Budziszewski, 123–40. Grand Rapids, MI: Baker Publishing Group, 2006.

"What Is the Target: Communism or Anti-Communists." *Christianity Today*, 22 May 1961, 22–23.

"What Protestant Ministers Believe." *Christianity Today*, 31 March 1958, 30.

White, Arthur H. "Philanthropic Giving." In *Philanthropic Giving: Studies in Varieties and Goals*, ed. Robert Magat, 65–71. New York: Oxford University Press, 1989.

White, Ronald C., Jr. *Liberty and Justice for All: Racial Reform and the Social Gospel (1877–1925).* San Francisco: Harper & Row, 1990.

Wilcox, Clyde. *Onward Christian Soldiers? The Religious Right in American Politics*. Boulder, CO: Westview Press, 1996.

Wilentz, Sean. *Chants Democratic: New York City and the Rise of the American Working Class, 1788–1850*. New York: Oxford University Press, 1984.

Williams, Daniel K. *God's Own Party: The Making of the Christian Right*. New York: Oxford University Press, 2010.

———. "Sex and the Evangelicals: Gender Issues, the Sexual Revolution, and Abortion in the 1960s." Paper presented at the David Bruce Centre for American Studies Colloquium "New Perspectives on American Evangelicalism and the 1960s." Keele University, UK, 16–19 April 2011.

Williams, Rhys H., ed. *Cultural Wars in American Politics: Critical Reviews of a Popular Myth*. New York: de Gruyter, 1997.

———. "Culture Wars, Social Movements, and Institutional Politics." In *Cultural Wars in American Politics: Critical Reviews of a Popular Myth*, ed. Rhys H. Williams, 283–95. New York: de Gruyter, 1997.

Wood, James R. "Liberal Protestant Action in a Period of Decline." In *Faith and Philanthropy in America: Exploring the Role of Religion in America's Voluntary Sector*, ed. Robert A. Wuthnow, Virginia Hodgkinson, and Associates, 165–86. San Francisco: Jossey-Bass, 1990.

Woodiwiss, Michael. *Crime, Crusades, and Corruption: Prohibitions in the United States, 1900–1987*. Totowa, NJ: Barnes & Noble, 1988.

Wuthnow, Robert. *After Heaven: Spirituality in America since the 1950s*. Berkeley: University of California Press, 1998.

———. *The Consciousness Reformation*. Berkeley: University of California Press, 1976.

———, ed. *Encyclopedia of Politics and Religion*. Washington, DC: Congressional Quarterly, 1998.

———. "Religious Commitment and Conservatism: In Search of an Elusive Relationship." In *Religion in Sociological Perspective*, ed. Charles Y. Glock, 117–32. Belmont, CA: Wadsworth, 1973.

———. *The Restructuring of American Religion: Society and Faith since World War II*. Princeton: Princeton University Press, 1988.

———. *The Struggle for America's Soul: Evangelicals, Liberals, and Secularism*. Grand Rapids, MI: Eerdmans, 1989.

Young, Neil J. "We Gather Together? Rethinking the Religious Right." Paper presented at the Policy History Conference, Columbus, Ohio, 3–6 June 2010.

Young, Shawn David. "From Hippies to Jesus Freaks: Christian Radicalism in Chicago's Inner-City." *Journal of Religion and Popular Culture* 22 (Summer 2010), http://www.usask.ca/relst/jrpc/pdfs/art22%282%29-jesusfreaks.pdf. 4 September 2010.

# Index

Italicized page numbers indicate illustrations.

213

institutional separatism: neo-evangelicals and, 10, 42–43, 48–55, 64; neo-evangelicals' and fundamentalists' separation and, 10, 32–33, 42–45, 48–51, 53, 57, 63, 66, 171n42, 172n58; separatism/engagement duality and, 5, 9, 10, 12, 40, 50, 64
institution building, 11–12, 30–31, 55–56, 79, 96. *See also* organizational issues
intellectual leadership, 46, 52–53, 63. *See also* ideological leadership; *specific leaders*
interdenominational evangelicals, 9, 20, 33, 34, 47–48, 129
internal backlash and marginalization, 112–20, 128, 130, 132, 145–46, 153–55
International Council on Biblical Inerrancy (ICBI), 115
Inter-Varsity Christian Fellowship (IVCF), 47, 58, 78, 97, 133
intramovement conflict mediation, 6, 71, 114, 137, 145, 158. *See also* New Christian Right

Jackson, Jesse, 18
Jellema, Dirk, 46, 52, 53
Jesus Movement, 97–101, 105, *106, 108, 109*. *See also* left-leaning evangelicalism
Jewett, Paul K., 11, 52, 79, 114
Jews: anti-Semitism and, 7, 10, 43, 53, 54, 63, 129–30, 146; conversionism and, 54; ecumenism and, 10, 21–22, 43, 129–30; inerrancy and, 21–22; partisan politics and, 23, 35
Jones, Rufus, 84–86, 89–90, 118

Kamm, S. Richie, 81, 82
Kantzer, Kenneth, 112
Kaus, Mickey, 38
Kazin, Michael, 20
Keillor, Garrison, 44
Klatch, Rebecca, 39, 128, 132

Lasch, Christopher, 38, 39, 123, 191n11
Layman, Geoffrey, 23, 24, 35, 37
LCMS (Lutheran Church-Missouri Synod), 16–17, 56, 78, 84, 140. *See also* Lutheranism

leadership issues, 46, 52–53, 63, 67, 112
left-leaning evangelicalism, 10–12, 69–71, 76–80, 102–5, 174n1; abortion issue and, 134, 181n147; alternative communities and, 83, 86–87, 98; anticommunism and, 103; antistatism and, 92, 96; church growth and disparity statistics and, 70; Cold War society contradictions and, 11, 46, 64, 76; conservative Protestants and, 21, 105; consumer capitalism and, 11, 13, 69–70, 72–73, 76, 77; conversionism and, 12, 74, 77, 79, 101; counterculture links with, 6, 11–12, 93–101, 103–4, 180n138, 181n147; doctrine and, 74, 76, 79–80, 95; ecumenism and, 13, 71, 85, 91, 93; evangelicals and, 59–60; family values and, 105; fragmentation of movement and, 11, 21, 70, 80–81, 91–92; inerrancy and, 13, 21, 79–80; Jesus Movement and, 97–101, 105, *106, 108, 109,* 134–35; liberalism and, 11, 96; libertarianism and, 159; military-industrial complex and, 83–84; moral issues and, 11, 80–83, 94–95, 97–104, 108, 178n75; NAE and, 80–81, 90–98, 103, 114; New Christian Right mobilization and, 6–7, 10, 13, 70–71, 128, 132, 149, 153–55; New Christian Right's organizational strategies and, 131–36, 154; organizational approach of, 11–12, 79, 96; Pentecostalism and, 99–102; pietism and, 77; political activism and, 21, 70, 78, 81–82, 85–87, 107, 154–55; poverty doctrine of, 77, 86, 176n43; race relations and, 70, 74–76, 81–83, 86, 88–90, 179n108; repoliticization/resocialization of former hippies and, 6, 12, 101–2, 109, 134–36, 155, 182n178; social action and, 10–11, 13, 21, 70, 77–80, 83–84, 86, 110, 179n95; social issues in the 1950s and, 71–76; the South and, 78–79; spiritual marketplace and, 77, 98; spiritual pluralism and, 80, 97–101, 105, 106, 107–9, 108–9; subcultural identity and, 12, 84, 104; superpatriotism and, 11; therapeutic Christianity and, 11, 12, 100–102; utilitarianism and, 94–95; welfare institutions and, 85–86; the West and, 78;

## ❖ STUDIES IN AMERICAN THOUGHT AND CULTURE ❖

*Back to the Land: The Enduring Dream of Self-Sufficiency in Modern America*
Dona Brown

*Margaret Fuller: Transatlantic Crossings in a Revolutionary Age*
Edited by Charles Capper and Cristina Giorcelli

*Creating the College Man: American Mass Magazines and Middle-Class Manhood,
1890–1915*
Daniel A. Clark

*Robert Koehler's "The Strike": The Improbable Story of an Iconic 1886 Painting
of Labor Protest*
James M. Dennis

*Emerson's Liberalism*
Neal Dolan

*Observing America: The Commentary of British Visitors to the United States,
1890–1950*
Robert P. Frankel

*Picturing Indians: Photographic Encounters and Tourist Fantasies in H. H. Bennett's
Wisconsin Dells*
Steven D. Hoelscher

*Cosmopolitanism and Solidarity: Studies in Ethnoracial, Religious, and Professional
Affiliation in the United States*
David A. Hollinger

*Thoreau's Democratic Withdrawal: Alienation, Participation, and Modernity*
Shannon L. Mariotti

*Seaway to the Future: American Social Visions and the Construction
of the Panama Canal*
Alexander Missal